W. H. Hall

Across Mexico in 1864-5

W. H. Hall

Across Mexico in 1864-5

ISBN/EAN: 9783337252908

Printed in Europe, USA, Canada, Australia, Japan

Cover: Foto ©Andreas Hilbeck / pixelio.de

More available books at **www.hansebooks.com**

ROSS MEXICO

IN

1864-5.

BY

W. H. BULLOCK.

London and Cambridge:
MACMILLAN AND CO.
1866.

LONDON:
R. CLAY, SON, AND TAYLOR, PRINTERS,
BREAD STREET HILL.

CONTENTS.

CHAPTER I.
VERA CRUZ

CHAPTER II.
VERA CRUZ TO ORIZABA

CHAPTER III.
ORIZABA TO PUEBLA

CHAPTER IV.
PUEBLA TO MEXICO

CHAPTER V.
CITY OF MEXICO

CHAPTER VI.
CITY LIFE IN MEXICO

CHAPTER VII.
LIFE IN THE CITY (*continued*)

CHAPTER VIII.
THE ENVIRONS

CHAPTER IX.
A RIDE ROUND THE LAKE OF TEZCUCO

CHAPTER X.
MEXICO TO MORELIA

CHAPTER XI.
MORELIA

CHAPTER XII.
MORELIA TO GUARACHA 211

CHAPTER XIII.
HACIENDA LIFE IN MEXICO 227

CHAPTER XIV.
GUARACHA TO GUADALAJARA 250

CHAPTER XV.
GUADALAJARA 266

CHAPTER XVI.
TEPIC 279

CHAPTER XVII.
TO THE PACIFIC AND BACK 289

CHAPTER XVIII.
A TRIP TO A COTTON PLANTATION ON THE RIO SANTIAGO 306

CHAPTER XIX.
THE CARNIVAL AT TEPIC 327

CHAPTER XX.
A VOYAGE OF SIX DAYS IN A DILIGENCE—GUADALAJARA TO MEXICO 338

CHAPTER XXI.
REAL DEL MONTE 352

CHAPTER XXII.
REAL DEL MONTE TO ZACUALTIPAN 369

CHAPTER XXIII.
THROUGH THE HUASTECA TO TAMPICO 379

LIST OF ILLUSTRATIONS.

	TO FACE PAGE
JUAREZ	10
INDIANS OF TIERRA CALIENTE	22
AZTEC CALENDAR STONE	85
AZTEC OLD WOMAN	88
MESTIZOS OR MIXED BREEDS	90
CHAPULTEPEC	146
RUINS OF TLALMANALCO	149
NATIVE SOLDIERS	264

ACROSS MEXICO IN 1864-5.

CHAPTER I.

VERA CRUZ.

NOT easily will any of us who, on the morning of November 29th, 1864, stood anxiously watching on the foredeck of the R.M.S. *Solent* forget the first glimpse of the snow-capped peak of Orizaba, as it revealed itself to us through the grey dawn, proclaiming that we were drawing nigh to the Mexican shore. All night long we had been floating through a sea of fire, not only phosphorescent in the track of our vessel, but all around as far as the eye could reach. With the earliest streaks of opening day a distant solitary snow peak became faintly visible like a phantom in the heavens, and we needed no telling that yonder snowy pyramid resting on a base of clouds was the peak of Orizaba, for the first sight of which we had been yearning so long. With increasing daylight we could make out the general outline of the mountains and the coast, and before long the towers and brown-red domes of Vera Cruz, overtopping its low sea-bleached wall, came into sight. As we drew nearer we could distinguish the once formidable island-citadel—the fortress of San Juan de Ulua, built on a low reef, and separated by a narrow channel from the mainland. In this treacherous roadstead some twenty vessels were lying at anchor in perpetual dread of the sudden springing up of the "Norte" or "Norther"— the signal to put out to sea on the instant; for no vessel can live in the roads of Vera Cruz while the *Norte* is blowing.

So it is in fear and trembling lest a *Norte* should spring up, and snatch away his chance of getting ashore, that the traveller passes the hours on shipboard which intervene between sighting the coast and anchoring in the roads. For the *Norte* may spring up when the sky looks least threatening, and woe be to those who are caught by its violence. Then the traveller, who has been rejoicing in the prospect of getting ashore in a few hours, must resign himself with the best grace he may to being tossed by the merciless waves until the *Norte* shall have spent his fury—it may be in two or it may be in fourteen days. But no *Norte* sprang up to intercept our landing.

In the meantime the appearance of our steamer on the horizon had created hardly less excitement among the Veracruzans, than the sight of land had occasioned on board. For at all times the arrival of the packet is a great event, and on this occasion she was known to have on board Monseigneur Meglia, Archbishop of Damascus in *partibus infidelibus*, the newly-appointed Nuncio to the court of Maximilian—the Nuncio who was fondly believed to be invested with full powers to bring about a settlement of the religious questions which had been so long pending.

Scarcely had we dropped anchor in the roads, when we were surrounded by a fleet of small craft, among which was conspicuous a stately boat conveying a pompous-looking individual in full evening costume, and whose breast was one dazzling expanse of orders. As soon as his boat was brought alongside, this hero stepping upon the gangway boarded us, and at once inquired for the Nuncio, who, as ill luck would have it, was still in his berth, and in no condition to receive a state visit. So the august party had to beat a precipitate retreat, and take up a position on deck, until such time as the Nuncio should be ready to present himself.

Now as it is said that no man can be a hero to his own valet, so was it with the Nuncio and us. For during the latter part of the voyage we had been brought into close contact with the holy man, having—by a great piece of good luck—been admitted to a select company of six, who messed at a little table a deck higher than the bulk of the passengers, whose meals were served on the lower deck in an atmosphere which was perfectly suffocating in the tropics. We who dined at this table were naturally the envy of the whole ship. The conversation, however, at our table was far from brilliant, for the Nuncio said but one thing worth remembering during the whole of our intercourse with him. My companion happened to be giving vent in somewhat unmeasured terms to his abhorrence of the monotony of life at sea when the Nuncio suddenly interrupted him, saying, "Vous qui êtes Anglais, vôus vous plaignez de la mer! La mer, c'est vôtre terre." Before the end of the voyage we had reached such a pitch of intimacy with the holy man as to be admitted to the privilege of sharing his bottle of light claret, while he was not backward in helping us to get through ours; so that when, on this eventful morning, he presently appeared on deck in the full glory of his violet and green ecclesiastical trappings, having laid aside the simple black habit and velvet skull cap which he had worn during the voyage, we felt that a great gulf was thenceforth fixed between him and us, and that our familiar intercourse was broken for ever. Could this be the Nuncio, whom, but a few days before, we had beheld engaged like the rest of us in chasing the cockroaches, which swarmed in all our cabins?

His interview with the wearer of many orders over,

Vera Cruz.

the Nuncio stepped down the gangway into the boat of state, his ecclesiastical aide-de-camp following, and the party was rowed ashore amid ringing of bells, and salvos of artillery from the forts on shore, answered by the French and Austrian men-of-war at anchor in the roads, and the fortress of San Juan de Ulua. Almost simultaneously we too took boat, and followed in the wake of the Nuncio, the chief engineer of the Imperial Mexican Railway Company, who was of our party, expressing the profane conviction that, waste what amount of powder they pleased upon the Nuncio, the arrival of his railway people was an event really much more worthy of being announced to the country by the thunder of cannon. From the landing-place the Nuncio proceeded to the church of San Francisco, and dispensed in a becoming manner to the assembled multitude, which was mostly composed of half-naked Indians, the blessing which he had received but a few weeks before from the hands of the Holy Father himself.

There being but a single hotel at Vera Cruz in any way respectable, the Casa de Diligencias, and that far from comfortable, inasmuch as, apart from other inconveniences, such as incessant gambling and "liquoring up" all over the premises, you have to share a brick-floored room with three or four strangers, if you happen to be alone; it is not wonderful that, on the arrival of the packet with upwards of 100 passengers, considerable confusion should arise.

While the hotel accommodation is thus inadequate, the means of transport up country are even more limited still. For although a train capable of carrying two or three hundred passengers runs daily from Vera Cruz to Camaron,* the present terminus of the railway some thirty-five miles distant across the hot unhealthy plain called the "Tierra Caliente," but a single diligence, constructed to carry nine inside and three out, is there in waiting to carry passengers onward. From this, it results that travellers are not unfrequently detained a week or ten days at Vera Cruz, always subjected to extreme discomfort, and, in the unhealthy season, exposed to the imminent risk of losing their lives. Not the least boon which the completion of the railway from Vera Cruz to the city of Mexico will confer upon the country, will be that of remedying this deplorable state of things.

We, however, enjoyed the singular good fortune of being received into a private house, where the unaffected hospitality of our host and hostess made us feel at our ease at once. Our entertainers, who were Americans, informed us, that having been constrained to fly from Butler's *régime* at New Orleans, they had

* Since these pages were written the line has been extended to Paso del Macho.

at length found a temporary resting-place at Vera Cruz. For the first time I found myself listening to invectives against the Yankees, poured forth with a very decided Yankee twang, from the lips of one of those captivating Southern ladies, against whose charms few travellers have been proof. Although differing considerably from my hostess in my views of the general merits of the American question, I must plead guilty to having felt quite unequal to doing battle for them then and there, especially against such agreeable and hospitable antagonists.

With regard to the state of the country, our host informed us that things were just as bad as they could possibly be. According to him, the French intervention in Mexico had only made matters ten times worse. Life was not safe outside the walls of the towns, and even the French had to submit to the indignity of paying a toll to the guerillas for the safe passage of their convoys of mules through the *Tierra Caliente*, which it was impossible to hold with French troops, owing to the deadliness of the climate. That all that the French attempted was to occupy Vera Cruz and a few other points with black troops from Martinique, and a few companies of Nubians, borrowed against all international usage from the Viceroy of Egypt, who, according to the Michel Chevalier, ought to have thought it an honour to mingle his troops with those of France. That on one occasion some Liberals had actually ridden up to the gates of Vera Cruz, lassoed the Nubian sentinel on duty, and carried him off with them.

Worse than all, our host went on to assure us that we had most to fear from the conduct of the French troops along the road, which consisted mainly of the Second African regiment and the foreign legion, of which the first was composed of men drafted into the regiment as a punishment on the expiration of their term of imprisonment, and the second of deserters from every army in Europe. That from these regiments the ranks of the brigands were freely recruited, and that only a few weeks before, five of them had been caught and executed for the murder of the driver of the diligence.

While drawing this doleful picture of the state of the country, our host did not attempt to conceal from us that his sympathies, in common with those of the majority of the inhabitants of Vera Cruz, whether native or foreign, were decidedly in favour of Juarez, whom he represented as a disinterested patriot. On the other hand, he drew the portrait of Miramon, and the leaders of the Church party generally, in the blackest colours, fully approving of the violent measures by which the secularisation of the property of the clergy had been brought about.

Now, inasmuch as during the voyage out from England I had been a good deal thrown into the society of Mexicans belonging to the Conservative or clerical party, who were taking advantage of the intervention to return home, and had been rather favourably impressed by them, I was not prepared to admit as just the violent abuse which my American host heaped on the party indiscriminately. Indeed my subsequent experience convinced me that the report of the state of the country which I had just received was no more trustworthy than the ordinary intelligence about Mexico which is derived from American sources. So offensive to Americans in general is the attempt to establish an empire in Mexico, that the least successes of the Juarists are invariably magnified into important victories by the American press, and eagerly believed in by the people. There was, however, something surprising in these sentiments proceeding from the mouth of a violent Southerner.

But, if the Americans lie in favour of Juarez and his party, the French, to say the least of it, have not been backward in displaying in equally false colours the merits of the clerical party. As for myself, I became more and more convinced, as my acquaintance with the country increased, that it was utterly impossible to sympathise, in the remotest degree, with either of the contending factions.

If Vera Cruz was a priest-ridden place ten years ago, as from the number of ruined churches, monasteries, and convents I should be inclined to argue it may have been, no such charge can be brought against it now. Indeed, if for a long period the Mexican clergy enjoyed the privilege of riding over the rest of the community, it is very evident that, in these latter days, there has been a deal of riding over them. Nowhere else has Juarez—that arch-destroyer of religious foundations—left his mark so unmistakeably. In fact, during his occupation of Vera Cruz from 1858 to 1860, he proved an epidemic many degrees more fatal to churches than the yellow fever, which decimates the population in the summer months. For the yellow fever merely takes off one in ten, whereas Juarez destroyed the nine and left the one.

As seen from the sea, Vera Cruz presents rather an imposing spectacle, which is to be accounted for by its long array of towers and domes. But, as at Constantinople—to compare small things with great—the traveller has but to set his foot within the walls to be dis-illusionized in an instant. Of all its churches, San Francisco alone has been left available for religious services. As for the rest, where the walls are left standing, they have, for the most part, been converted into warehouses, and bales of cotton and hardware were to be seen piled up on the high altar. One church had been converted to a less profane use and was doing duty as a school.

He who has seen one town in New Spain has seen all. There is but one thing to be said in their favour, which is this, that they have the air of having been built to live in and not to be looked at.

They are hopelessly regular. The streets all cut each other at right angles, and it is the boast of Spaniards and Mexicans that you can see the country at the end of every street. The houses are mostly one-storied, and apparently substantially built, though the material generally used in their construction is simply a mud brick, called "adobe," baked in the sun. When coated with plaster, this brick has all the appearance of stone-work, and the traveller, unless he were informed of the contrary, would carry away the erroneous impression that the Mexican towns were built of stone. Carlyle's description of Mendoza, which he calls "cheerful, mud-built, whitewashed," will apply to every town in Mexico, Central and South America. The same author is equally happy in his delineation of Spanish Americans in general, who, according to him, are a set of "laughing, leathery, lying, sooty fellows."

However, beyond its whitewash there is little cheerfulness at Vera Cruz; for the grass grows in all the streets, and the rattle of a wheel over the stones is a sound quite unknown. A silence as of the tomb reigns, and you would suppose the place plague-stricken if you did not know that it was. An open gutter—manifestly with the view of harbouring the yellow-fever, or "vomito" as it is called—runs down the centre of every street, affording savory meat and drink to the "zopilotes," or vultures—the black scavengers of Mexican cities. As for these birds, it is a crime to kill one of them, and you can read in their deportment the consciousness of being the subject of legislation.

As for the shops in Vera Cruz, they are fairly supplied with an inferior quality of almost every article of which you can stand in need, though the principle on which a tradesman carries on business strikes a new-comer as somewhat strange. For instance, you go into a bookseller's store, and ask for a book which we will suppose is not to be had. With many expressions of regret, the shopman suggests that you may be in want of a pair of boots, or a piece of soap, which you probably end by buying.

I have read in a German work, which professes to give a faithful account of the manners and customs of the Mexicans, that, in the event of his running short of small change, a tradesman will not uncommonly request his customer to take his change out in a drink of brandy, a bundle of cigarettes, or even a ride on a mule kept saddled at the door for the purpose; but I never had the luck to meet with a case where this occurred. However I know that a somewhat similar proceeding prevails at Malta, where, in a religious book-store, I actually received a Chinese New Testament in lieu of threepence change due to me.

What little life of any sort exists at Vera Cruz, is divided between the market-place and the theatre—for even plague-stricken Vera Cruz has its theatre. A stroll through the market in the morning, "liquoring up" in the afternoon, and a visit to the theatre in the evening,—these are the excitements of the day at Vera Cruz.

In the market-place the traveller will enjoy a favourable opportunity of observing at his leisure the true type of Mexican Indian—the copper-coloured skin, the high cheek-bones, low forehead, the small slits, which do duty for eyes, and the straight black hair. The first thing that strikes you about these Indians is their extreme squalor and poverty-stricken appearance. If however, disregarding their miserable exterior, you watch them more nearly, you can scacely fail to be struck by a certain amount of refinement, and gentleness of manner, which seems at once to raise them above the negro, from whom they are also remarkably distinguished by their wiry slender build, and by the melancholy air, which seems so innate in them that they can hardly shake it off in the fits of drunkenness which are habitual with most of them. Only in the remote outlying provinces of the empire are the Indians of the savage scalping sort. In the accessible parts of the country, luckily for the rest of the population, of which the pure Indians make up nearly two-thirds, they are for the most part harmless; and only dangerous when their passions are excited by the priests, who exercise an extraordinary influence over them. As a rule, the Indians take no part nor interest in politics, though from time to time they follow chieftains of their own, such as Mejia, Lozada, and Alvarez into the field.

As for what is sold in the market-place, I will at once confess myself quite incompetent to enumerate the names of the strange fruits and vegetables, which are produced in lavish profusion by the tropical heat of the surrounding *Tierra Caliente*, and exposed in great heaps for sale in the markets of Vera Cruz. In the tropics—inasmuch as one lives perpetually in the atmosphere of a hot-house—one should by rights be a botanist, but if one is not, the unbotanical reader will perhaps overlook it. The lament of Columbus as to his own shortcomings in this respect is soothing to the unscientific traveller: "As I arrived at this Cape (Exumeta)," said he, "there came thence a fragrance so good and soft of the flowers and trees of the land, that it was the sweetest thing in the world. I believe there are here many herbs and trees which would be of great price in Spain for tinctures, medicines, and spices, but I know nothing of them, which gives me great concern."* However, as one cannot make one's way through a thicket without a certain number of prickly substances attaching themselves to one's clothes, so, in spite of oneself, the names of a few strange fruits will remain in one's memory; such, for instance, are the *chirimoya*, or custard-apple, the *zapotes*, and *granaditas*, which are daily set before the traveller in Mexico, in addition to apples, oranges, pine-apples, strawberries, mostly of a very inferior quality.

In the midst of huge piles of fruits and vegetables, you come upon stalls where half-naked Indians offer for sale rosaries and images of the Virgin, among which those of " Nuestra Señora de Guadalupe," of which I shall have occasion to speak later on, are always in immense request.

Not so much for what is to be seen on the stage, as for the grotesque appearance of the audience, is the theatre at Vera Cruz worth a visit. Men and women alike were for the most part dressed in white; a shirt and a pair of white trousers being considered full dress for gentlemen, while the ladies were attired in white muslin. Standing out in relief against this white back-ground was a sprinkling of black-coated individuals, who looked exceedingly hot and uncomfortable. For the sake of coolness, the sides and fronts of the boxes consist of open trellis work, so

* Washington Irving's "Life and Voyages of Columbus," vol. i. p. 102.

that you enjoy an uninterrupted view into your neighbours' premises. As we had paid six dollars (twenty-four shillings) for a box in the dress-circle, we were not a little surprised to find ourselves next to a party who could not boast of a pair of shoes or stockings among them. In spite of a very feeble performance, the theatre was crammed to overflowing, and the audience displayed extraordinary animation. From the aspect of its theatre, you would find it difficult to believe that Vera Cruz was the head-quarters of yellow fever.

I could not wish for my bitterest enemy a worse fate than to sleep at Vera Cruz without a mosquito-curtain, by an open window, with a "sereno" or watchman immediately below, whose duty it is to spring his rattle violently every quarter of an hour, and shout out into the night the state of the weather —a most senseless arrangement in a country where it never rains for eight months in the year, and rains continually for the other four. Such, alas! was my own lot, which, bad in itself, was aggravated by the annoyance of listening to the regular breathing of my companion, who, within his curtain, bade defiance to the mosquitos, which, after a few vain efforts to get at so promising a body, devoted their undivided energies to me. Two such nights, I am sure, would have driven me wild.

But before I have done with Vera Cruz, I must say

one word about its baths, which are deserving of the most unqualified praise. For cleanliness and general excellence of arrangement, they are quite unequalled in any place with which I am acquainted. Round three sides of a small garden plot, over which the broad plantain leaves throw a pleasant shade, are ranged the bathrooms, each fitted with its own marble basin, where you pass a delicious quarter of an hour in each day. If anything could, surely the baths should reconcile one to life at Vera Cruz.

Reconcile one! Yes, perhaps, if the *Norte* did not catch you as you emerge from the bathroom, filling your mouth, eyes, and ears with sand, and undoing in an instant all that the bath has done for you. While the *Norte* blows, all doors, windows, and apertures of every kind in the house must be closed, or it will fill with sand. So suddenly does the *Norte* spring up, that residents of Vera Cruz never go abroad in winter without spectacles, to save themselves from being blinded by the driving sand.

Woe to the washerwoman who has clothes out to dry when the *Norte* comes on to blow. Woe too to the traveller, who has given his clothes to be washed, and has to start on the morrow with his shirts turned into sandbags.

Yet, with all its concomitant ills, the *Norte* is welcomed at Vera Cruz, for it is the *Norte* alone which clears the air of the pestilential vapours with which it would otherwise be perpetually laden. It is the *Norte* to which Vera Cruz is indebted for its comparative immunity from *vomito* during the winter months.

And so, like the conversation there, my chapter on Vera Cruz ends, as it began, with the *Norte*.

CHAPTER II.

VERA CRUZ TO ORIZABA.

ON the passage out from England I had been fortunate enough to make the acquaintance of Don Antonio Escandon, who in 1861 had obtained from the government of Juarez a concession to construct a railway from Vera Cruz to the city of Mexico. Owing, however, to the disturbed state of the country, which was at first only made worse by foreign intervention, Don A. had been compelled to take temporary refuge with his family in Europe, and only the small portion of the line from Vera Cruz to Camaron, mentioned in the last chapter, had been completed as yet. During his residence in Europe, Don Antonio Escandon, foreseeing the impossibility of getting his railway satisfactorily constructed by a Mexican firm, had adopted the somewhat bold expedient of transferring his unconfirmed concession to an English company, only reserving certain rights and interests to himself and his heirs. Don A. E. was now returning to Mexico to get his concession confirmed by the Emperor's government, in which object he ultimately succeeded.

Thanks to this gentleman's kindness, after two days' detention at Vera Cruz, I obtained a seat in the special train, which was in waiting to convey his party and our old friend the Nuncio to Camaron, where private diligences were to be in readiness to carry us up the country. We had been cut down to the most meagre allowance of baggage, each passenger being restricted to 20 lbs. owing to the absolute impossibility of getting over Mexican roads at that season in a heavily-laden carriage. The rest of our baggage was to follow by slow stages, but no hope was held out of our receiving it before Christmas, which was sufficiently provoking, as it would involve the necessity either of missing the Christmas festivities, or of providing ourselves over again—at the exorbitant rate which Mexican tradesmen charge for everything—with necessary articles of dress, which we possessed already packed in our portmanteaux.

On Dec. 1, at 7 A.M. our train, consisting of three American cars, one for our party, one for the Nuncio, and one for his Nubian escort, drew out of the station at Vera Cruz, the locomotive giving vent to its feelings in a series of shrill bellowings, which on the other side of the Atlantic replace the European railway-whistle. Even at that early hour the sun was burning with a fierce heat, and I pitied the military and municipal authorities of Vera Cruz, who had turned out to do honour to the Nuncio, and stood exposed to its scorching rays.

On leaving Vera Cruz, the railway makes a detour to the southward, in order to avoid the sand hills, which hold the city in their cruel embrace—cruel because, but for them, Vera Cruz might be as comparatively healthy as the other towns along the coast. Such formidable sand-dams have been piled up to the landward of Vera Cruz, by the instrumentality of the *Nortes*, that no water can escape through into the sea. From this it results that the tract of country outside the sand-hills is in the rainy season converted into a pestilential marsh, which exhales those deadly miasmas which make Vera Cruz the grave of so many Europeans.

And now we had fairly entered upon the famous *Tierra Caliente*—a flowery wilderness of acacia, convolvulus, cactus, oleander, and a thousand other shrubs and plants, which I am incompetent to name—a region not so unlike what the Roman Campagna might develop into, were sufficient heat applied; but a Campagna without shepherds, ruins, or any kind of human interest. Not that the district is quite without inhabitants, for from time to time the traveller comes upon villages, tenanted by Indians, living, however, in such squalor and degradation, that they seem almost to belong to the brute creation. Over this desolate region the distant mysterious Peak of Orizaba holds his silent reign, and serves as a guiding star to the traveller on his way from the coast to the capital. Just such a scene as we were gazing upon then must Cortes have had stretched out before him, when, after burning his ships, he set out with his handful of followers to brave the Aztec monarch, enthroned beyond the mountains.

The journey from Vera Cruz to the city of Mexico —a distance of some 250 English miles—divides itself naturally into three stages, corresponding with the three climates of the country—which answer roughly to the three zones, into which the terrestrial globe is divided. Its *Tierra Caliente*, or hot region, extends from the sea to an elevation of some 3,000 ft.; its *Tierra Templada*, or temperate region, between the elevations of 3,000 and 5,000 ft.; and its *Tierra Fria*, or cold region, from 5,000 ft. upwards, attaining in the valley of Mexico 7,190 ft.; and in the valley of Toluca, the highest story of the country, 8,450. The mean temperature of the *Tierra Caliente* is 77° Fahrenheit; of the *Tierra Templada*, 68° to 70°; in the city of Mexico (*Tierra Fria*) the mean temperature is 64.° Each of these districts is distinguished by its own peculiar vegetation, and where the transition

* Chevalier's "Mexico, Ancient and Modern," vol. ii. pp. 102–104.

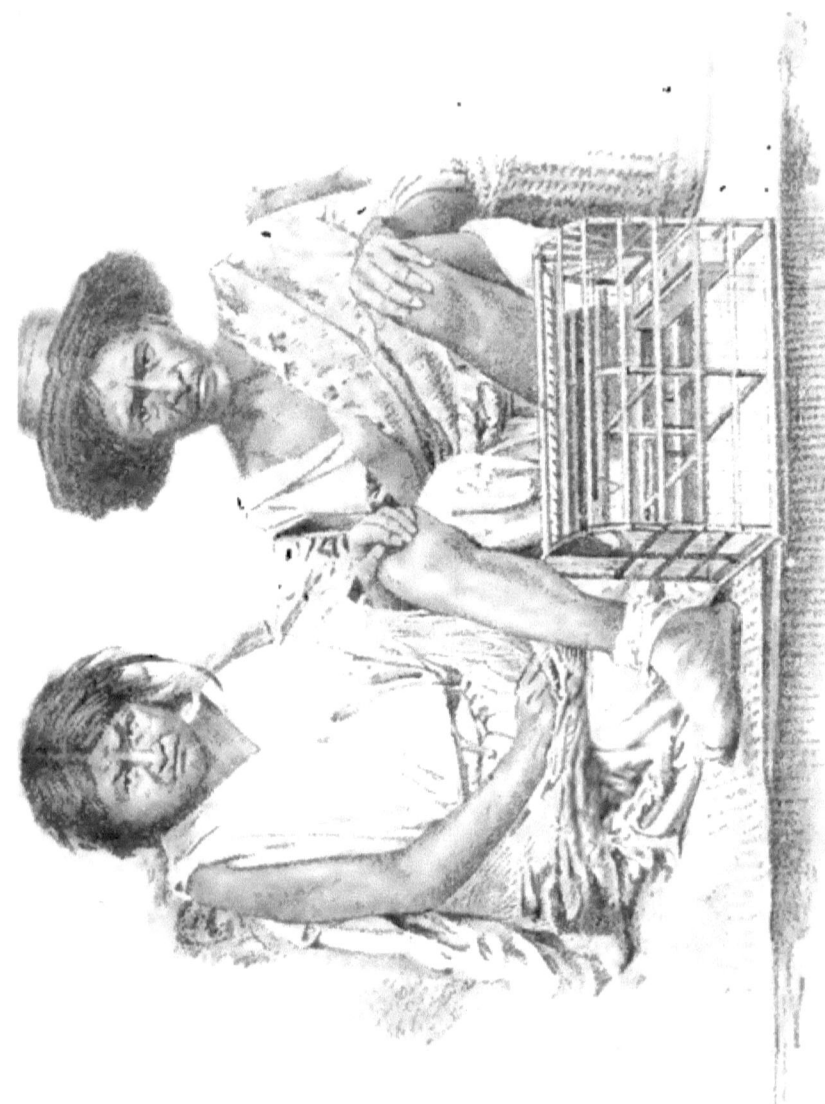

from one to the other is sudden, the effect is very striking. Unhappily, however, this is not the case on the most frequented road in the country—that from Vera Cruz to the city of Mexico; so that travellers, whose experience is confined to this single road, have little conception of the wonderful effects produced by the sudden contrasts of climate in other parts of the country. For instance, the traveller going down from Mexico to Acapulco, on the Pacific coast, from the summit of the pass, which leads out of the valley of Mexico, a region of almost perpetual snow, beholds in the valley of Cuernavaca, which is stretched out at his feet, a tropical vegetation, and a few hours of descent bring him into the midst of sugar and coffee plantations.

In M. Chevalier's "Mexico, Ancient and Modern" —a work which was evidently inspired by the French Imperial Government—the following passage occurs (Vol. ii. p. 144): "To the traveller desiring to pass through Mexico after landing at Vera Cruz, on his way to Acapulco, which is at the foot of the other slope, the distance (*as the crow flies*) is but 345 miles, nearly that between Paris and Bordeaux." Now this passage is, to say the least of it, misleading, for by the shortest cut, at the lowest computation, it is quite impossible to reduce the distance from Vera Cruz to Acapulco, *viâ* the city of Mexico, to less than 500 miles. In this computation, 97 leagues are allowed from Vera Cruz to the city of Mexico, and 103 from the city of Mexico to Acapulco, the two distances together making a total of 200 leagues, which is over 500 miles, for the usual reckoning of $2\frac{1}{2}$ miles to the league is slightly below the mark.

Some thirty miles from Vera Cruz—with difficulty accomplished in two hours, owing to the slippery state of the rails, occasioned by the tremendous fall of dew—stands La Soledad, the principal settlement in that portion of the *Tierra Caliente*, and the centre of the French military operations. Perched high on the abrupt banks of the River Jamapa, which has there cut itself a deep bed in the crumbling rock, La Soledad, with its pleasant shade, presents a most inviting aspect, as seen from the rickety wooden railway bridge, which has there been thrown across the stream as a makeshift. For some reason best known to itself, our train, after safely traversing this frail structure—which, like all other bridges on the line, was only built to last six months—suddenly ran back again, as if to give the bridge another chance, and halted for at least ten minutes in the very centre, to the no small consternation of the female members of our party. Nor were their fears by any means groundless; for, only three months after we passed the spot, one of these bridges actually gave way, occasioning great loss of life and limb to a battalion of Zouaves, which, after distinguished service, was returning to Vera Cruz for the purpose of embarking for France.

However, we had the luck to get safely over the bridge a second time, and in less than an hour found ourselves landed high and dry at Camaron, the then terminus of the railway, consisting of an extemporary collection of wooden huts, which have since moved on with the railway to its present terminus, Paso del Macho, at the foot of the Chiquihuite Pass. A less promising place to find oneself stranded, and left to one's own resources, I could not imagine; but such was very far from being our lot, for we were at once taken charge of by the contractors of the line, and conducted by them to their wooden dwelling, and there entertained by them with a hospitality so extraordinary that one could not help regarding it as intended as a set-off against the imminent risk of our lives to which they had subjected us.

As for the *Nuncio*, on his arrival at Camaron he was hurried into a "volante," a sort of gig with elongated shafts, got over from Havana for the purpose, and whirled off towards the capital in the midst of a black cloud of Nubians—the Crescent doing homage to the Cross in lending true believers to form the escort of the envoy of the Pope; and here, for the present, we will take leave of the *Nuncio*.

On the conclusion of our magnificent repast, we were informed that the diligences were in waiting to convey us on our way, and, on issuing from our wooden banquet hall, we found a couple of unwieldy red coaches drawn up outside. To each coach were yoked eight mules—two in the shafts, then four abreast, and two leaders. On nearer inspection, the bloated appearance of the vehicles was accounted for by the discovery that each contained three seats inside, instead of two, like ordinary diligences, a broad leathern strap being slung across the carriage to serve as a back to the middle seat.

Now the question arose, how to stow away our numerous party, for Don Antonio Escandon was not returning to Mexico unattended. The Don himself had stayed behind at Vera Cruz, and was to follow on the morrow with the bearer of his privy purse—late Minister of Justice in Miramon's cabinet—and the light division of his retinue. The heavy division, to which I found myself attached, consisted of Don Vincente Escandon, Don Antonio's brother, the Donna Catalina, and her five young children—the youngest, a baby in arms, Carlotta, to whom the Empress had given her name, a very paragon of a baby, for it was never once heard to cry from the day we left Southampton to the day we reached Mexico. Then there were two Mexican Indian maids with a wonderful capacity for making the most delicious chocolate at odd times, and a French *bonne*, who astonished us one day by declaring her opinion that

England must be a miserable country to live in, because the land was entirely in the hands of the rich. Then there was the English governess, the English valet, the French tutor, and the Spanish financial secretary, with his wife, daughter, and two sons, the whole in charge of Mr. Grandison of Orizaba, aided by a French courier endowed with a genius for contriving sumptuous repasts in wild places. The Belgian gardener, the English coachman and groom, with four horses and two terriers, were to follow by slow stages. Finally, a Spanish hidalgo in reduced circumstances was to bring up the rear, with the convoy of waggons in which the heavy baggage was stowed away.

After holding a council of war, it was decided to convert one of the diligences into a nursery, which arrangement met with very general approbation, and by dint of close packing, the other diligence was got to hold the rest of the party. However, being anxious to see a little more of the country than would be feasible from the inside of a diligence, I gladly availed myself of the offer of one of our hosts to lend me a horse to ride. The beast, however, had to be caught, and a "mozo," or farm servant, was sent into the bush with a lasso for the purpose.

In the meantime the diligences set off without me, so I had nothing for it but to resign myself to a second glass of whisky and water, and the amusing conversation of my host, whom, from his way of talking, I at once set down for an Irishman, but learnt afterwards that he was a British Canadian. In the course of conversation he informed me that, previous to undertaking the contract for the railway, on which he was then engaged, he had edited an English newspaper in Mexico called The *Mexican Extraordinary*, which, under the circumstances, I could not help thinking an admirable name, for no ordinary journal could have had a ghost of a chance of success in a country where English is so little read or understood. The *Mexican Extraordinary*, of course, turned out a failure, and so the ex-newspaper editor took to railway making.

My host informed me that, having lately received insulting letters from the railway superintendent, he had taken the liberty of giving the fellow a horse-whipping, which had unfortunately brought the French authorities down about his ears. For that, instead of calling him out like a man, the cowardly superintendent had gone and told Colonel Marechal, the French commandant at Vera Cruz.

Now, as ill luck would have it, my host had unfortunately already incurred the displeasure of this gallant officer by opposing himself to a little plan by which the colonel thought to immortalise himself. For it appears that, struck by the impropriety of the name "La Soledad," "the waste," for the spot, which, from its salubrity and charming position, the French had selected for their headquarters in that unhealthy district, Colonel Marechal had entertained the ambitious project of changing its name from "La Soledad" to "Marechal," and had actually obtained the requisite authorisation from the government. None the less, however, my host would insist in calling the place "La Soledad."

Here then was the Colonel's opportunity, and he was not slow to profit by it. For, summoning his Nubian myrmidons around him, he at once ordered an express train, and proceeded in high dudgeon to Camaron to wreak his vengeance on him who had had the audacity to oppose his ambitious scheme. Arrived at Camaron, the infuriated Colonel at once marched to the enemy's quarters, where he found his foe, and arrested him on the charge of disturbing the public peace. Then, forcing his prisoner into the train, he carried him off to Vera Cruz, and threw him into prison. The matter, however, coming to the ears of Mr. Ledward, the English consul, representations were made in the proper quarter, and, at the expiration of two or three days, an order was sent down from Mexico by telegraph to release the prisoner at once.

On my suggesting to my host, that his life at Camaron could hardly be an agreeable one, exposed as he was on the one hand to the insults of the authorities, and on the other to the constant danger of falling a victim to the deadly climate of the *Tierra Caliente*, like a second Mark Tapley, he would not admit for a moment that he had anything to complain of, declaring with some warmth that his life was a very jolly one.

At this point our conversation was broken in upon by the arrival of a couple of hot and dusty English engineers, who had ridden down from Orizaba on their way to Vera Cruz to meet some friends, who had just arrived from England. On their road down these gentlemen had encountered the *cortège* of the Nuncio, which the sight of their revolvers had thrown into a state of great alarm. Being taken by the escort for brigands, they were at once arrested and brought before the Nuncio, who, on satisfying himself of the mistake, ordered them to be discharged.

In the meantime my steed had been led in captive, and was brought round to the door fully caparisoned with the bran new saddlery which I had brought out from England. The poor little beast—for it was nothing more than a pony—seemed quite crushed by the amount of trappings which hung about him a world too big for his slender proportions. Listening to the advice of my London saddler, I had provided myself with every conceivable article of saddlery which could be required on a riding tour in a hilly country. In addition to saddle and bridle, my pony was rigged out with crupper; valise, with pad to prevent the valise from galling the animal's back; a pair of enormous holsters, one to hold pistols, the other fitted with a tin to hold water; hunting breast-plate, to prevent the saddle slipping off behind, while going up steep places; and finally a long halter wound round his neck. This last article gave the beast so forlorn an appearance, that it looked for all the world as if it had been mercifully added to provide the animal with a means of putting an end to his existence by hanging, should life become a burden to him.

On such a beast and so accoutred I launched forth alone into the wilds in pursuit of the diligences. My road lay across a level plain overgrown with dwarf acacia and low underwood quite incapable of affording any kind of shade—on the whole as uninteresting a tract of country as one could wish to ride over. The heat too became intense, and I began to regret having declined a seat in the diligence. However I was drawing nigh to the hills, which lay stretched out before me, clothed to their very tops with a dense matted vegetation.

From time to time the stony track, dignified by the name of road, which I was following, suddenly dived down into a deep gully, called in Mexico "barranca," of which the banks are so abrupt that you have no notice of them till you find yourself pulled up on the very brink. At the bottom of these *barrancas* you generally find a sluggish muddy stream, blocked up with boulders, on which scantily-clad Indian women may be often seen kneeling, and going through the form of washing their clothes.

Whether Mexicans are by nature brigands, or whether they were tempted to become so by the configuration of the country, I will not presume to decide, but this much is certain, that no country in the world could be more admirably adapted for this purpose than Mexico. The sides of these *barrancas*, which are for the most part densely wooded, are the favourite lurking-place of brigands, and just as the beggars used to avail themselves of the steepness of the hill at Aricia, as Juvenal tells us, up which vehicles could only go at a foot pace, so Mexican brigands spring out upon their prey, as they begin to climb the opposite bank of the *barranca*.

Having been informed at Vera Cruz that this portion of the *Tierra Caliente* was infested by "guerilleros," I was in constant expectation of falling in with them, and when I came suddenly upon a party of wild-looking horsemen, I gave myself up for lost. When I learnt that these fellows were Mexican lancers, and had formed part of the escort of the Nuncio, I was lost in astonishment that such slovenly ill-conditioned looking villains could make a pretence of belonging to any army in the world.

A fifteen mile ride, which I accomplished in two

hours and a half, brought me to Paso del Macho, a small town at the foot of the hills. Here, to my no small satisfaction, I found the diligences drawn up in front of the inn—the very inn at the entrance of which a few weeks before the regular diligence had stopped with the driver shot dead upon the box.

It was now 3 P.M. and Potrero, the next possible sleeping-place, being, owing to the infamous state of the roads, at least five hours distant, it was decided to pass the night at Paso del Macho, and accordingly we took possession of the whole of the inn, which was kept by a very knowing fellow, who was reported to have made a fortune as captain of a slaver. To explain his present position, he informed me that, although he had plenty of money to live upon anywhere, he could not stand a do-nothing life, and had set up as a Mexican innkeeper simply as a means of amusing himself.

However, whatever his past history may have been, it soon became evident that the fellow understood his business; for, to the general surprise of us all, who had been prepared for any amount of roughing it on the road, we found our dinner spread with an air of taste and luxury which would have done credit to a Parisian restaurant. If the dinner itself did not quite reach the excellence of the *Café Riche* or *Les Trois Frères*, it was wonderfully good considering all things; and the champagne was first-rate. Nor do I think the bill of

20*l.* which included the board and lodging of the whole party, was under the circumstances extravagant.

The lodging, however, turned out very inferior to the board, which was altogether an exceptional phenomenon at a Mexican roadside inn. As we had to get up at 3 A.M. we thought it prudent to retire early; so, after a stroll in the town, during which we stumbled upon a telegraph office in a street which was like a ploughed field, to bed we went at 9 P.M. but not to sleep, for what with rats, mosquitos, and jackals it was well nigh impossible to close one's eyes.

After a night spent in continual dread lest the huge black rats, which chased one another wildly about the room, should get into one's bed, and in listening to the whining bark of the jackals outside, it was a relief when the *mozo* appeared with a light, and declared it was time to get up.

By 4 A.M. we had swallowed the chocolate, without which no Mexican ever thinks of making a start, and soon after, the diligences rolled away into the darkness. I mounted my pony and followed, but to my dismay the diligences, after floundering through the mud for about a hundred yards, suddenly went off in opposite directions, leaving me in the mire, and strangely perplexed to know which to follow when I should have emerged on to dry ground. For the moment I thought that my pony and I would have been quite overwhelmed by the mud, but the little beast made a gallant and successful effort to extricate himself, and I started off in pursuit of the diligence which had last disappeared in the darkness. As soon as I came up with it, the driver applied to me to inform him what had become of the other diligence—a piece of information which I was utterly unable to afford. So we had nothing for it, but to halt till day-break.

Soon after day had dawned the second diligence joined us, and all went on comparatively smoothly. We had now fairly commenced the ascent of the hills leading to the *Tierra Templada*, or temperate region, in which Cordova and Orizaba are both situate. The heat, however, was by no means tempered, for the sun scorched us more unmercifully than the preceding day as we toiled up the steep zig-zags of the Chiquihuite Pass—a well-known position in the annals of Mexican warfare. Cannon—eloquent of past struggles—were still lying by the roadside, half overgrown by the rank vegetation. As we stood gazing at the view from the summit of the pass, the torrent roaring a thousand feet below us, Mr. G. remarked to me that, from his painful experience of the deadliness of the climate, he could affirm with certainty, that of the labourers who were about to commence the work of carrying the railway through the pass, but a very small percentage would be alive at the end of the period requisite to complete the undertaking.

The Chiquihuite is the pass behind which the allies bound themselves to retire in case the peace negotiations should break down, when the Mexican Government allowed them to pass unmolested to take up a more healthy position in the hills. It is only fair to add, that in this instance the French did keep their word to the letter, in spite of the unfairness and dishonesty which characterized their first proceedings in Mexico. Strange to say, no opposition was offered to their second passage.

From Chiquihuite to Potrero the road is so bad, that in the rainy season the diligence is sometimes compelled to cease running for a month together; and men and mules are not unfrequently overwhelmed in the slush. Col. Van der Smissen, of the Belgian legion, whom I met subsequently in Mexico, informed me that on their march up to the capital some of his men had actually been forced to resort to swimming to save their lives. So notoriously infamous is one portion of the road, that it has been christened "Sal si puedes," "get out of it if you can." Get out of it our diligences did, but how they managed it will be to me for ever a mystery.

The subjoined extract, from an account of a journey from Vera Cruz to the capital, which recently appeared in the *Indépendance Belge*, shows that the condition of this road has not improved:—

"M. Langlais, the French deputy who was sent over

to Mexico, to inspect the finances, has had rather a rough time of it. He started from Vera Cruz for the capital on the 12th of October by rail, and arrived safely at Paso del Macho, a wretched hole, where the line ends for the present. That dismal locality was encumbered by 400 soldiers, and M. le Deputé had to wander about, without bed or supper, and finally esteemed himself lucky in finding a resting place under a barn. On the following day he started under an escort of six soldiers, but he had barely travelled seven miles and a half when his carriage was upset in a bog. He was fortunate enough to extricate himself; the carriage gradually sank and disappeared. He procured another, and on the 14th resumed his journey; but the same ill-luck attended him; the vehicle was smashed in the bad roads of the Cumbres, and on the 16th he was still at 80 leagues (200 miles) from the capital, under drenching rain and bad roads. An ancient Roman would have turned back after all these adverse signs, but M. Langlais went on. Let us hope his perseverance may be rewarded with success."

After five hours' toiling through a forest jungle, along what I sincerely hope to be the most execrable high road in the world, we at length emerged into the open, where, surrounded by a magnificent amphitheatre of hills, stands the straggling *hacienda* of Potrero. Here we found a battalion of the 99th

French regiment of the line encamped upon the grass in front of the *hacienda*, engaged upon their midday meal, which the officers were enjoying at a table spread under the portico of the *hacienda*. The colonel, who was exceedingly affable, informed us that he was on his march to Vera Cruz, to re-embark his men for France.

Notwithstanding the presence of the French, the gentleman whom I took to be the proprietor received us with great *empressement;* which was explained when I learned that he merely farmed the *hacienda*, which, like most other things on the road thus far belonged to the Escandon family. At the end of a most substantial breakfast, our host, Herr Fink, informed us that nothing had been set before us which had not been produced on the estate, even down to the rum, coffee, and sugar.

After breakfast, Herr Fink showed us over his *hacienda*, which seemed admirably conducted. He informed us that the land on which he was now raising crops of coffee, sugar, cotton, tobacco, &c. with equal success, had been but a few years previously reclaimed from the surrounding jungle, and insisted upon it that Anglo-Saxon industry and enterprise alone were wanting to make the country one of the most productive in the world. The best proof of the truth of this remark was certainly to be found in the success with which his own industry had been crowned. What would M. Chevalier, with his Latin race theory, have said to this?

It seems now to be generally agreed that of the three Mexican climates the *Tierra Templada*, or temperate region, alone is adapted for European colonisation on a large scale. If the reader will take the trouble to glance at the map at the beginning of the volume, he will at once see the region I refer to. On either slope of the treeless Mexican table-land runs, at the elevation of from 3,000 to 5,000 feet above the sea, a green zone of surprising fertility, about 1,000 English miles long, and of the average breadth of 70 miles. Here such crops as quinine, vanille, cochineal, jalap, coffee, sugar, cotton, tobacco, &c. which will always find a ready sale in the markets of Europe, can be produced probably to greater advantage than in any district in the known world.

As for the *Tierra Fria*, or cold region, it produces certainly every kind of cereal where water is to be had for irrigation; but, except in the mining districts, there are no fortunes to be carved out of it; and the climate of the *Tierra Caliente* will always render it uninhabitable to Europeans.

From Potrero to Cordova—the first town of any importance on the road from Vera Cruz to Mexico— is an easy ride of a couple of hours. The road, with the exception of one infamous bit at the entrance of

Cordova, is, for Mexico, wonderfully good. About a mile before reaching Cordova, we suddenly came upon a covey of huge church bells, which, to the number of twenty-nine, were lying high and dry in the middle of the road. Unable to destroy the churches altogether, as at Vera Cruz, the Liberals had contented themselves with maiming them by cutting their tongues out.

The position of Cordova, encircled by belts of orange groves and surrounded on every side by mountains, is as strikingly fine as the aspect of the town is dreary. After following an ill-paved street, with an open drain running down the middle, for nearly half a mile, you find yourself landed in the Plaza Mayor, a dreary open space surrounded on three sides by shabby one-storied houses, while the fourth side is taken up by the cathedral—a huge straggling building a world too big for the place. Neither in the market-place, nor in the streets leading out of its four corners, was any sign of life except such as was given by some swaggering French soldiers, who informed me that they were invalided home, and seemed to avail themselves of the circumstance to get drunk with impunity.

However, thanks to the hospitality of one of the principal citizens, who as usual turned out to be a vassal of Don Antonio Escandon, we were entertained at a banquet, at which the delicacies of every season and either hemisphere were combined. While we were feasting upon the fat of the land, it gave an additional relish to everything to learn that the Emperor and Empress, on their arrival at Cordova half starved, had been hardly able to get a cup of chocolate and a piece of dry bread, as it could not be settled to whom the privilege of entertaining their majesties rightfully belonged.

After the banquet, we adjourned to the balcony to enjoy the view of the mountains, and I think I never witnessed anything so magnificent as the appearance of the Peak of Orizaba bathed in the moonlight.

Next morning, which was Saturday, we continued our journey, having an easy day's work before us. For the distance from Cordova to Orizaba, where we intended to pass the Sunday, is barely eight leagues (or twenty English miles, reckoning two and a half miles to the league), which might easily be accomplished in three hours were the road moderately good. As it turned out, the diligences occupied six hours in the transit.

But if the road itself is bad, its badness is amply atoned for by the beauty of the scenery, and you felt that it would have been a thousand pities to get over the ground at a quicker rate.

Orizaba, which lies some 4,000 feet above the level of the sea, is reached by two distinct ladders of zig-zags, with a plateau several miles broad intervening between the two. Till within a few hundred feet of the summit of the second zig-zag, the hill-sides are overgrown to their very summits with the same dense matted jungle with which the traveller is first struck on the Chiquihuite pass. When this rank vegetation ceases, the hills are either quite bare, or only scantily clothed with dwarf shrubs.

Landed on the plateau on which lies the town of Orizaba, the traveller sees stretched out before him a large grassy plain, bordered on the right by a bold mountain block. Beyond this plain, in a dip of the ground, lies Orizaba, quite embedded in orange groves.

CHAPTER III.

ORIZABA TO PUEBLA.

THE traveller whose main object is fine scenery should go no further than Orizaba. Were he, instead of climbing the Cumbres, which lead to the bare, unsightly table-land, to turn to the right, and keep in the green zone along the slope of the hills till he reached Jalapa, and return thence *viâ* Tampico or Vera Cruz to Europe, he would declare, when he got home, that Mexico was the most enchanting country in the world. The beautiful approach to the Mexican table-land through the *Tierra Caliente* and the *Tierra Templada* is as deceptive as the magnificent facades to their poor cathedrals, or the handsome stone gateways, leading absolutely to nothing, on which you often stumble in different parts of the country.

When you have reached Orizaba, you may reckon that you have accomplished one-third of the journey to the city of Mexico. If the sun has been scorching, you could, at any rate, escape from him temporarily at any time by diving into the woods which line the road so far, at the risk, however, of getting covered with venomous insects. Henceforward, the sun will burn with a scarcely less fierce heat, and you may seek in vain for a bit of shade for leagues upon leagues. At the most you may find an overgrown cactus, under whose oval, prickly, fingerless hands—suggestive of flesh-scrapers used to produce friction after a bath—you may crouch for an hour at midday, in imminent danger of lacerating your person. This lamentable absence of trees extends over the whole length and breadth of the Mexican table-land, which may be compared to a yellowish-brown table-cloth, from which the *Tierras Templada* and *Caliente* hang down like a green fringe. On this point Prescott remarks: "In the time of the Aztecs the table-land was thickly covered with larch, oaks, cypress, and other forest trees, the extraordinary dimensions of some of which, remaining to the present day, show that the curse of barrenness in later times is chargeable more on man than on nature. Indeed, the early Spaniards made as indiscriminate war on the forests as did our Puritan ancestors, though with much less reason. After once conquering the country they had no lurking ambush to fear from the submissive semicivilized Indians, and were not, like our ancestors, obliged to keep watch and ward for a century. This spoliation of the ground, however, is said to have been pleasing to their imaginations, as it reminded them of the plains of their own Castile, the table-land of Europe; where the nakedness of the landscape forms the burden of every traveller's lament who visits that country." *

However dull a place Orizaba might prove to live in, it would be hard to find a more ideal place to repose at for a Sunday after a fatiguing week. And when I speak of Orizaba, I mean Cocolapam, just without the town, where Mr. Grandison, the manager and part owner of the contiguous, cotton, calico and paper factories, entertained us with a truly Scotch hospitality. The reader by this time will take it for granted that the greater part of the factories belonged to the Escandon family.

If there is more life at Orizaba than at Cordova, the factories at Cocolapam are the cause of it. Attached to the factories are large blocks of dwellings for the workpeople, who are mostly Indians. As compared with the Indians who work in the fields, these operatives, although as much addicted to drunkenness, are certainly raised a step—or perhaps only half a step—higher in civilization. From the appearance of their dwellings, you could see that they were beginning to feel more wants, and supply themselves with little comforts as yet unknown to the agricultural labourers.

Sunday being market day all over Mexico, we had

* Book i. cap. i.

an excellent opportunity of observing the country-people, who flocked into Orizaba in great numbers. Compared with the costume of the peasantry in any part of Europe, the dress of the Indians is singularly unpicturesque. Indeed, they can hardly be said to dress at all, for in the hot country they go nearly naked, and even in the cold region the men wear nothing but a calico shirt and drawers, and on their heads a straw hat, with brim sufficiently broad to serve as a sun-shade to their wives and children, who invariably go bare-headed. If you look down on a crowd of Indians collected in the market-place, you see nothing but a waving sea of straw hats.

A wholesome custom prevails in Mexico of exposing the criminals to the gaze of the people assembled in the market-place. With this end in view, a conspicuous spot is chosen for the prison, where the prisoners are stared at through the iron bars, like wild beasts in a cage. As we moved along with the crowd, we too took our peep at the prisoners; but I must confess that I failed to discover any one among them with an expression of countenance at all approaching in villainy that of the sentinel on guard over them.

A little further on we came upon a booth, where "pulque," the celebrated drink of the Mexican table-land, was being dispensed to the thirsty multitude. *Pulque* is to the Mexican what his beer is to the

Englishman, and, when Cortes conquered the country, it was the ordinary beverage of the Aztecs. Indeed, it is the most genuine relic of them that remains. Perhaps, when everything else English has disappeared, Lord Macaulay's New Zealander may find our small beer still surviving. Having heard the wholesome qualities of *pulque* much extolled, we determined to give it a trial. In appearance it is something like the milk of the cocoa nut, but its smell is suggestive of rotten eggs. First attempts at drinking *pulque* are invariably failures, and so was ours, but we were assured we had only to persevere, and we should end by drinking nothing else. This prophecy turned out so far true in my case, that subsequently I drank *pulque* whenever I could get it; but so I did every other drink one came across, for the highly rarified air of the table-land induces insatiable thirst.

Pulque is a milky juice, extracted from the American agave or maguey, of which you find the finest specimens in the Llanos de Apam, some thirty miles to the north-east of the city of Mexico. If the plant is left unmilked, a stem some fifteen feet high, exactly like a Brobdignag asparagus stalk, will shoot up out of the middle of the bunch of broad, pointed leaves, like sword blades, which form its base.

In order to milk the plant, you must wait till it is ready to flower, and then cut the heart out, when the juice, which would have otherwise fed the main stem of the plant, will run into the hollow thus formed. From this hollow the liquid is drawn off by suction into skins. Before the process of fermentation sets in, the *pulque* is sweet and scentless, and in this state is generally preferred by beginners, although inveterate *pulque* drinkers consider it insipid. To aid the process of fermentation, a little " madre pulque," or " pulque mother," is added, and the *pulque* gradually acquires its intoxicating properties, and flavour of rotten eggs.

The Indians being for the most part deeply engaged all Sunday morning in buying and selling, the priest dispenses with their attendance at mass, requiring of them only to dip their fingers in the holy water, and kiss the crucifix which is handed round the market-place, and to fall down on their knees whenever they shall hear the tinkle of the bell in the church announcing the elevation of the host.

Orizaba, which is already a considerable town, will soon become a place of great importance, as it has been fixed upon by the engineers of the Imperial Mexican Railway Company as their principal station between Vera Cruz and the capital. To be ready for the expected influx of visitors, Mr. Grandison is erecting an elegant theatre from his own designs.

During the Orizaba conferences, which terminated in the breaking up of the triple alliance between France, England, and Spain, Sir Charles Wyke and

Commodore Dunlop were, as a matter of course lodged at Cocolapam. During their stay, an amusing incident occurred. It appears that, one fine morning, a French officer passing that way was, naturally enough, struck by the pleasant airy look of the place; and, unaware that it was already occupied by the English, was proceeding to march his men in at the gates, with a view to establishing himself there, when he was considerably taken aback by hearing himself rated in good round terms, in bad French, from an open window. Looking up, he perceived an officer in the English naval uniform; this officer was Commodore Dunlop, who had just ridden up from Vera Cruz, with a dozen mounted marines, horse marines thus becoming a reality for once. The affair, which was described as throughout extremely ludicrous, ended by the French beating a precipitate retreat.

At Orizaba I made my first investment in Mexican horseflesh, giving ninety dollars for an animal which was barely worth forty. On this animal, whose subsequent performances by no means came up to the great promise which he evinced on trial, I continued my journey to Mexico, in the company of a young Pole, who was about to take service in the Imperial army.

As had been arranged before starting, Don Antonio and the light division overtook us at Orizaba; but our company was already so thinned by sickness and other causes that two diligences still sufficed to carry on the combined forces.

With daylight on Monday morning we made our start for Puebla, proposing to accomplish the 38 leagues (95 English miles) in two days, halting for the night at San Augustin del Palmar. Just outside the western *garita* (barrier) of Orizaba rises up abruptly the hill of Borrego, celebrated for a dashing episode, by which the French in a great measure retrieved the *prestige* which they lost by the repulse of their first attack on Puebla. Consequent on that disastrous event, the French found themselves compelled to retreat upon Orizaba to await reinforcements from France. Upon this the Mexican general Zaragoza made bold to take the initiative; and, marching down with the greater part of his forces to Orizaba, took up a position to the rear of the hill of Borrego, and summoned the French general Lawrencez to surrender. This summons was, of course, treated with contempt, and, night having set in, both sides prepared for battle on the morrow, the Mexicans from their recent success and superior numbers being quite confident of gaining the victory. At 2 A.M. a company of the 99th French infantry was sent up the steep face of the hill to reconnoitre the enemy's position. Unaware that the Mexicans had meanwhile pushed forward their advanced posts over the crest of the hill, and thrown up a battery on the townward side, the French were advancing quite unsuspiciously, when they suddenly found themselves under the muzzles of the enemy's guns. The gunners, however, were fast asleep, and no sentries posted to give the alarm, the Mexicans considering their position on that side inaccessible. To get possession of the battery, and to turn the guns on the enemy, was the work of a few minutes, and Orizaba was awakened from its slumbers by the roar of artillery.

Taken completely by surprise, the Mexicans offered little or no resistance, and their whole army (according to the French version of the story) fled before a single company. The Mexicans, however, assert that the main body of their army was encamped at a village two leagues off, where General Zaragoza had established his head-quarters, and that only their vanguard was put to flight in the manner above related. However, whatever be the truth of the story, the Mexicans at any rate beat a hasty retreat to Puebla, and confined themselves thenceforward to the defensive.

At Aculzingo, a small village near the foot of the Cumbres, the first of two tremendous mountain staircases by which you ascend from the plateau of Orizaba to that of Puebla, we overtook the diligences, and found the party sitting down to breakfast under a tumble-down portico clinging on to the ruins of a straggling mud-brick building, which called itself a "fonda" or *restaurant*.

Throughout Mexico the kind of road-side accommodation which a traveller finds is as follows:—In the Indian villages he will see exposed for sale at the windows of many of the cottages "aguardiente," a fiery kind of whisky, "pan dolce" (bread cakes), onions, oranges, and cigarettes. In cases of emergency he may pass the night in one of these cottages, where a guest's chamber is sometimes set apart.

In the small towns the traveller will find a dirty "meson," more like an Oriental caravansery than an European inn, where he can be accommodated with a windowless cell with a wooden arrangement in the corner, a few planks raised above the floor, intended to do duty as a bed. With more than this the *meson* will not furnish him. To get anything to eat or drink the traveller must go to the *fonda*, or *restaurant*, which is an institution quite distinct. The *fonda* in its turn is supplied from the adjoining "tienda," or general store. This threefold arrangement of *meson, fonda, tienda*, exists all over the country.

However, along the roads over which their diligences run the proprietors have established "casas de diligentias," diligence houses, where, for the most part, very fair accommodation is to be had. But if the traveller fails to keep step with this arrangement, *i.e.* if, being on horseback and unable to accomplish the great distances which the diligence gets over in a day, he attempts to sleep at a breakfasting place, or anywhere but at the appointed sleeping place, he will generally find himself as badly off as in the least frequented parts of the country.

If nothing else is to be got at the *fonda*, "frijoles," a kind of broad bean, peculiar to Mexico and universal there, eggs, rice, "tortillas," leathery pancakes made of Indian corn, and a general substitute for bread, and chocolate are always to be had. On these articles of food the traveller will soon learn to make a very hearty meal. Milk is hardly ever to be had,* and cheese and butter are almost unknown luxuries.

Being somewhat tired after my twenty miles ride before breakfast, I was not sorry to accept the offer of a seat in the diligence for the next stage, but I soon had cause to repent of this arrangement.

The ascent of the Cumbres of Aculcingo is tremendously difficult. To avoid it the engineers of the railway company intend to carry their line up a side valley, and reach the plateau of Puebla by the more gradual ascent of the Maltratta Pass. In this pass the most formidable obstacle to be surmounted is a deep ravine or *barranca*, across which the company is throwing a bridge 300 feet high, with three arches, each 300 feet wide. In Switzerland I know of no bit of road, which can compare in steep-

* The Aztecs were quite unacquainted with the use of milk.

ness with the ascent of the Cumbres. Hardly by putting forth their utmost strength can the wretched mules drag a carriage up the precipitous zig-zags. But when it comes to heavily-laden waggons, whole days are taken up in the ascent.

Half way up we overtook some machinery on its way to the great mining establishment at Real del Monte, which lies in a delightful region 60 miles to the northeast of the city of Mexico. To watch the desperate efforts of the mules, of which I counted twenty-eight attached to one waggon, to move the heavy loads, their eyes almost starting out of their heads as they strained every nerve, was painful in the extreme. The difficulty was of course to get them to pull all together. If cracking of whips and loud shoutings could have made the wheels turn round, the thing would have been soon done, for if Bedlam had broken loose, the noise and confusion could not have been wilder.

On reaching the summit of Cumbres No. 1, instead of finding yourself on the expected plateau, you perceive that you have but come up the hill to go down again, and before you know where you are, the diligence is whirling you at a tremendous pace downhill, making a succession of wild bounds from rock to rock. If your skull is not of more than ordinary thickness, it will probably be fractured during the descent, with such tremendous violence is your head brought into contact with the roof of the diligence. I hardly know which is more painful, the blow to your head, or the violence done to your stomach by the jarring thump with which you subside again into your seat. If you are in rude health at the time, the process is unpleasant enough, but if you happen to be suffering from diarrhœa or dysentery, which commonly attacks Europeans in the *Tierra Caliente*, I could hardly imagine more exquisite torture.

When you have reached the summit of Cumbres No. 2, you are fairly landed on the plateau of Puebla, nearly 7,000 feet above the level of the sea. Anything more dreary than the first aspect of this plateau it would be impossible to conceive. As far as the eye can reach, you see a boundless uncultivated plain stretched out before you—a wilderness of wild cactus and maguey, which no soil is apparently too poor to produce. This abandoned region is traversed by a mere wheel track, into which the high road degenerates, as if exhausted by the fatigue of climbing the Cumbres. Nothing was wanting to complete the sense of desolation which came over us, for the sky became overcast, and a heavy rain set in—quite contrary to all precedent, for it has no right to rain on the Mexican table-land between the months of October and June.

As bad luck would have it, I had remounted my horse, which was by this time dead tired, and so, wet through and weary, we plodded on towards San Augustin del Palmar. Already from the summit of the Cumbres we had descried its gleaming church and white walls, and fondly hoped that in a couple of hours we should have reached our destination. But it turned out far otherwise, for at the end of four we were still ploughing our way painfully through the slush. At nightfall we seemed to be no nearer our journey's end, and the prospect of supper and a bed to be getting more and more remote. The night, however, was surpassingly lovely, for the clouds had cleared away, and the moon shone forth with extraordinary brilliancy. The road, which the rains had converted into a river of mud, showed ahead of us like a silver thread. In boats we should have got along capitally, and a row by moonlight would have been much pleasanter than our plunging progress in carriages or on horseback.

At length we caught sight of the white walls of San Augustin gleaming in the moonlight, and pushed on eagerly to get within the precincts of the town. When we reached the place, to our astonishment it seemed to be nothing but wall. For there was no appearance of houses—only never-ending whitewashed walls thirty feet high, with here and there small doors and occasional barred windows opening on to the street, but no sign of any sort of roof.

These walls, however, turned out to be inhabited,

for on the inside clusters of low dwellings clung to them, like swallows' nests attached to the eaves of a house. But inasmuch as nearly all the windows, for security's sake, opened on to the interior inclosure, and the walls did not reach half way up the lofty outside wall, there was little indication from without of the place being inhabited.

Diving under an archway in one of these walls, we found a kind of caravansery inside, where we were accommodated for the night in a long cold stone-floored chamber, down which ran a double row of beds, as in the ward of a hospital.

Next morning, an hour before daybreak, we were on the road again, and but for the altered position of the constellations I could not have believed we had been to bed at all. Sirius, Orion, and Aldebaram—the guiding star of the gipsies—to which we had had our backs turned the night before, now stood ahead of us, and the Great Bear, which was then below the horizon, was now conspicuous on our right. After the rain of yesterday, the atmosphere was perfectly transparent, and the air was so keen that I was glad to get off my horse, and warm myself by walking. While it was still dark with us, we chanced to turn round, and beheld the Peak of Orizaba already suffused with rosy tints, just as I remember to have seen the Matterhorn blood red, when the valley of Zermatt still lay in darkness.

As the day dawned, we became aware that the aspect of the country had changed. The uninhabited waste, which had made such a melancholy impression on us the day before, had given place to well cultivated fields, and the landscape was pleasantly dotted by white *haciendas*.

On our right, the serrated outline of Malinche—so called after Cortes' Indian mistress—cut clear against the sky, and right ahead of us, nearly a hundred miles distant, the shadowy outlines of Popocatapetl and Iztaccihuatl, the volcanos, which stand sentinel over the valley of Mexico, became faintly visible on the horizon.

For four hours we followed the highway, which leads from San Augustin del Palmar to Acacingo, where we were to halt for breakfast. Then, as the road made a great detour, and we could see Acacingo conspicuous on a hill to the left of us, we determined to try a short cut across country. In the course of this steeple-chase over newly-reaped fields of Indian corn, we came upon a *hacienda*; and, being anxious to see the inside of a Mexican country house, requested half-an-hour's shelter from the scorching sun. I think from the miscellaneous way in which we rode over their fields, the inmates took us for brigands; but, nevertheless, they received us civilly enough, though they made us no offer of refreshments.

Being desparately hot and thirsty, we after a time

made bold to ask for glasses of water, which were produced in their naked simplicity. Having a brandy flask with us, we produced it, and having mixed a little with the water, went through the form of inviting our hosts to drink. To our considerable amusement, they showed no sort of reluctance to accept of our hospitality, and finished the whole glass between them. From their extremely youthful appearance, we supposed our hosts to be brother and sister, and were not a little astonished when they told us they were man and wife. They were the youngest couple I ever came across—he seventeen, and she not yet fourteen.

As we were about to set off for Acacingo, my host suggested that he had a capital horse to sell, much stronger than the animal I was riding. I went to look at it, and was so much pleased with its appearance that I at once agreed to the proposal that I should ride it on trial as far as Acacingo, and if I did not like it, send it back by the *mozo*, who was to ride my own animal to that town.

Notwithstanding our delay we got into Acacingo before the diligences, which had been detained by the heaviness of the roads, the wheels sinking half a foot deep into the sand at every revolution. On their arrival, the new horse was generally approved of, and my English friend agreed to buy him on my recommendation. The price, seventy dollars (14*l.*)

was paid to the *mozo* in the presence of the *alcalde*, or mayor of the town.

Who shall say how many leagues it is from Acacingo to Puebla? Leaving Acacingo at noon, we reached Puebla at 9 P.M. so that if the distance be really only 12 leagues (30 miles), we travelled at about the rate of 3½ miles per hour, allowing for a brief delay at Amozoque, celebrated for its manufacture of the huge spurs, of which Mexicans are so fond.

Some two miles before the city proper begins, stands the *garita* or outer barrier of La Puebla. At this point, the ragged escort which had accompanied us from Acacingo thought proper to leave us, and we were not sorry to see them turn their backs, for a more good-for-nothing looking set of fellows I never beheld. In less than half-an-hour we were safely landed in the *Casa di Diligencias* in the centre of the city.

CHAPTER IV.

PUEBLA TO MEXICO.

Puebla is a cheerful, well-built city, containing close upon a hundred thousand inhabitants. From its appearance, I should never have supposed that the place had recently stood a severe siege. In the heart of the city there is absolutely no trace of the bombardment to which the place was subjected at the hands of the French; and even in the suburbs you scarcely find more than the ordinary amount of ruin and devastation which characterises the outskirts of all Mexican cities.

If you walk through the streets of Puebla in the morning, you won't meet in the course of an hour with a dozen persons who look as if they had any right to be out of prison. As for the soldiers, of whom I met with a good many hanging about, words would quite fail to give anything like an adequate idea of their filthy and slovenly appearance.

In the afternoon, when the wealthier inhabitants take their carriage exercise, the impression made upon you is certainly less painful. Still, among the upper classes of Mexican society, the prevailing expression of countenance is so listless, that you cannot believe that it ever occurs to them that they have any duties in the world, beyond leaning back in a carriage.

On strolling into the cathedral, which is one of the few really fine specimens of architecture in the country, I found it thronged with people. High mass was being performed, and the building was set off to great advantage by the picturesque groups of black-veiled women scattered about the stone floor; for in Mexican churches no woman is allowed the luxury of sitting on a chair or bench.

It was hardly possible not to feel some kind of emotion at finding the gorgeous Roman ritual so exactly reproduced beyond the Atlantic. One could not help feeling that, in spite of its corrupt practices —nowhere carried so far as in Mexico—there was yet something admirable in the indomitable energy which the Roman Church must have displayed, to establish itself so firmly in the New World. Still, when one reflected what the country might have become, had the people been taught to believe in a purer and more exalting faith, one could not refrain from laying a large measure of the guilt of the national degradation at the doors of the religion, which has mainly exercised a corrupting influence over its votaries.

Except the cathedral, we could not hear that Puebla had anything of interest to offer. Accordingly, at sunset on the day after our arrival, we mounted our horses, and took the road for Mexico, preceding the rest of the party, who followed by instalments in the diligence. Almost before we reached the *garita*, the brief Mexican twilight had changed into night; and, as we passed through the barrier, the guards regarded us with unfeigned astonishment, wondering at our boldness in travelling after sunset. We, however, having weighed the matter well, had decided that the certain advantage of escaping from the scorching sun quite overbalanced the mere probability of falling among thieves.

The night was beautiful beyond description, and, as if the light of the moon and the stars was not sufficient, the earth too became alive on every side with fires. These at first we supposed to proceed from factories or smelting houses, till, on approaching an Indian village, we found the church a blaze of light, and learnt that on that night—the eve of the festival of the Immaculate Conception—it was the custom throughout Mexico to illuminate the churches. Presently too, rockets began to shoot up into the air in all directions, falling in fiery showers. On our left, glimmering ghost-like in the moonlight, rose up the snow-capped summits of the volcanos themselves now extinct, but seeming to have bequeathed their fire-breathing properties to the surrounding plain.

So strangely beautiful was the whole scene, that for the first three or four hours we went on our way rejoicing, and congratulating ourselves that we had decided in favour of moonlight travelling. When, however, at the end of five hours there were no signs of San Martin,—a village reported to be eight leagues from Puebla, where we proposed passing the night—and the cold blasts from the snow mountains began to chill us through, we found to our cost that night travelling too had its drawbacks. It was now eleven P.M. and we were alone without a guide in a boundless plain, following a sandy track, which led we knew not whither. By this time the artificial lights had all died out, and the moon herself was on the point of setting; so we felt as a man does who, having gone to sleep by his comfortable fireside, wakes up in the small hours of the night to find the fire gone out, and all around cold and comfortless.

From time to time we passed a few tumble-down mud hovels, in reconnoitering one of which we were naturally enough taken by the inhabitants for brigands, and pursued accordingly. This did not encourage us to repeat the experiment, so we plodded on in silence, ploughing our way painfully through the sand.

It was past midnight when at length we reached San Martin. A death-like stillness reigned in the place, and we rode on through the streets, in the hope of finding the *Casa de Diligencias*, where we had been informed at Puebla that decent accommodation was to be had. In looking for the inn, we stumbled upon a couple of French soldiers, one of whom was very drunk indeed, and the other a good deal the worse for liquor. The latter, with drunken gestures, at once invited us to repair with him to the quarters of his lieutenant, declaring solemnly that, for amiability and generosity, that officer was without an equal in the French army. We, however, did not particularly care to test the accuracy of this statement at so unseasonable an hour, and continued our search for the inn. At the expiration of a few minutes we were attracted by an oil lamp hanging in front of a doorway, and by its flickering light could just make out the magic words, "Casa de Diligencias." There, sure enough, was the inn, but then arose the question, "How to get into it?" for every entrance was carefully barred, and a silence as of the tomb reigned within. After ten minutes of fruitless knocking and shouting, which only resulted in bringing the drunken soldiers to our aid, we became quite desperate, and as a last resource hurled a great stone with all our force against the main entrance. Breaking in a panel, the stone fell with a crash in the courtyard, and effectually woke up the inmates, who from sheer terror received us with great civility, congratulating themselves that we did not begin by cutting their throats. On looking round, we perceived that our drunken friends had rolled into the courtyard after us; but, being by no means desirous of their company, we summarily expelled them.

With his "scrape," a kind of striped woollen blanket, carefully wrapped over his mouth to keep out the cold night air, the wretched-looking *mozo*, a kind of Indian "boots," proceeded to show us into an apartment, furnished, in the simple fashion of the country, with a couple of wooden bedsteads, two chairs, and a table.

There being no possibility of supper at that hour, we were only too glad to get a cup of hot chocolate and a piece of dry bread before turning into bed. This was prepared for us by a copper-coloured individual, who astonished us by addressing us in a strange dialect of broken English, which he told us he had picked up in California. Taking the precaution to lock the door before going to sleep, we then became aware for the first time that there was no vestige of a window anywhere—an arrangement which has this advantage in a country like Mexico, that it restricts robbers to breaking in by the door, to which you are free to devote your undivided attention.

There is, however, this drawback to having no window to your room, that, the daylight being quite excluded, you are apt to sleep far into the day, which is fatal to travellers in tropical regions, where it is indispensable to start at dawn of day. On the present occasion it happened, that when the *mozo* brought us our chocolate at 9 A.M. he found us still fast asleep. For this indulgence we afterwards paid severely, for the mid-day sun punished us most unmercifully, and compelled us to halt for several hours at Puente de Tesmelucan, at the foot of the Rio Frio Pass, over which the carriage-road from Puente to Mexico passes.

As soon as the heat of the day had somewhat abated, we commenced the ascent of the beautiful pass of Rio Frio. After a hundred miles or more of glaring plain without a bit of shade, it was inexpressibly refreshing to find the road mounting by zigzags through a magnificent pine forest, reminding one pleasantly of Europe—suggestive, too, of brigands, who abound there at all times.

A gradual climb of from two to three hours brings you to the station of Rio Frio, which lies at an elevation of upwards of 9,000 feet above the level of the sea. Planted on a grassy plateau, and surrounded by an amphitheatre of wooded hills, the settlement of Rio Frio has so completely the air of an Alpine village that the thoughts of the traveller are in an instant transplanted to Switzerland or the Tyrol. Through the centre of the valley meanders, glistening in the sunshine like a silver thread, the running stream, which gives its name of "Cold River" to this mountain-valley, so called from the fact—strange from its lying just five degrees within the tropics—of its edges being seen covered with a thin coating of ice at morning and evening.

On entering the place, we found it thrown into confusion by the simultaneous arrival of a French baggage train from San Martin, and a convoy of horses and mules from Mexico, which an officer of the Mexican Imperial Guard was escorting to Vera Cruz to be in readiness for the Austrian military contingent, which was expected to arrive towards the end of the month. In despair of getting any separate accommodation, we threw ourselves on the hospitality of the French, and had no reason to regret the step we had taken. In the officer in charge of the military train, we were amused to recognise the amiable lieutenant, of whom we had heard so much in our midnight rencontre with the drunken soldiers at San Martin. And amiable he certainly did his best to prove himself by inviting us on the spot to perform the rest of our journey to Mexico in his company, and share "pot luck" with him, or "le sort du pot" as he expressed it. There were, however, two considerations, which made us hesitate to accept his offer. In the first place he was to start at an extravagantly early hour next morning, and in the second place the wine, which he continually pressed upon us with the assurance that he received it direct from France, and which one could not refuse without directly offending him, was the nearest approach to vinegar of any liquid I ever tasted professing to be anything else. So we avoided giving a decided answer, and on waking at daybreak next morning were somewhat relieved to learn that the lieutenant had started several hours before.

Having heard much of the nipping cold of Rio Frio, we were not surprised on going out of doors to find the fir woods silvered with hoar-frost, and a thin coating of ice along the edge of the running brook. Having no time to lose, we ordered our horses; and, having paid our bill, in which we were amused to find ourselves charged a couple of dollars for the supper for which we had fondly supposed ourselves indebted to French hospitality, pushed forwards on the road to Mexico.

In less than an hour we reached the summit of the pass, but from the thickness of the wood no view was to be had. For this, however, we had been prepared, so that we were not disappointed, and pressed on eagerly to the point a few miles down the slope, where the first view of the far-famed valley of Mexico bursts upon the traveller. This view was very far from coming up to my expectations.

Admitting, as I do willingly, that it would be well nigh impossible for one at all acquainted with the real history of Mexico, and especially with Prescott's highly-coloured picture of the conquest of the country by the Spaniards, its most brilliant if not its most authentic page, to look upon the valley of Mexico for the first time without some kind of emotion, I cannot but attribute this far more to the influence of its historical associations than to its intrinsic beauty. Of the city of Mexico itself you get not a glimpse, for it is completely concealed by a range of bare hills, which crop up in the centre of the valley. Of the much vaunted lakes you see almost nothing, and the mountains which surround the valley are of that yellowish-brown complexion which characterises the whole Mexican table-land, and are for the most part quite bare of trees. As for the valley itself, a large portion of it is neither land nor water, but an unsightly expanse of marsh and bog. Of the dry land barely one-third is under cultivation, the remaining two-thirds consisting chiefly of square grass fields, hedged round by impenetrable fences of maguey.

Where, then, are the elements of beauty here? With the most earnest desire to find them—for I had no other purpose in going out to Mexico than, by looking on the things themselves, to slake at the fountain head the thirst occasioned by Prescott's gorgeous images—I can only say that I sought for them in vain, yet till the end of the world I suppose people will go on talking of the beautiful valley of Anahuac, the Indian name of Mexico. However, it must be borne in mind that the traveller approaching from the east has his back turned upon the snow-capped volcanos Popocatapetl and Iztaccihuatl, which lend whatever of grandeur it possesses to the valley of Mexico. Constantly at morning and evening to behold these two mountains lighted up by the rays of the rising and setting sun is the most beautiful sight in the world. Take them away, and, in spite of the deep blue sky, it would not be easy to match the rest of the picture in ugliness.

Proceeding an hour further down the slope we descried a great cloud of dust ahead of us, in which we conjectured the French convoy to be enveloped. For in Mexico every wheeled carriage which passes along the road throws up such a cloud of dust, that it is quite concealed from view at even a very short distance.

A brisk canter soon brought us alongside, and in less than a quarter of an hour we reached the dilapidated *hacienda* of Buena Vista, where the amiable lieutenant invited us to take breakfast with him. When we proceeded to investigate the premises, not a human being was to be found anywhere, and most of the rooms were completely gutted. At length a wretched copper-coloured *mozo* appeared, and undertook to get some maize for our horses at the neighbouring *tienda*, while a couple of French soldiers in attendance on our lieutenant set about preparing breakfast.

In the course of our wanderings through deserted chambers, we came upon an apartment, which looked as if it might have done duty as the drawing-room in the palmy days of the *hacienda*. On the walls were still hanging four oil paintings, representing St. Peter, with enormous cross-keys, and three other apostles less easily recognisable than their chief. About the room were scattered several articles of furniture, and, in one corner, was the wreck of a sofa. Here then we determined to establish ourselves, and proceeded to avail ourselves of our discovery. The chairs, however, on the first attempt to sit down on them, went all asunder, and a wooden table, on which we proposed to lay our breakfast, literally crumbled away under our touch, collapsing altogether into a shapeless heap of dust and ruin. Luckily our lieutenant had a camp table and a couple of chairs with him, and the sofa resisted the weight of him who was bold enough to make the experiment.

Ere long breakfast made its appearance, and the *vin aigre* was duly produced, and pressed upon us with the usual eulogium. To mix it with water was unfortunately out of the question, for the water of the place had the appearance and consistency of thick soup, and was so impregnated with chalk and lime as to be quite undrinkable. However, in spite of these drawbacks, and sundry admonitory symptoms, on the part of the sofa, of an approaching crisis, we got through our meal in a most satisfactory manner.

After breakfast, we strolled down to the *tienda*, and whiled away the time in watching the customers going in and out. Taking them one with another, I never beheld so low a type of human nature, as they presented.

First came a squalid Indian woman, with matted raven hair, and a half-naked child lolling out of her hood. Calling for *aguardiente*, she swallowed a glass or two, and, squatting down on the mud floor, then and there proceeded to give suck to her infant. After her came a dust-begrimed French soldier, whose entire clothing consisted of a seedy great-coat, a ragged pair of trowsers, and boots from which the toes protruded. Linen he had none, neither shirt, drawers, nor socks. The poor fellow looked half-starved, and was buying some potatoes, when I asked him his history. To my surprise, he answered me in German, and told me that he had belonged to the French Foreign legion, which then had its head-quarters at Puebla; that before joining the Foreign legion, he had deserted from the Prussian army with a comrade who had also joined the Foreign legion; that his comrade, who had again deserted in Mexico and taken to brigandage, had been captured and shot the week before in pursuance of sentence of death passed on him by court martial.

While the soldier was buying his potatoes, a slouching hairy ruffian, accompanied by a degraded-looking woman in rags, came into the shop, and began begging in vain for a drink of spirits on credit, for they apparently had not a copper between them. The complexions of both man and woman were about the colour of untanned leather; and, had not the fact of his face being hideously marked with the small-pox happily decided the point in favour of the man, one would have been hopelessly perplexed to say which of the two countenances wore the deeper expression of villainy.

While this well-matched couple were engaged in earnest dialogue with the store-keeper, in rolled a slip-shod fellow in shirt sleeves, wearing a pair of leathern breeches open down the side, in the Mexican fashion, from which protruded most offensively a pair of very dirty drawers. On inquiring what might be the meaning of the cartridge-belt which he wore round his waist, I was astonished to learn that the uncouth being before me belonged to the rural police force!

From the *tienda* we returned to the *hacienda*, and in the cool of the evening continued our journey to Ayotla, where we found fair accommodation at the *meson* or inn. Being quite unprovided with books, I sent an Indian woman to beg of the landlord to lend me any he might happen to have in the house. After a short time she returned with a Virgil with Spanish footnotes, from which I derived much entertainment. What should I have thought in my school days, if any one had told me that I should one day be reading Virgil for pleasure in Mexico?

From Ayotla we continued our journey, on the following day, to the capital, now only twenty miles distant. At the present day the city of Mexico is approached from the east by a broad dusty causeway about fifteen miles long, carried over an unsightly expanse of morass, which extends, on the north, as far as the salt-water lake of Tezcuco, and on the south, up to the fresh-water lake of Chalco, of both of which, by keeping a sharp look out, you may get rare glimpses. A little beyond Santa Martha, the last post station, the traveller catches sight, for the first time, of the towers and domes of Mexico, only just visible above the unsavoury marshes by which the city is surrounded. At the period of the Conquest, the waters of the lake of Tezcuco extended right up to the city, which was unapproachable from the east, except by water, and could never have been completely invested but for the brigantines, which were so marvellously built and more marvellously transported across the mountains. When Cortes set fire to his ships, he knew very well what he was about, and only burned the wood, which could be replaced at any moment, carefully preserving the iron bolts and tackle against the time when he might have occasion for them.

When the day appointed for the assault arrived, Olid advanced against the city along the great southern causeway from Cojohuacan, by which the Spaniards had originally entered the city unmolested; Pedro de Alvarado from Tacuba, on the west; and Sandoval from Tepejacac, on the north; while Cortes directed the movements of the brigantines in person. Never before or since, I suppose, was a flotilla seen at such an altitude, for the level of the lake of Tezcuco is upwards of 7,000 feet above the sea. As the brigantines got under weigh, the Spaniards on board beheld the flames shoot up from the summit of the Peñon—a hog-backed isolated hill at the foot of which the modern causeway runs, but which was then an island. This was the signal for the advance of the fleet of Indian canoes, which, although so numerous as almost to cover the surface of the lake, availed little against the brigantines. Cortes' first exploit was to dislodge the enemy from this island-fortress, an operation which was effected without losing a single man. Curiously enough, it was the ugly look of this very Peñon, which had been strongly fortified by Santa Anna, which determined General Scott to make a *détour* to the southward, and give up his intention of attacking the city by the direct approach from the east.

The entrance to the modern city is quite in keeping with the uninviting approach, and consists simply of a gap in a mud wall, dignified by the name of "La Garita de San Lazaro." Once within the walls the traveller finds himself in a waste place half a foot deep in sand, bounded on one side by a stinking ditch, on the other by ruined churches and convents, and tenanted by dogs and vultures preying on the offal which is left there to rot. Sometimes a vulture may be seen daintily picking the eye—the tit-bit—out of the head of a dead horse or mule, in the carcase of which a dog may be descried buried up to his tail.

Such is the spectacle which meets the eye of the traveller as he enters the city by its eastern gate, and it can hardly be without a painful feeling of disenchantment that he threads his way through the filthy streets across the great square to the inhabitable quarter of the city, which has for its centre the Calle de Plateros, and its continuation the Calle de San Francisco.

CHAPTER V.

CITY OF MEXICO.

Perhaps I cannot commence this chapter more appropriately than by quoting a passage from the introduction to the only handbook on the city of Mexico, which I believe exists, and which came into my possession at the last moment by the merest accident. The book professes to be written by one Marcos Arroniz, and is remarkable throughout for the extraordinarily patriotic spirit in which it is written.

After informing us that he does not write for the statesman, which is his apology for not touching upon political and financial questions, Don Marcos goes on to state his more humble aim, which he explains to consist in "laying before the traveller everything bearing upon the useful and ornamental that can be of interest to him, at the same time refuting, by incontrovertible proofs, those authors who have treated lightly or malevolently our dear country, which, with all its faults and misfortunes, is after all deserving of the admiration and respect of the civilized world." Now, should I be destined to fall under the lash of this enthusiastic and patriotic writer, I shall endeavour to bear my punishment with that resignation, which a feeling that it is undeserved, is said always to impart to the sufferer. For during my whole residence in Mexico, I made a constant effort to find the city as beautiful as travellers, from Humboldt downwards, describe it as being. Under one aspect alone could I find anything at all to admire about it. When seen by moonlight, it was impossible not to be struck by the faultless symmetry of the streets. But by the broad light of day, I could find nothing more to admire about Mexico than about Mannheim, or any other city built at right angles with itself. It is however necessary to bear in mind, that at the beginning of the present century, when Humboldt visited Mexico, the city may well have presented a much more flourishing appearance than it does now. For the country was at that period still under the Spanish yoke, which was not finally cast off till the year 1821. And the Spaniards, although they monopolized all the higher offices in Church and State, and generally misgoverned the country in a most shameful manner, at any rate deserve some credit for having kept everything in an excellent state of repair. As under most tyrannical governments, the aedilés department alone was administered in such a way as to make itself regretted.

Even before they had achieved their independence, the Mexicans began to indulge in the luxury of knocking down public buildings, destroying bridges, and actually tearing up the roads, which had been constructed, on the principle of the Roman roads, at an enormous expense by the Spanish government. For those portions of the high-road which are now quite impassable in the rainy season, were formerly traversed by stone causeways, similar to those which are carried across the marshes into the city of Mexico.

No wonder then that, after fifty years of unbridled licence, during which every Mexican has thought to give proof of his manliness by knocking or kicking down something, the country should bear the appearance of having been bombarded from one end to the other. The real wonder is that anything at all should be left standing upright.

In the city of Mexico itself, more than anywhere else in the country, is the traveller struck with the general want of repair into which the place has been allowed to fall. No sooner has he entered the city, than the most painful evidence of this neglect is forced upon his senses by the network of open black drains, which, with a tropical sun constantly pouring down upon them, fill the air with the most poisonous exhalations. Dig wherever you will in Mexico, and within two or three feet of the surface you come upon liquid black mud. With this mud the drains mingle, and flow with an united stream down the centre of all the back streets.

This is the first and most glaring evidence of the general carelessness. The next fact which forces itself on the notice of the wanderer through the streets of Mexico, is the extraordinary number of ruined churches and convents.

Now in Humboldt's day, and even when the late Sir Henry Ward and Madame Calderon de la Barca wrote about Mexico, the city could boast of a show of churches and religious edifices, such as, in point of size and number, if not of beauty, was to be found in few European capitals.

The convent of San Francisco alone, which was perhaps the wealthiest religious establishment in the New World, contained at least five separate churches, and extended over about half a square mile of ground. Now its principal church stands a shapeless ruin, facing the street to which it gives its name, and which will soon know it no more, for it is to be cleared away altogether to make room for the new blocks of houses which are to be built on its site. What formerly was the garden of the convent has been now let to a Belgian for a nursery garden, and one of the churches has been turned into a *café*. It seemed droll to see "Café et Billard" written up over a church door, and to see French soldiers drinking and playing dominoes in the inside, which had undergone little or no alteration.

I was more interested in the ruins of the convent of San Francisco than in those of any other religious edifice, because I learnt the particulars of its destruction from an eye-witness—a young Mexican, who had been educated in England. This gentleman informed me that he had with his own eyes seen President Juarez arrive with a party of soldiers, and give his orders for the work of demolition to commence; that as it proceeded several lives were lost in consequence of the thoughtless and precipitate manner, in which the workmen laid about them in their eagerness to attract the favourable notice of the President.

From another eye-witness—an American—I learnt that, during the early part of the year 1861, it was quite common to see President Juarez making his round of the churches, and superintending the work of destruction.

So hard-pressed for ready money was the Government of Juarez at this period—the beginning of the year 1861—that the sites of the ruined churches—sometimes including the sacred edifice itself—were sold for the most trifling sums. I even heard of one case in the provinces, where a Belgian bought a piece of ground—church and all—for nineteen pounds ten shillings! Indeed the Government rarely refused a bid, however small, provided payment were offered in money down. For there was a great lack of buyers. In Mexico in those days, persons who had money invariably belonged to the Conservative party, or in other words, wanted to keep what they had; and as the priests had most, they were of course ultra-Conservatives. Those on the other hand who had nothing, belonged to the Liberal party, which was really only liberal in the sense of wishing to make free with other people's property. So when Juarez put the property of the clergy up to public auction, the Conservatives as a rule would not bid for it, for if they had done so, they would have been excommunicated by the priests, and it was either knocked down to the Liberals, who rather liked being excommunicated than not, or to such foreigners as were willing to pocket their scruples and invest in it. In this way, many Frenchmen and Belgians, and some English, realized considerable fortunes.

In the absence of all reliable statistics, it would be vain to attempt to estimate what amount of property was squandered away in this manner. All that is certain is, that so little of the purchase money found its way into the public treasury, that in the same year the Government had to effect a loan of one million dollars to satisfy its most pressing wants. The apologists of Juarez, however, declare, that it was not the object of his Government to enrich the public treasury by the sale of the property of the clergy, but only to wrest that property out of the hands of the priests, and hand it over to those who would work it to the greater advantage of the state. This I could not but consider as an exceedingly lame apology, for the needy adventurers, without capital, to whom much of the property fell, were hardly likely to make a use of it which would be profitable to the country at large.

Much has been written of the striking effect of the Plaza Mayor, or great square of Mexico; but, like the rest of the city, it seemed to me that only when viewed by moonlight was there anything at all attractive about it. What Charity is in the moral, that is the Moon in the material world, and as Charity is said to cover a multitude of sins, so does the Moon shed her light so tenderly over the deformities, which by day are so offensive to the sojourner in the capital of Montezuma, that she even makes things of beauty out of hideous objects. The open black drains, for instance, which are so uninviting by daylight, by moonlight positively assume an attractive appearance, and their unsavoury odour alone betrays their disguise.

The cathedral, of which the Mexicans make so much boast, occupies the north side of the Plaza Mayor. It is a huge straggling building in that

debased style of Spanish ecclesiastical architecture which is commonly found in New Spain. Its most striking features externally are a pair of square towers, and a florid façade towards the Plaza. I call the present cathedral huge, but it merely occupies one corner of the former site of the colossal *teocalli*, or pyramidical temple of Huitxilopotchli—the terrible war god of the Aztecs—the precincts of which extended as far back as the Plaza de Santo Domingo, which derives its name from the ruined church at its northern extremity.

Contiguous to the church of Santo Domingo, stood formerly the tribunal and subterraneous prisons of the dreaded Inquisition—curiously enough, near the very spot where the horrid banquets of the Aztec priests took place, at which were served up the bodies of the Spanish prisoners, who had been offered up as victims on the sacrificial stone on the summit of the teocalli. (In Mr. Barron's villa at Tacubaya is preserved a painting and the mystic symbol of the Inquisition, with its blasphemous motto, "Exsurge, Domine, causam judica tuam.") The Inquisition buildings are now converted into a medical college, and the dissecting room occupies the site of the chambers where formerly living bodies were tortured. It would seem that the place is for ever destined to bloody associations.

It is, perhaps, after all not wonderful that the

Mexicans should think their cathedral beautiful, as they are exempt from the disadvantage of instituting unfavourable comparisons between it and the cathedrals of Europe. If there is little to admire about it outside, inside there is still less. The roof is of the ordinary tawdry description which characterises second-rate Roman Catholic churches; and the floor is only so far remarkable, that it consists of dirty wooden planks loosely joined together. The choir, about which is a good deal of handsome oak carving and silver ornamentation, is in the centre of the building.

On Sundays, at 8 A.M. a military mass is now performed for the French army of occupation. This service is regularly attended by Marshal Bazaine and his staff. At a few minutes before eight, he rides up on his grey charger, followed by a splendid staff, the brilliancy of which works, I would venture to affirm, far more than the rumour of a victory over the Juarists upon the imaginations of the crowds of Indians, who invariably flock into Mexico on a Sunday. Inside, the cathedral is lined with French troops, between whose ranks the Marshal marches in state to his seat near the high altar, in front of which are stationed three Zouaves in the form of a triangle, whose chief occupation consists in presenting arms to the Host, whenever an opportunity occurs.

As I watched this ceremony, I could not help being struck with the ubiquity of these French soldiers. I had seen them in St. Peter's at Rome; I had seen them in the Church of the Holy Sepulchre at Jerusalem at the time of the French intervention in Syria; and here they were now in the cathedral of Mexico. And all this in the space of four years! Of a truth Napoleon III. understands how to govern the French nation.

As soon as the military mass was over, the Indians flocked in in great numbers, and a spiritual repast was served up suited to their tastes. For just as the Indian population and the lower orders in Mexico in general like their rice and tortillas to be highly spiced with the inevitable chile, so they consider even the Roman ritual insipid, without an unusually strong admixture of the sensational element.

However uninteresting the cathedral of Mexico may appear from an architectural point of view, I suppose that in no religious edifice in the world would you find on a Sunday morning so strange a congregation. The great body of worshippers are pure Indians—the direct but degenerate descendants of the warlike Aztecs; who at the present day—strange to say—stand upon a decidedly lower level than the descendants of the Otomi, and other Indian tribes still found in the country. The appearance of men and women alike is painfully squalid. The women, most of them, carry a half naked infant in the hood of their "rebozo," a coarse kind of striped shawl, which is worn like a Spanish mantilla. For nether garments, they wear a dark petticoat called " enagua," wrapped so tightly about them as to be continually suggestive of the lower portion of a mummy. I never once saw an Indian girl who could be said to have the slightest pretensions to beauty; and the pitch of ugliness to which the old women reach is quite unparalleled on this side the Atlantic.

Turning from the women to the men, one was even more struck with their wild uncouth mien. As I regarded them devoutly kneeling, with their tawny faces, on which their raven hair hung down in matted tufts, directed in adoration towards a tawdry image of the Virgin, one could not help thinking that after all it might be better that they should thus be exhausting their energies in the harmless amusement of crossing themselves, than in scalping and eating their enemies. From the vigour with which they set to work, it was easy to see that they were trying to crowd a deal of devotion into the few minutes, which they could spare from the more important business of the market, which was going on outside.

Great as is the influence exercised over the Indians by the Roman Catholic priests of the present day, it yet falls very far short of the hold which the Aztec

religion had over the minds of the people. Now-a-days, such of the Indians as feel disposed to leave their business in the market-place may with difficulty get a glimpse of the mysterious figure of the priest gesticulating in front of the altar.

Formerly religious associations were continually forced upon them day and night. In the day-time, the crowd in the market-place had but to lift up their eyes to behold the sacred procession winding up the spiral ascent to the summit of the teocalli, where the victim was sacrificed, and his bleeding heart exposed to public gaze. By night fires were kept continually burning on 600 altars, which shed a lurid glare over the whole city. Once every fifty-two years the sacred fires were let out, and the multitude went forth from the city at sunset to the summit of a neighbouring mountain, having previously smashed up all the furniture and utensils in their temples and houses, acting —with a consistency beyond Dr. Cumming—on the supposition that the whole world would be destroyed that night, because their own cycle of fifty-two years had come to an end. Waiting patiently on the mountain till such time as the Pleiades should have reached the zenith, the priests then would call upon the gods, who never refused to send down a fresh supply of the sacred fire, with which they returned to the city rejoicing.

Besides the Indians collected in the cathedral, there

was a considerable crowd of Mestizos, or mixed breeds of Indians and whites, often more easily distinguishable from the pure Indians by their European costume than by the colour of their skins, which exhausts every shade of yellowish-brown.

Of pure whites there were very few, only here and there among the crowd you might come across a kneeling female figure with a marble face, set off against that most graceful of costumes—the mantilla, or long black veil worn by Spanish ladies at their devotions.

And here I hope I shall be pardoned if I make a general observation to the disparagement of my own countrywomen. When I see the sober dresses almost universally worn by foreign ladies in church, I never ail to be struck with the better taste they display in this respect than English ladies, who are so much addicted to smart dresses and fashionable bonnets.

Along the eastern side of the Plaza Mayor runs the low façade of the now Imperial—formerly National—Palace, more like a long grange than a royal residence. The length of the building, which exceeds 200 English yards, is out of all proportion to its height. This modern grange is poetically spoken of by American writers as "the halls of Montezuma."

Up to the year 1862 the "Palacio Nacional" belonged to the family of Cortes, of whom it was purchased by the Spanish Government as a residence

for the viceroys for the sum of 38,300 pesos de oro, probably equal to about half a million silver dollars.

Round the southern and western sides of the Plaza run low one-storied houses, with rows of shops on the ground floor. In front of these shops are arcades, called "Portales," where loungers gossip all day long, and where inferior saddlery, cutlery, Mexican hats, boots, spurs, gingerbread, cigarettes, the silver trinkets of the country, and every other conceivable thing that you don't want are exposed for sale on stalls that would hardly have passed muster in Greenwich fair. Here, too, newsvendors thrust their journals upon you, and feeble attempts at political caricatures are posted up in conspicuous places. In short, whatever life there is in Mexico—and there is uncommonly little—is to be found under the shade of the *portales*.

In the centre of the Plaza Mayor is—nothing. Take your stand in the middle, and you cannot fail to be struck with the poverty of the buildings which your eye rests upon. The Plaza is a world too big for the buildings which surround it, and has more the air of an overgrown Indian encampment turned into stone than of the great square of a city. Yet no wonder that hitherto the appearance of the Plaza has been quite neglected, as it has been chiefly employed so far as the principal scene of the ever-recurring revolutions. To get possession of the Plaza Mayor was generally the first move of the revolutionary leaders. Here they would plant their artillery, and proceed to bombard, or threaten to bombard, the Palacio Nacional.

But if there is nothing attractive about the Plaza itself, it is inexpressibly refreshing to look up from it to the snowy summits of the volcanos, which in their unchangeableness seem to rebuke the fickle passions of the Mexicans of to-day.

In the whole city of Mexico there is but one strikingly fine building, the "Mineria," or School of Mines, which, for its imposing massiveness, it would be difficult to match in any city in the world. Commenced in the year 1793 from the designs of Don Manuel Tolsa, who was appointed director of the works with a yearly salary of 2,000 piastres, the building was completed some twenty-five years later, shortly before the termination of the War of Independence, and was the last legacy left by the Spanish Government to the Mexican nation.

Perhaps the "Douana," or custom-house, would come next in importance as a public building after the Mineria. Like everything else in the country it is immediately under the protection of the Virgin of Guadalupe, whose picture hangs over the principal staircase, with the motto, "Non taliter fecit omni nationi." On the occasion of my visit, the court-yards were thronged with pack-mules, lading and unlading.

Inasmuch as the British consul in Mexico informed me that he had of late years been unable to send in his annual report of the state of trade in Mexico owing to the entire absence of all reliable statistics, I think the general reader will agree with me that it would be highly unbecoming on my part to hazard any unofficial statement at all on the subject. Statistics of any kind are not very palatable things to most people, but there can be no possible apology for offering unreliable figures. A recent writer on Mexico has favoured the public with about 100 pages of this edifying mental food in a volume of less than 500 pages, but I do not hesitate for a moment to say that the irritation produced by the stings of all the venomous insects of the *Tierra Caliente* combined is as nothing compared with that which results from a conscientious attempt to grapple with those figures. I sincerely hope and believe that I am the only individual in the world who ever made such an attempt.

The University is perhaps, take it all in all, the most contemptible thing in the city. As a building, it is insignificant to the last degree, and it seems conscious of its delinquency in this respect, by attempting to hide itself behind the Indian covered vegetable market. Its position is only betrayed by a forlorn flag-staff, which may be descried over the roof of the above-mentioned market. It is the peculiarity of the University of Mexico, that at present it can neither boast of students nor of professors, but it is satisfactory to know that this singular institution has known better days. Hear on this point our old friend Señor Marcos Arroniz. Writing of the University, the author remarks:—"During the whole period that its renown lasted, the University produced men distinguished in all branches. But—like *everything human*—it went to decay, and for twenty-five years its importance has been insignificant. Since 1833, it has only existed to give degrees, and the building has served for a hundred different purposes. In short, you may say that the University has existed for everything, but to give instruction in the sciences."

For the benefit of any one who may be curious to know where the candidates for degrees come from, I may add, that they are chiefly supplied by the secular College of San Ildefonso and the religious seminary of San Camillo. The first of these is a huge building, and is in this respect particularly interesting to an Englishman, inasmuch as the students have rooms in college as at Oxford and Cambridge. About the furnishing of the rooms, there was enough to remind one of our English universities, though everything was on a far more frugal scale. I was amused to find the habit of hanging photographs of their sisters on their walls, for the benefit of their friends, as common among Mexicans as among English students. The College of San Ildefonso was built by the Jesuits immediately after their arrival in the country in 1574. Turned out of all the Spanish dominions by a decree of Charles III. the Jesuits were brought back during Santa Anna's first administration in 1833, expelled again under Comonfort in 1856, and are now gradually creeping back again.

Among the purposes alluded to by Señor Arroniz to which the University building is put, is that of serving as the Museum of Antiquities. The collection, however, is a very poor one. This extraordinary poverty is chiefly to be explained by the extreme zeal displayed by the Spanish missionaries in destroying every relic of antiquity, which might have served to carry the minds of the Indians back to the idolatry of the past. Believing the uncouth symbols which occur in their picture writings, which were absolutely unconnected with religion, to be representations of their idols, Zummaraga, first Bishop of Mexico, caused as many of them, as he could lay hands on, to be collected in a heap, and publicly burnt. The excellent bishop, who conceived that by this act he had removed a great obstacle to the conversion of the Mexicans to Christianity, actually cut off the only possible source, from which a satisfactory knowledge of Mexican history prior to the conquest might have been derived. The meagre information, which we at present possess on the subject, is almost entirely derived from the few specimens of picture-writing, which survived the general destruction. The art of picture-writing naturally fell into disuse when the Spaniards introduced their simpler method of writing.

Robertson, who wrote his history of America prior to the discovery of the ruined cities of Yucatan and Central America, is inclined to argue, from the total absence of architectural remains in the valley of Mexico, that the common accounts of the advanced state of Mexican civilization must have been much exaggerated.

Prescott, on the other hand, who was evidently much influenced by the remarkable work of his fellow-countryman, Stephens, could only read in the discovery of Palenque and Copan an indirect confirmation of the traditional splendour and magnificence of the Aztec capital.

And now at the end of the chapter it occurs to me, that I may have been somewhat unkind in criticising the shortcomings of the city of Mexico, seeing that it is perhaps more wonderful that the city exists at all than that it should not be beautiful. In her struggles for bare life, Mexico has had little time to thinking of adorning herself. For what between floods, earthquakes, and revolutions, the city has indeed had a hard time of it. Resting upon a marsh, the foundations of the principal buildings in the city are constantly sinking, and you can recognise in the waving outline of some of the houses the heaving motion of the waters underneath.

CHAPTER VI.

CITY LIFE IN MEXICO.

THE Hotel Iturbide—a lofty, three-storied building, with a decorated façade, originally intended to serve as the palace of the Emperor Don Augustin Iturbide—receives most travellers on their arrival in the capital. It is situated in the best part of the city, in the Calle San Francisco, a little below its junction with its continuation the Calle de Plateros (Street of the Silversmiths), which leads westward out of the Plaza Mayor. At the bottom of the Calle San Francisco is the Alameda—a seedy kind of public promenade, where the band plays three mornings a week.

The hotel itself is about as comfortable as a second-rate hotel in Italy, and constructed on the same airy principles. One half of the ground-floor of the building is occupied by the *fonda* or restaurant, which is kept by a Frenchman, and is quite distinct from the hotel, and the other half by a huge upholsterer's shop and dingy show rooms. A wide stone staircase, reached by crossing a stone yard, which is laid under water during the floods, conducts you to the upper regions, and access is gained to the bed-rooms by means of exterior galleries carried round the courtyard on each flat. The doors of the rooms which open on to these galleries serve at the same time for windows, the upper panels being fitted with glass.

We, however, owing to the kindness of Don Antonio Escandon, to whom we looked—and never in vain—as to a kind of Mexican Providence, were saved from the necessity of lodging in the hotel. This gentleman was good enough to place at our disposal a couple of rooms in a spare house of his own, into which he intended to remove with his family as soon as it should have been properly furnished. The furniture, which had been purchased in London and Paris, formed the chief part of the heavy baggage, which was coming up from Vera Cruz in charge of the above-mentioned hidalgo.

The house — I had almost written palace — in which we found ourselves lodged was one of the most elegant in the whole city. Like most Mexican houses, it was one-storied, although a sort of encampment on the *azoeta*, or flat-terraced roof, where the servants were stowed away, answered the purpose of a second story. The house was built in the form of a double quadrangle, the ground-floor of the outer one, towards the street, being let for shops, and of the inner being devoted to stables, coach-house, and harness-room. The first-floor alone was occupied by the rooms of the family. One long drawing-room, with a smaller one at each end, which were temporarily converted into bedrooms for our benefit, took up the whole face of the house towards the street. The rest of the principal rooms opened into the front quadrangle, while schoolrooms, nurseries, and kitchen ran round the back quadrangle over the stables, in which we kept our horses. During the whole period of our residence in these excellent quarters, we were entertained by the spectacle of a couple of workmen, busied all day long with cutting and sewing carpets in the long drawing-room, which separated our rooms, while a third individual always sat by, solemnly smoking, watching their proceedings. In Mexico, nobody ever does anything without somebody else standing or sitting by, doing nothing.

Our daily *régime*, during our stay in the capital, was pretty much as follows. At 7 A.M. we took our "desayáno," consisting of a cup of tea or chocolate, in our bedrooms. This was followed by a ride in the Paseo—the Rotten Row of Mexico—which, although a little monotonous, was by far the most enjoyable part of the day. At 11 A.M. we breakfasted, and dined at 6.30, devoting the intervening hours to reading, writing, strolling, or sitting—sometimes almost shivering in great coats—in fireless rooms, waiting for the dinner hour.

Persons who think of Mexico as of an altogether wild and uncivilized country, would be surprised at the amount of tea drinking which goes on there in a quiet way—chiefly among the English, of whom there is a considerable sprinkling all over the country. So that, whenever there was no more exciting amusement in the wind, we were always sure of a welcome at some one or other hospitable tea-table. The prevalence of this habit of dropping in in a miscellaneous way to drink a cup of tea, without any sort of invitation, seemed to me to prove that our countrymen settled in Mexico had made a step in advance of us at home in the art of living.

In order to keep ourselves *au courant des événements*, we took an *abonnement* to the two leading journals of the capital, *L'Estafette* and *La Sociedad*, for Mexico is not without its full allowance of daily papers. Besides the two above mentioned, many others exist, such as *La Chronista*, *La Monarquia*, *L'Ere Nouvelle*, &c. &c.

Deserving of special notice is the organ of the ultra-clerical party, which, from the wonderful flights it is wont to take, and the airiness of its articles, bears the appropriate title of *El Pajaro Verde*, or *The Green Bird*. The circulation of this religious journal is enormous, and for some inexplicable reason the Imperial Government, some months before our visit, took the unwise step of suspending it for a period of six months. So for six months the singing of the bird was put a stop to, but at the expiration of its period of enforced silence it poured forth such a flood of melody as positively to overflow the whole city. In all conspicuous places, on the walls of churches and public buildings, the eye fell upon the picture of a large green bird with a long tail, perched upon a bough.

La Sociedad is the organ of the moderate clerical party, and is, on the whole, a respectable and well-conducted paper. For Mexican news, *La Sociedad* is far superior to *L'Estafette*, but the foreign news and leading articles of *L'Estafette*, its French rival, are decidedly to be preferred. Indeed, the *L'Estafette* is edited with an amount of sprightliness and ability which is really surprising in a country like Mexico. From late accounts which have reached me from Mexico, I learn that *L'Estafette* has brought down upon itself the wrath of the authorities, and has received an *avertissement*.

Besides this multitude of journals, Mexico can boast of at least one circulating library and public reading room.

In the way of clubs the Lonja, in the Plaza Mayor, is the principal place of public resort. At the Lonja, to which I was introduced by the kindness of Mr. Barron, the principal banker in Mexico, the reading room is supplied with most of the principal journals of both hemispheres, and adjoining the reading room are billiard and smoking rooms. The hall of the Lonja is said to be employed by the principal merchants as an exchange, but I do not believe that you would often find half-a-dozen persons collected there for any purpose whatsoever. On the occasion of my first visit, I found a single individual, my banker's clerk, haunting its precincts, and the desolation of the place made such an impression upon me, that I never went near it again, except for the great ball which was given there in honour of the Emperor and Empress.

On that occasion there were upwards of a thousand persons present, in rooms which would only hold five hundred with any degree of comfort. The heat was perfectly stifling, and it was almost impossible to move, much less dance. A certain number of couples might have been observed each revolving on its own axis, but they invariably left off dancing where they began.

The Emperor and Empress and their suite were roped off from the pressure of the crowd, and, in their crimson velvet chairs, looked for all the world like a group of wax-work figures at Madame Tussaud's. The looks of the Emperor, who is on all hands admitted to be by no means deficient in capacity, belie him altogether, for it would be difficult to conceive of a less intelligent face. Physically, he is a strikingly fine-looking man, and, were he not Emperor, would be admirably fitted to make one of his Palatine Guard. The Empress is said by all who know her to be an exceedingly clever and agreeable woman, but she did not appear to me to have any claims to beauty.

To meet their Majesties, not only the cream, but also the milk, of Mexican society was invited, and when one reflected that almost every article of ladies' or gentlemen's dress had been brought nearly 5,000 miles across the ocean, and then 250 on mule-back up country, one could not but regard the display as wonderful. Nor was there by any means a deficiency of female beauty, for the Mexican ladies belonging to the best families are many of them strikingly handsome, and there was a fair sprinkling of good-looking foreign ladies.

Where only the pen of a Madame Calderon de la Barca, who has been happily described as a "lively observer of men, manners, and millinery," could do anything like justice to the scene, it would be presumptuous on my part to attempt it. I shall, therefore, confine myself to enumerating a few of the more noticeable personages in the room. Amongst these was conspicuous by his *distingué* appearance, with which the Yankee twang with which he spoke English contrasted strangely, the French Minister, Monsieur de Montholon, son of him well known to fame as the latest friend and executor of Napoleon I.

and his legatee to the substantial amount of 4,000,000 francs. In attendance on him was Monsieur le Comte Chateaubriand, an elegant youth, who has inherited the name without the talent of his famous relative. Then there was the Mexican savant *par excellence*, Señor Ramirez, Curator of the Museum, Minister of Foreign Affairs, and, at the same time, legal adviser of the Imperial Mexican Railway Company, a post which is probably worth more to him than all the others put together.

Not the least remarkable person present was Señor Raphael Beraza, who has filled the post of special courier to the British Embassy for upwards of forty years, to the satisfaction of everybody. Señor Beraza, who is now, I believe, upwards of eighty years of age, is, without doubt, the most active individual in Mexico. He informed me that he had run up from Vera Cruz expressly for the ball, and had arrived in the capital at six o'clock that evening; that, after the ball, he proposed taking the return diligence at four A.M. in order to reach Vera Cruz in time to receive Mr. Scarlett, the newly-appointed British Minister, who was expected out by the next steamer.

Amongst others pointed out to me as notorieties was Señor Iturbide, remarkable as being the son of him who, by his pardonable treason in deserting with the troops under his command to the insurgents, was mainly instrumental in achieving the independence of his country; but, as far as I could learn, remarkable for nothing else in the world.

Nor must I omit to mention the American judge O'Sullivan, who was bidding high for the imperial favour against a rival who, according to the judge, was such a good-for-nothing fellow, that he wondered how Maximilian could tolerate his presence in his capital. Eventually the efforts of the judge were crowned with success, and he succeeded in obtaining the consent of the Mexican Government to pay an annual subsidy of 80,000 dollars to his employers —the firm of Benjamin Halliday and Co. of New York—who had applied for a concession to establish a steam service for carrying the mails and passengers between San Francisco and Mexican ports of the Pacific.

While the Lonja is the general meeting-place of all the merchants in Mexico, whether native or foreign, the Spaniards and Germans, who are settled in greater numbers than any other foreigners in Mexico, have established separate club-houses of their own. The German club, of which I was admitted an honorary member, bears the name of "Das Deutsche Haus," and is a much less dreary place than the Lonja in its every-day dress. At the Lonja you can get no sort of refreshment, but at the Deutsche Haus the visitor who has a taste for such things can regale himself to his heart's content on "Leber-Wurst," "Raue Schinken," and "Lager-bier."

Preparatory to my journey into the interior and to the Pacific coast, where I was informed that I should not get on at all without some knowledge of the Spanish language, I applied to a German friend to recommend me a teacher. Now, unfortunately for me, it occurred to this gentleman that here was a splendid opportunity of shifting a distressed countryman of his own, who was then a burden to himself, on to my shoulders. He assured me that his *protégé* was a man of first-rate education, hinted that he was a nobleman in disguise, could vouch for his speaking the purest " Castillano," and finally promised to send him to me next day. When, however, my teacher presented himself at our residence next morning, he was peremptorily refused admittance by the porter, who had the sagacity to perceive that it was as much as his place was worth to let into the house an individual of so doubtful a character, as my would-be teacher turned out to bear. However, as I was more or less bound to him, and found he understood his business, I repaired with him next day to the Alameda,—the Kensington Gardens of Mexico,— and took my lesson in public on a stone bench. In appearance my teacher was still a fine-looking fellow, in spite of his broken-down air, which was partly owing to his seedy dress, but perhaps more to a suspicion of *delirium tremens* which hung about him. He was apparently about forty years of age, was nearly bald, but made up for the lack of hair on his head by the length of his beard and mustachios, which he was continually stroking. His dress consisted of a brown wide-awake, a dirty shirt, with a loose handkerchief round his neck, a long greasy threadbare brown great-coat, a dilapidated pair of trousers, and an old pair of slippers, in which he glided about noiselessly with a ghost-like movement.

In the course of my interview with this strange individual, who conducted himself throughout with remarkable *hauteur*, he informed me that he had already been upwards of twenty years in the country, and had formerly been employed as commercial traveller to a firm, which had since failed; that in Sant Anna's time his employers had purchased him a captaincy in one of the regiments of the State of Jalisco, in order that, in the course of his travels in the interest of their house, he might not, officer as he was, be amenable to the civil tribunals. For the keynote of Sant Anna's policy was to gain the support of the army and the church by granting all kinds of unconstitutional privileges to the military and ecclesiastics.

Among other things which struck me as I wandered through the streets of Mexico, were the wonderful illustrated signboards over the doors, and especially over the *pulque* shops. Of these I noted down a few; such as "The Daughter of the Sun," "The

Colossus of Rhodes," a very favourite one, where a ship is represented sailing into harbour between the legs of a giant, who is just tall enough to admit of the main-mast passing under without causing him inconvenience; "The Aurora Borealis," "The Loves of the Sultan," "Mount Olympus," where goddesses in short petticoats are represented as scouring the mountains, while the gods show their superior sense by reclining luxuriously in the shade.

An event of the day, which caused us a good deal of amusement, was the arrival of the postman. I know not if all the Mexican postmen are mounted on sorry hacks, and wear spectacles, but this is certainly the case with the particular individual in whose beat the Calle de Plateros lies. I am not able to say whether the postman or his steed wore the more slipshod appearance, for I never saw them apart, so it was impossible to say, which contributed most to the miserable *tout ensemble*. I presume that the postman is mounted with a view to a more expeditious delivery of letters, but I could hardly fancy an arrangement less likely to answer the end in view. For in the first place the nature of the Mexican streets is such as to render riding over them a highly dangerous operation at all times; and in the second place it is exceedingly rare for any one to be at the door to receive letters, so that the postman, who has never been known to dismount, may be seen waiting any length of time at the entrance till somebody should either go in or go out, when he will feebly stretch out his hand, and request any casual visitor to take charge of the letters for the whole house.

Another remarkable feature of the Mexican streets are the "aguadores," or water-carriers, who may be recognised by their huge leathern helmets and aprons, and the moist atmosphere with which they are surrounded. These must not be confounded with the vendors of *pulque*, which, like the water-carriers of Egypt, they carry in pig-skins, to which the liquor inside lends a quivering motion horribly suggestive of convulsive movements of the muscles of the animal, which you might suppose to be within.

Then there is the perambulating butcher, who in Mexico, instead of setting up shop and becoming a nuisance to his neighbours (as butchers' shops are apt to be even out of the tropics), invests in a hack, which may be had good enough for his purpose for the moderate sum of from five and twenty to thirty shillings, rigs it up with a skilful arrangement of hooks, from which the carcases of several sheep and pigs, and large joints of beef and veal, are suspended, and drives it before him through the streets.

His will be a very exceptional case, who, in the course of his wanderings through the city, does not sooner or later encounter the mystic gilded coach, preceded by an attendant ringing the well-known bell, which announces the approach of the Host. If it happens to be in a frequented part of the city, or on a market-day, the effect produced by the unwonted spectacle of the whole multitude suddenly dropping upon their knees is very striking. I was informed that formerly natives or foreigners who neglected to show their respect for the Church in this marked manner, abstained from doing so at their peril. In these latter days, however, it is optional with all classes to do as they think fit; but the custom is still very generally observed, proving what an extraordinary hold Roman Catholicism still retains over the mass of the people. As far as I am aware, this custom of falling down before the Host is peculiar to Spain and her present and former possessions.

The Citadel at Mexico is an institution of which one hears and reads a good deal; but one may sojourn a long time in the city without having the remotest inkling of its whereabouts. Few strangers, who ride down the Paseo, have any idea that that low straggling building to their left, immediately they get outside the city, whose walls seem scarcely to emerge from the surrounding bog, is a spot so crowded with historical associations as the Citadel of Mexico. When I use the term "historical associations," I perhaps ought to explain that I do not mean that events of world-wide interest have there happened; but that the Citadel has played an important part in the Mexican revolutions, as being the retreat to which the President, for the time being, was wont to retire while the usurper had "his fling." The big chimney cropping up in the middle of it points to the fact that the building was formerly a tobacco factory.

On my way home from the Citadel after my visit, I took a turning which brought me into a hitherto undiscovered part of the city, and learnt, from a playbill over a theatre, that the quarter was called "New Mexico." Conceive a portion of Shoreditch with two stories taken off the houses, and the remainder left roofless and painted blue, pea-green, or whitewashed, all the drains opened and exposed to view with a tropical sun perpetually pouring down upon them, and you will have some faint notion of what New Mexico is like.

In this promising neighbourhood is one of the chief fruit and vegetable markets, of which there are several in the city. About the articles exposed for sale there was very little that was suggestive of the tropics, the stalls being, for the most part, stocked with potatoes, cabbages, carrots, turnips, cauliflower, onions, parsnips, and other vegetables with which the London markets are supplied daily.

Adjoining the market is, as a matter of course,

a church. Indeed, if I remember right, there are two. Into one of these, San Juan de la Penitencia, to which a convent is attached, I wandered, as is my usual custom, and found the congregation assembling for mass. Through gratings before the upper galleries glimpses might be caught of the veiled figures of the nuns.

Inasmuch as the convent of San Juan de la Penitencia was one of the few spared by the arch-destroyer Juarez, I was anxious to learn a little about it, and made bold to ask a bystander how many nuns there might be. With the extreme politeness and gentleness of manner which characterises Mexicans, he regretted that he could not tell me, and soon after I left the precincts of the building. A quarter of an hour or twenty minutes later, when I had nearly reached home, I suddenly was aware of an individual addressing me from behind, and, supposing that he was a beggar, was hurrying on to be rid of him, when I caught the words, *Cien tantas monjas* (a hundred odd nuns). The polite stranger, of whom I had asked the question in the church, had taken the trouble, first to inform himself, and then pursue me for a mile or more to give me the information I required. Really the politeness of Mexicans should cover a multitude of their sins.

It was our ordinary habit to breakfast and dine daily at the restaurant attached to the Hotel Itur-

bide. You can, if you please, take a monthly
abonnement for twenty-five dollars (5*l.*), which is
certainly a very moderate charge for two substantial
meals a day. I should highly recommend travellers
to follow this arrangement. It is at your peril that
you swerve from it. I followed it for a month, at the
end of which time I felt a yearning for a little more
liberty, for which I paid very dear. As an instance
of this, I cannot refrain from inserting a bill which
was presented me for a plain dinner without wine—

	Doll.	Cents.
Potage	0	50
Poulet	1	0
Pouding de Riz	2	50
	4	0

or 16*s.* English money. When I sent for the proprietor
of the restaurant, and objected to the charge of half a
sovereign for a plain rice pudding, the only consolation
I got was that, had I dined in my room, he should
have charged me three dollars and a half (14*s.*); that
a rice pudding was a thing that gave an infinity of
trouble, and had taken up so much of the chef's time
that, for himself, he hoped I should not order it again.
Finally he consented to take half a dollar off the bill,
which I then paid. My companion, who was on one
occasion rash enough to invite five friends to dinner,
was charged the sum of one hundred dollars (20*l.*),
being at the moderate rate of 3*l.* 6*s.* 8*d.* per head.

I

Nothing strikes a stranger in Mexico so much as the limpness of the natives. You feel an irresistible longing to put a little starch into them, but it is not to be done. Their limpness is apparent in their whole behaviour, whether engaged in business or pleasure. The only thing the Mexicans are not limp about is their gambling. This limpness often however takes a very amusing turn, as in the following incident. My companion and I were invited to dine one evening with one of the principal Mexican families. When the day came it occurred to us that no hour was fixed, so we took it for granted that the dinner would come off soon after seven—the hour at which the most fashionable people dine in Mexico. So, at a quarter-past seven, we repaired to the house in full evening costume, and were rather surprised to meet our host crossing the "patio" in morning dress. Thinking that perhaps we had mistaken the day, we made the suggestion to our host, upon which he rejoined gaily, "Oh dear no, walk up, I am only just going to make a call, and shall be back directly." So up stairs we walked; but, instead of finding any signs of dinner or our hostess, we were amused to find the servants dancing in the corridors, and a great deal of merry-making going on. We had dropped in upon what is called a "Posada"—a kind of carnival, which takes place during the days immediately preceding Christmas-day, during which an inordinate amount of sweetmeats is consumed, and families parade in procession to commemorate the fruitless search of the Virgin Mary and Joseph for quarters at the inn at Bethlehem. After regarding the merry-making for a little, our hostess not having yet appeared, we bethought ourselves that we had friends near, and accordingly went and paid them a visit. At the end of an hour we returned, and finally dinner was served.

CHAPTER VII.

LIFE IN THE CITY (*continued*).

In taking care that the important items of roast beef, plum-pudding, and mince-pies shall not be absent from their dinner-table, the English in Mexico observe Christmas-day as religiously as we do at home. But English church service there is none—only a feeble imitation of it in the shape of a French Protestant service, instituted I suppose for such of the French soldiers as belonged to the Protestant religion, but frequented in the most praiseworthy manner by English ladies, whether they understand French or not. Only once before was a Protestant service ever held in the city of Mexico—when General Scott established one for his soldiers, during the occupation of the city by the Americans.

While the English ladies pay a graceful compliment to the French by attending their service, the gentlemen, who are for the most part engaged in business all the week, devote the Sunday to the healthy recreation of cricket, by which means alone they lay in a sufficient stock of health, to keep them going through the week.

But to return to the subject of Christmas-day in Mexico. Not for mince-pies, plum-puddings, cricket, nor any kind of religious service, will that day be thenceforth memorable to me, but as being the first occasion on which I witnessed a bull-fight. Now, in spite of its being on the whole a revolting and demoralizing spectacle, a bull-fight is certainly a thing to be seen once in one's life, but by no means twice. It was the following advertisement, which seems to me to be worthy of being laid before the reader in its entirety, which drew our attention, in common with that of the rest of the Mexican public, to the subject of bull-fights:—

"On the first of the current month, I had the honour to avail myself of the leading journals of the capital to direct an invitation to the renowned (matador) Bernardo Gavino and other dexterous performers, in order to give as much *éclat* as possible to the entertainment which I propose to give in the amphitheatre in the New Paseo. At the same time you will be pleased to take notice that I do not intend to exclude amateurs from trying their hand.

" Now that definite arrangements have been made with Señor Gavino and his troop for the first entertainments, to take place on the 25th and 26th of the present month, it is indispensable that the public should be informed by anticipation of my desires, which are simply to serve it to the utmost of my ability, and to enable it to enjoy the traditional recreation of our country, for the moderate entrance-fee of one dollar in the shade, and three reals (eighteen-pence) in the sun.

"As this is a duty to which I devote myself cheerfully for the sake of my fellow-citizens, I confidently expect that the order, which is indispensable to such exhibitions, may not be disturbed, and that by this means society, which judges of all our actions, may be impressed in our favour.

"It being impossible for a mortal to fulfil to the letter all that he proposes, it is for this reason that I beg of the public, to whom I have the honour to address myself, to deign to take a lenient view of such trifling blemishes as may be independent of my volition. "JOSÉ JORGE ARELLANO.

"MEXICO, *December* 19, 1864."

Attracted by the above notice, we repaired to the Plaza de Toros in the Pasco Nuevo, at 4 P.M. on Christmas-day. Having paid our dollars for seats in the *sombra* or shade, on entering we found the spectacle in full swing. A little dark brown angry bull, gaily decked out with garlands and many-coloured rosettes, was in the act of rushing at a *banderillero*, whose agility in swerving on one side, and at the same moment planting another fish-hook with rosette attached in the flesh of the animal, the multitude greeted with vehement applause. In the arena, besides the *banderilleros* or rosette-planters, who were provided with red and green flags to wave before the bull, were several *picadores* or prickers, armed with lances and mounted on very sorry steeds, whose breasts were protected by metal plates, and their hinder quarters completely encased in armour, which gave them the appearance of hobby-horses.

The amphitheatre itself was crammed to overflowing, and presented a very gay spectacle. Each box was tastefully decorated with the Mexican colours, red, white, and green, and there was a good sprinkling of fashionable toilettes. In the centre of the dress-circle was the box of the *juez* or umpire, in the decoration of which very great taste was displayed. On one side the band, and *vis-à-vis* to it on the other side a company of Mexican infantry, separated the *élite* in the *sombra* from the rabble in the *sol*, who, I must say, behaved with great decency throughout.

At the first *coup d'œil* the spectacle appeared very attractive, and there seemed nothing at all revolting about it. Not till one saw the blood trickling down the sides of the bull, did one become aware that the gay rosettes were fastened in his flesh by means of a kind of fish-hook. But in spite of this, from time to time, by dint of tremendous shaking, the poor beast would contrive to rid himself of one occasionally; at which, as it lay on the ground, he would butt furiously, and try to toss it with his horns. Then a *banderillero* would approach, and drawing off the bull's attention from the rosette by waving his scarf in front of him, would fly before him to the shelter of a boarding, between which and the side of the arena was left just sufficient space to admit of a man's body. In consequence of this arrangement, you very soon felt convinced that the men on foot ran no sort of danger.

It is now the turn of the mounted *picador* to approach. At first the bull seems to take no notice of his assailant. When this happens, the *picador* knows that he has a desperate customer to deal with, and must look out for himself. The bull is only pausing to gather himself up for a desperate charge. Lowering his head, he rushes headlong, and bowls over rider and horse. The rider may extricate himself as best he may from his steed, for the bull doesn't care for him. It is the unfortunate horse on which he is bent on wreaking his vengeance, and does not desist until he has ripped the belly open. Then delicate ladies clap their hands, as the poor horse, if he has strength to rise, limps out of the arena with his entrails hanging down and trailing along the ground.

But the hour of the bull has now come. He has had his allotted fifteen minutes of torment crowned by his bloody revenge, and must now die. While the *banderilleros* and *picadores* retire, the *matador* or slayer steps forward into the arena, approaches the judge's box, and makes his obeisance—more fortunate he than the Roman gladiators, with their "Ave, Cæsar, morituri te salutant."

Armed with a rapier in his right hand, and a red scarf in his left, the *matador* approaches his prey. Then follows a momentary pause, and a silence that may be felt pervades the multitude. The first time that the *matador* waves his scarf before the bull, provoking him to charge, the *habitués* know that the death blow will not be dealt. But the second time that the bull exposes his broad side in charging past the executioner, who swerves with the utmost ease on one side, then his fate is sealed. At a single blow, the *matador* plunges the sword up to the hilt in the heart of the animal, with such dexterity that untrained eyes hardly know what has happened. Then is the moment that a Roman crowd would have shouted out, "Habet!" (he has got his death-blow); the full force of which expression flashes, for the first time, across the mind.

At this juncture the *banderilleros* again approach, and wave their scarves before the bull on all sides to make him turn and pursue them; in order, by this means, to aggravate the dizziness brought on by the loss of blood. The poor beast, clinging to life, makes one or two feeble efforts to get at his foes. Then dreadful moments follow as the giddiness increases, and you can feel that the death agony is approaching. Finally the bull, keeping his legs to the last, and describing smaller and smaller circles—the last vanishing into a point—gathers himself together, and sinks down all of a heap to die.

Then the trumpets bray out, the gates of the arena are flung open, and a yoke of gaily caparisoned mules, with nodding plumes of green, red, and white, are driven up to where the bull lies weltering in his own blood; a lasso is thrown round his legs, and the carcase is dragged out of the arena amid the plaudits of the multitude.

In the short period which intervenes before the appearance of the second bull, a couple of clowns entertain the multitude by cutting capers. Of these capers the most genuine and involuntary are the last, to get out of the way of the fresh bull; who is infuriated at the outset by a rosette dexterously planted on the nape of his neck, as he is in the act of rushing from his den into the arena.

In much the same fashion as his predecessor, the second bull was worried and finally slain; and after him three more—five bulls and five horses being sacrificed to make a Mexican holiday; but no man received a scratch. In the death of one of the bulls, the interest was much increased by the feat which he performed of shaking the sword right out of his heart among the audience in the lower tier of boxes.

As I left the amphitheatre reflecting on the cruelty of the spectacle I had just witnessed, I could not help thinking, as my eyes fell on the snow-capped summits of Popocatapetl and Iztaccihuatl, that it would have served the people right had these volcanos resumed their activity, and, Vesuvius-like, buried the amphitheatre with ashes.

The Plaza de Toros stands at the head of the Paseo Nuevo, where the show of carriages on Sundays and feast days is certainly the most remarkable sight which the city of Mexico has to offer to strangers. There is no sacrifice to which a Mexican will not willingly submit during the week, in order to put in an appearance in some sort of a vehicle in the Paseo on Sunday. Food, clothing, education, are one and all considerations which are not to be weighed for a moment against the all-important Sunday drive. Society, which inexorably requires of its votaries to appear in the Paseo on Sunday, is by no means exacting as to the nature of that appearance. Indeed, in Mexico, it is a generally received maxim that no person need be deterred from showing him or herself in the Paseo because of the shabbiness of their clothes, or the humble nature of their equipage.

About half an hour before sunset, the Mexican world, which, for fear of exposing itself to the heat of the sun, boxes itself up till that time, begins to stream down the Calle de Plateros and Calle de San Francisco, through the Alameda into the Paseo Nuevo; which is very soon thronged with a double procession of carriages at the sides, and of horsemen in the centre.

It is worth while to visit the Paseo half an hour before the world makes its appearance, in order to observe the Indians at work watering it. The business of watering the roads in and about the city of Mexico is carried on upon two distinct principles, which are applied according to circumstances. The first of these principles consists of shovelling the water out of an aqueduct down on the road from above, and the second in pitching up bucketsful out of a ditch from below. In whatever direction you turn in the neighbourhood of the city of Mexico, you are certain to find a ditch or an aqueduct by the roadside, and not unfrequently both. I think, of the two methods, the pitching up from below is preferable, as the unwary traveller is less likely to get a ducking, than where the shovelling-down system is applied. If both should be going on at the same time, there is no help for it, but to put spurs to your horse, and run the gauntlet between the two fires.

The Paseo Nuevo is a strip of dry land, some two miles long, reaching from the Plaza de Toros to La Piedad, an outlying church, which was formerly remarkable for the richness of its ornaments, but which now presents a most forlorn appearance. This long slip of dry land, called the Paseo, is, flanked by wide, unsavoury ditches, which separate it from the surrounding expanse of spongy meadows. If there is anything at all attractive about the appearance of the Paseo, it is entirely to be attributed to the avenue of Mexican poplars, which more or less conceal the deformities of the above-mentioned ditches.

At about four P.M. the Indians, whose duty it is to water the Paseo, make their appearance upon the scene. They find the road some six inches deep in sand, and leave it six inches deep in mud. They set to work without any kind of method. Instead of appointing some of their number to stand down by the ditch and fill the buckets, and then hand them up to others ready to receive them, each man works entirely on his own account. Bucket in hand, he goes down into the ditch, fills his bucket with water, spills about half of its contents in scrambling up again, and pitches the remainder with a great splash all in one spot on the road. This process of watering goes on till the company begins to appear.

In the Mexican Paseo on a gala day, you may see, I suppose, a greater variety of carriages than you would meet with in any European capital. By the side of the cumbrous family coaches of the Mexican aristocracy, mostly drawn by richly caparisoned mules, you may see neat English broughams, elegant barouches from Paris and Vienna, light outrigger carriages of wonderful construction from New York and San Francisco, at least one four-in-hand drag, and every kind of humbler native and foreign conveyance.

But the most striking feature of the whole is certainly the costume of the riders, and the trappings of the horses. Each horseman looks as if he were returning home with trophies of the chase, such a display of skins is hung about himself and his steed.

As for the rider, on his head he wears a felt hat with an outrageously broad brim, called, significantly, *sombrero,* or sun-shade. The *sombreros* worn by Mexican dandies are worked with such a mass of gold and silver embroidery that the prices they reach are something fabulous. Under the hat is an embroidered jacket, and the rider's legs and breeches are encased in leopard's skin overalls, called *chaparcros.* Finally, an enormous pair of spurs jingle at his heels. So much for the rider.

As for the horse, it is managed by a cord, which is as slender as the bit, with which it communicates is severe. A sudden jerk of the rein causes a round plate in the centre of the bit to spring with such violence against the roof of the animal's mouth, as to pull it up on the instant, at whatever pace it be going. Mexicans, however, will never admit the severity of the national bit. If such a bit could be put in the mouths of the men, I suspect that we should hear no more of Mexican revolutions.

The saddle-cloth commonly in use in Mexico is a wonderful arrangement of skins and fringes, which lends the horse a wild appearance, which is as picturesque as it is unpractical. The saddle itself, like all barbaric saddles, is provided with a huge peak behind and before ; the front peak, round which the lasso is wound, terminating in a round silver plate. The stirrups—of which the leathers are some six inches wide, and the irons capacious boxes to hold the feet—are of so intricate a construction, that without long apprenticeship it is impossible to understand how they are worked. It appeared to me to take at least two men to take them up or let them down a hole. The seat of the saddle is made of wood, over which a shiny coating of leather is sometimes stretched, and an aperture is slit down the centre, to prevent the seat from getting hot. The arrangement has its decided advantages, and it is remarked that after the first few months, Europeans generally take to the Mexican saddles and bridles in the same way they do to *pulque*, which is nauseous to most people at first.

So careful are the Mexican ladies of their complexions, that they take what they are pleased to call their "airing" boxed up in the family coach, an arrangement which, in the most provoking manner, hides the charms of the señoras, who may be discovered indolently leaning back in the corners, as if they did not come out to see and be seen. However, by a kind of instinct, they are said to know the right moment to lean forward, when the looked-for cavalier approaches, who, on his side, understands when to show his horsemanship off to advantage.

In the evening of Christmas-day we dined with Mr. Barron, at his magnificent house in the Calle San Francisco, and so *recherché* a dinner was served up, that we were not surprised to learn that the Emperor had petitioned for the loan of Mr. Barron's cook during his master's contemplated absence in Europe. The dinner was followed by a ball, which was the most brilliant affair. At midnight the guests were conducted into a supper-room, where a wonderful banquet was laid out. What astonished me more than anything else was the profuse display of slender-stemmed wine-glasses, cut-glass decanters, &c.; for only residents in Mexico can form any notion of the frightful mortality which rages among these fragile articles in the course of transport on mule-back up from the coast. It so happened that Mr. Barron received several cases of glass from Europe one day when we were dining with him, and on opening them he found that, on an average, hardly three out of each dozen had arrived unbroken.

Having been fêted on Christmas-day with such magnificence by Mr. Barron, I may add that we were guests at a hardly less sumptuous entertainment, given by Mr. D—— on New Year's eve. However as we clinked our glasses at the stroke of midnight, it seemed to take something off the glossiness of the New Year to reflect that it was already five hours old to those near and dear to us in England. When we here in England are gathered round the death-bed of the Old Year, who shall say what day it is at the antipodes? Of course the hour is twelve o'clock at noon, but is it December 31st or January 1st? I will leave the reader to decide for himself. Lord Dundreary would, I suspect, class the difficulty among those things "which no feller can understand."

Before leaving the city of Mexico, I went to visit the cemetery of San Pablo, understanding that it was a curious sight in its way. On entering the porch, I saw a large waste piece of ground before me, quite free of gravestones, and, but for a chapel in the centre, showing no signs of serving as a burial-ground. On one side of the chapel stood a few trees, from among which a three-legged cur made its appearance, and barked violently at me.

All round the ground ran a wall, fitted with niches to receive the coffins of such persons, as could afford the luxury of being buried high and dry out of the reach of the black mud, into which the bodies of poor persons are lowered in the "patio," or graveyard in the centre. After looking about me for a short time, my attention was attracted by a knot of persons on my left. Supposing that a funeral was taking place, I approached slowly, and was astonished to observe a photographic lens directed towards an open coffin, in which the corpse of a middle-aged woman was exposed to public gaze. Turning away from this spectacle, I struck across the ground to a spot, where some labourers were engaged digging a grave, which was already half-a-foot deep in slush. I had not long to wait here before I saw a funeral *cortége*, if I may so call it, approaching, for neither priest nor mourners followed the corpse, which was borne to the grave by a couple of ruffianly-looking fellows in shirt sleeves, accompanied by a crowd of idlers. Having reached the brink of the grave, the bearers deposited the coffin on the heap of earth thrown up out of it, and proceeded to inspect the grave itself. While they were thus engaged I had leisure to observe the corpse, which I found to be that of a woman, and apparently not a very poor person.

In the meantime, the bearers had come to the conclusion that the grave would not do, and passed on to another, which contained rather less water. Into this they lowered the corpse, having first pitched in a few broken planks for the coffin to rest on.

This operation was hardly completed when a second burying-party arrived with the corpse of the woman who had been photographed. Her body was lowered into the grave which had been rejected by the first comers, with as little ceremony as if they had been burying a dog. The same knot of persons who had witnessed the photographic performance accompanied the corpse to the grave. Among them, a tall stout woman, with grey hair, who seemed more than anybody else to take the lead in the proceedings, particularly attracted my attention. While the rest of the assemblage watched the operation of lowering the body into the grave, this old woman deliberately sat down on a heap of earth mingled with human bones, and quietly lighted a cigarette, which she proceeded to smoke with the utmost unconcern.

During the half hour that I remained in the cemetery, three funerals took place—in every case without a vestige of religious observance of any kind. Whether the absence of a priest was to be explained by the fact that the persons interred had forfeited their privilege of Christian burial from having been declared heretics, or implicated in the purchase of Church property, or whether they were too poor to pay for the attendance of a priest, I was unable to find out.

CHAPTER VIII.

THE ENVIRONS.

It is sufficiently characteristic of the country, that until within the last few years the only bit of railway existing in Mexico was that which conveys pilgrims from the capital to the celebrated shrine of our Lady of Guadalupe. In order to make the thing quite complete, the line, which is some two miles and a half long, is portioned out into twelve praying stations, analogous to those which one so frequently meets with, leading to some shrine on the summit of a hill, in the Catholic parts of Europe. The locomotive, however, which is of American construction, has not been trained to stop at the stations, and never pulls up till it reaches the terminus at Mexico, or Guadalupe.

December 12*th*.—The anniversary of the appearance of the Virgin Mary to the blessed Indian Juan Diego—an event which, having been invented for the purpose, of course led to the immediate conversion of the Aztecs to Christianity—is to the Mexicans what the Derby-day is to Londoners. It is the one day in the year on which the whole population of the city turns out into the country—if, indeed, one is justified in applying the term "country" to the miserable tract which is traversed by the road leading from the capital to Guadalupe.

The shrine of Guadalupe, conspicuously built on a projecting spur of the dreary treeless mountain-chain which bounds the valley of Mexico to the north, lies some two miles and a half distant from the city of Mexico. The present road which connects La Villa de Guadalupe—as it is called in common parlance—with the capital, is perhaps identical with that by which Cortes and his followers left Mexico on the "Noche Triste" (the sad night), of which such a graphic description is given in Prescott. At the period of the conquest, the prospect on either side the causeway must have been considerably less dreary than it is now, for then the eye wandered over an expanse of water reaching right up to the foot of the hills, which at that period are reported to have been well wooded. But since those days the scene has entirely changed, and the aspect which this portion of the valley of Mexico has presented since the draining off of the waters of the lake of Tezcuco is unutterably desolate. Were this region merely an unsightly tract of bog and marsh land, tenanted only by wild-fowl, like the larger portion of the valley, immediately surrounding the city, it would be bad enough, but I should have taken it as a matter of course. Here, however, scabby mounds of earth, standing forlorn amidst mud ruins of abandoned villages, lend an air of desolation quite peculiar to itself to this portion of what travellers will persist in calling the beautiful valley of Anahuac. On inquiring what could have induced human beings to settle on these marshes, I was informed, that when the waters of the lake of Tezcuco were drained off, the soil was found to be so impregnated with salt, that the poverty-stricken Indians found that they could support for a time a precarious existence on the slender profits derivable from washing the earth for salt. But their settlements have been long since abandoned, and are now only marked by the ruins of their mud hovels, and huge heaps of earth from which the salt has been extracted.

As on the Derby-day, the momentous question of going by road or by rail has first to be settled. We should probably have chosen the rail, had not Mr. Barron offered us seats in his drag, in which we performed the journey with as much comfort as is compatible with the state of Mexican roads.

Our first difficulty was to find our way out of the city, for the infamous road, along which we had been bumping at first, vanished altogether before we reached the northern *garita*, to which we were left to find our way, as best we might, by crossing waste places at haphazard, and dodging in and out among ruined churches, standing forlorn in the midst of sandy wildernesses.

After an exciting steeple-chase through the extremities of the city, we at last reached the Garita de Guadalupe, and were soon fairly on the high road, where the scene, in many of its features, was eminently suggestive of the roads leading to Epsom on a Derby-day. That one-horse van crowded with boisterous dust-begrimed merry-makers—the women arrayed in bright yellow and green dresses—might have taken its place with perfect propriety in the ruck of vehicles on the road to Epsom; and there was something peculiarly suggestive of the Downs in the appearance of yonder steed, out of which the man and woman on its back are trying to get an expiring canter.

In less than an hour we had reached La Villa, where a vast crowd of Indians was surging to and fro in front of the church, in which high mass was being performed by our ancient friend the Nuncio in the presence of the Emperor and Empress, and all the dignitaries of State. As soon as the religious service was over, the procession, for which the crowd had been waiting long and patiently, issued from the church, and the Emperor and Empress, surrounded by a brilliant court, showed themselves to the multitude.

So far the poor Indians had been exposed for hours to a broiling sun, and had seen little or nothing. The religious ceremony had, of course, been performed inside the church, to which a very limited number could be admitted.

I wonder if any one of that crowd of Indians had any inkling of the fact that any other than the Roman Catholic religion ever existed in the country. If he had, he might have reflected that, however bloody and barbarous were the observances of the worship of his ancestors, that religion had this great advantage, that it was conducted entirely in the open air. This was the secret of the extraordinary hold it obtained over the minds of its votaries.

The most striking feature in the Imperial *cortège* was the Emperor's Palatine Guard—a phalanx of giants averaging at least six feet six inches per man, who, in their flashing cuirasses, and helmets surmounted by golden eagles, must have appeared to the Indians as very gods. For myself, I could not help thinking it was but fair that these giants should be engrossing popular admiration, when I reflected to what inconvenience they must have been put on the voyage out from Europe. What penance walking between decks must have been to them! and where did they ever find berths in which to stretch themselves at full length?

While the royal party retire to the residence of the

Canons to take breakfast—the Canons, a large portion of whose income is derived from the profits of their lottery, which has its ramifications all over Mexico—the crowd outside also devotes itself to the important business of feasting upon the provisions, which each party has brought with it from home. There are no Derby luncheons here. The Indians, even on this gala day, do not depart from their usual fare of tortillas and chilis, while the groups of middle-class holiday-makers produce their scraggy smoke-dried legs of mutton, hams, or strips of sun-dried beef.

Near me is seated rather a pretty creole, who has walked out from the capital with husband and children. As they produce their meagre luncheon, a hungry priest approaches and eyes the tempting-looking viands wistfully, but in vain.

In the mean time I took the opportunity of looking into the church, which was still crammed with pilgrims, and redolent of incense, for the fumes of which the Indians have an especial weakness. Over the altar hangs the celebrated miracle-working painting of the Virgin, copies of which are scattered by millions all over Mexico. To the profane eye there is nothing remarkable about the picture, nor about the church as a whole, except the massive silver rails which surround the choir.

Besides this, the principal, church there is a smaller

one on the hill some two or three hundred feet above it, reached by a steep pathway hewn out of the rock. The upper one is, I believe, regarded as the original church, which the Virgin Mary ordered to be built, three hundred years ago, on the spot where she manifested herself to the Indian. No devotee will go home with a clear conscience unless he has mounted to the shrine on the hill, and said his prayers there, as well as in the church below.

Although there is absolutely nothing worth seeing about the church itself, it is worth while mounting for the sake of the view, provided you can get past the jostling crowd of Indians, which makes the ascent a work of some danger and difficulty.

As soon as the breakfast was over, the carriages of the various dignitaries in Church and State rolled up to the entrance of the Canonry, and took up their respective loads.

Among the earliest to take his departure was Archbishop Labastida, who, in his robes of lavender and green, rich lace skirt, shoes with silver buckles, and three-corned hat ornamented with green and gold, seemed bent on eclipsing the Nuncio, who followed him immediately, attended by his priestly aides-de-camp.

As soon as the Nuncio had been whirled off, Marshal Bazaine appeared upon the scene, stepped into his carriage, and was driven off. After him came

Monsieur de Montholon, and then General Uraga, General Ampudia, Señor Escudero y Echanove (Minister of Justice), and the rest of the great people.

Last of all, and from the simplicity of their morning costume in striking contrast to the dignitaries in their court dresses, whose heavy coaches had just rolled off, appeared the Emperor and Empress. Stepping into a light open phaeton, drawn by six mules with nodding plumes and jingling bells, they drive off in an unpretending manner, attended by a single aide-de-camp and a couple of Mexican outriders.

While the Villa de Guadalupe, where nobody but the lazy luxurious canons live, may be reached in a few minutes by rail, Tacubaya, where the wealthier citizens and foreign merchants have their country villas, is only connected with the capital by a mule tramway.

Were one condemned to end one's days in Mexico, one could perhaps hardly fix on a better place than Tacubaya to live in, though I have little doubt that even there life would soon become a burden to one. For there is that in the atmosphere of Mexico which renders "living" as opposed to "vegetating" something like an impossibility. Let a man come from Europe with what amount of energy he will, and mix for a year or two with a people, the mass of whom are, perhaps, rather destitute of any character at all, than vicious, and in their lives display an absolute indifference on all subjects, gambling excepted, and let us see what will become of his energy.

However, I should be guilty of the blackest ingratitude were I not to allow that Tacubaya has its charms. I will even go the length of admitting, that to one lately escaped from the city of Mexico Tacubaya may well appear a kind of Paradise; and I have little doubt that strangers who are fortunate enough to enjoy the friendship of Don Antonio Escandon and Mr. Barron will look back to the hours spent in their villas at Tacubaya, as the most enjoyable portion of their stay in Mexico.

Connoisseurs of paintings will find a great deal to admire and interest them in Mr. Barron's collection. Having never heard of a Mexican School of Art, I was much surprised to find the entrance-hall and several rooms hung with the works of native artists, arranged in chronological order for the convenience of the student. In the upper rooms are several very fine Murillos, a most remarkable head by Velasquez, and a number of less striking pictures by artists belonging to the Italian school.

Of native Mexican paintings, those of Echavi the Elder—the founder of the school—seemed to me to be the most finished, though perhaps the most remarkable were the works of an Indian called "Mendoza el Indio," to distinguish him from another painter of the same name. Besides these, the names of Cabrera, Carreno, Spañolleto, are deserving of mention. Most of these artists flourished in the latter half of the seventeenth and first half of the eighteenth centuries. Since the achievement of their independence, I am not aware that Mexico has produced a painter of any note.

The city and valley of Mexico are seen to greater advantage from the terrace in front of Mr. Barron's villa than from any other point that I know of. For there the beautiful gardens in front of the villa furnish an attractive foreground to the picture, and at the same time conceal, in a great measure, much that is unsightly in the valley of Mexico as seen from other points. In the middle distance the city with its domes and towers is stretched before you, not very unlike Oxford as seen from Bagley Wood; while the snow-capped volcanos form a magnificent background.

The tram-way which connects Tacubaya with the capital is carried for its entire length of three miles over an unsightly expanse of bog. But once you reach Tacubaya the ground begins to rise, and the soft bog-land is exchanged for a barren crumbling formation of tufa, as dry and arid as the other was wet and spongy. With such a soil to contend against, it is really wonderful that the gardeners of Tacubaya can produce anything so creditable in the way of lawns as you meet with there.

Had one been asked to name the thing, with which there was the least chance of meeting in a country like Mexico, one might very well have fixed on a game of croquet. Yet at Tacubaya you now find the inevitable hoops arranged on at least one lawn, and I believe I had the honour of taking part in the first game of croquet that was ever played in the land of Montezuma.

While croquet goes on at Tacubaya, the neighbouring village of Napoles is the head-quarters of cricket. Napoles is reached from Tacubaya by a deep sandy road, shaded in places by the elegant Peru tree, which is rather like the weeping-willow. The district which it traverses consists of meadows as hard as iron, surrounded by hedges of cactus and maguey, or meadows as soft as a sponge, surrounded by ditches. On one of the meadows, as hard as iron, the cricket takes place.

During the voyage out from England I had heard that cricket was played in the country, but supposed it would turn out to be cricket of that degenerate sort which one finds occasionally played by the English residents in different parts of Europe. So that when I got on to the ground, and found an excellent pavilion, a scoring-box, visitors' tent, the field marked out with flags, with the well-known letters M.C.C. (Mexico, not Marylebone, Cricket Club) marked upon them, and some eighteen or twenty players in flannels and cricket shoes, I was not a little astonished, and soon found out that I had to do with a very different sort of cricket to what I had expected.

Perhaps the most surprising part of the performance was that the best player on the ground was a Mexican, whose bowling and batting did infinite credit to the training which he received at Bruce Castle school.

Among the English players were several gentlemen close upon sixty years of age, who all expressed to me their conviction that they owed much of the health and energy which they still possessed, in spite of a forty years' residence in Mexico, to having stuck, through thick and thin, to their Sunday cricket. They assured me that they had never allowed political events to interfere with their game, which they had pursued unconcernedly, more than once, in view of the fighting going on in the hills around them.

Being fully alive to the fact that cricket is nothing without beer, there is always a liberal supply on the ground, of a very excellent quality, supplied by the firm of Blackmore — a name revered, beyond all others, by Englishmen in Mexico.

Midway between the city of Mexico and Tacubaya, conspicuous on a rocky eminence which rises out of a dark grove of primeval cypresses, stands the Castle of Chapultepec, a spot more than any other in the whole valley of Mexico associated with the memory of Montezuma. In the recesses of this grove of bearded sacred "ahuahuetes," the Aztec name for the *cupressus distichas* stood the temple where Montezuma used to offer up chosen human victims in private, whenever he stood in special need of counsel from heaven. It was to this shady retreat that the Aztec monarch retired, to commune with the deity, and to meditate upon the course to be pursued, when the tidings of the landing of the Spaniards reached him—an event which exercised from the beginning, an extraordinary spell over him. It was there, too, that he convinced himself that the white men could be none other than the descendants of the beneficent Quetzalcoatl; to whose return the oracles darkly pointed.

In their crusade against all relics of antiquity, and in their zeal to blot out everything associated with the past history and idolatrous worship of the Aztecs, it is surprising that the Spaniards should have left Chapultepec untouched. As it is, Chapultepec stands alone—the sole link connecting the Mexico of the Spaniards with the Tenochtitlan of the Aztecs, and the only spot where the memory of the past seems to linger.

Finding no other substance to feed upon, the imagination of the traveller, which will probably have been cruelly whetted by glowing descriptions of the country, will seize greedily upon this one spot, and cling to it in despair of finding any other place of rest.

In this feeling of respect for Chapultepec, the Emperor, who has made it his summer palace, is said to participate very strongly, and is as much bent on preserving every relic of the past, as the Spaniards were in obliterating them. Whether in pursuing this course the Emperor is influenced more by sentiment or policy, I will not presume to decide. If he be actuated by political motives, he could hardly have made a more successful bid for the sympathies of the Indians; for to no other spot would the monarchical leanings of the mass of the population so naturally attach, as to the rock and grove of Chapultepec; about which there seems to be an air of royalty, as inherent as in our own Windsor.

There are two roads from the city to Chapultepec; the one private, the other public. On the private road, the hoofs of your horse bury themselves in gravel; on the public road, in sand. For their whole length, both roads are skirted by ditches of black mud; and, for the latter half, by aqueducts— favourable for the double process of watering. Until it reaches the aqueduct, where it turns to the right, the public road is identical with the Paseo; and by

a figure of speech, may be said to be shady so far; but is exposed to the full heat of the sun for the rest of its course. The private road is shady all the way, and so it became our favourite morning ride. Whether we had any right to be there, I could never exactly make out; but I am inclined to think we had not, as we never met anybody, except the Emperor and Empress, and their suite.

Some six miles due south of the city, lies the picturesque village of St. Angel, a smaller and more retired Tacubaya. A little beyond St. Angel, and almost at the foot of Ajusco—the most conspicuous of the mountains which shut in the valley of Mexico on the south—lies the hamlet of Tizapan, celebrated for its cotton factory, and the hospitality of its late proprietor, Mr. Lowe; who—alas! for future travellers—has just bade farewell to Mexico for ever.

In the immediate neighbourhood of Tizapan is a curious lava formation, called the "Pedregal," which is pronounced by geologists to be of great scientific interest. To the unscientific eye, however, the Pedregal, except in those spots where it is traversed by running streams, which descend from Ajusco, presents a most unattractive appearance; and the prickly dwarf cactus, which crops here and there in the midst of the excoriated rock, rather adds to, than detracts from, the thirsty barren air which characterises the district, and makes itself so oppressively felt.

A visit to the Pedregal is not unattended with danger, as it abounds in caves and lurking-places for brigands, who are apt to spring out upon the unwary traveller. In order to put me on my guard, my hostess at Tizapan was good enough to describe to me in detail an encounter with robbers, with which two English gentlemen—guests of theirs—had met some time previously. It appeared that these gentlemen had started from Tizapan in the morning, on a sketching expedition, and were brought back in the afternoon in a most lamentable condition, from injuries received about the head. What made their case all the more aggravating was, that the blows had been inflicted with the butt end of their own revolvers, which had been wrested from them by the robbers at the outset.

A few miles beyond the Pedregal, up the slope of Ajusco, lies a wooded ravine called La Cañada—a scene which forms a most agreeable contrast with the gloomy sterility of the Pedregal. Right in the mouth of the ravine, down which a mountain torrent rushes, stands, buried in a wilderness of orchards and flower-gardens, a villa, which it is impossible to behold without coveting.

To the east of San Angel, lies San Augustin—

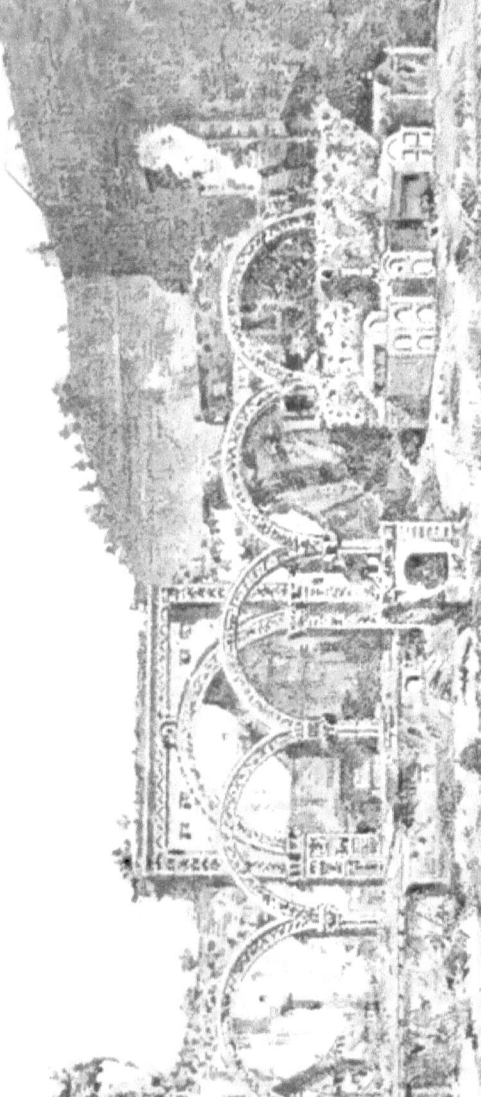

celebrated for its Midsummer festivities. During these days, no business is transacted in the capital, and judges, generals, and cabinet ministers, give themselves up to unlimited gambling.

The ruins of Tlalmanalco, which form the subject of the engraving on the opposite page, are situated near the hamlet of Amcca, which lies at the foot of Popocatapetl. Little more than the bare fact, that they are of Spanish origin, appears to be known about them.

CHAPTER IX.

A RIDE ROUND THE LAKE OF TEZCUCO.

No reader of Prescott will be content to leave Mexico without visiting Tezcuco, a city which, at at the time of the conquest, rivalled the Aztec capital in splendour. Accordingly, with this object in view, I started, on January 18th, at daybreak, determined to make the tour of the lake of Tezcuco. As I rode out of the *porte cochère* into the Calle de Plateros, my attention was attracted by the heavy rumble of artillery passing down the street. On inquiring of a French soldier what was about to take place, I learnt that four brigands were to be shot at 6 A.M. in the Plaza Mescalco, and that the guns were intended to keep the populace in awe during the execution. As the Plaza Mescalco lay but a hundred yards out of my road, I determined to turn aside and witness the proceedings.

On reaching the place of execution, I found a file of Mexican infantry drawn up in front of a blank wall, which bore ample traces of bullet marks, cloquent of previous executions. Behind the Mexicans, who were appointed to carry out the sentence of death, was drawn up a company of French Zouaves doubtless with a view of keeping the Mexicans up to the mark. In the rear the artillery took up position, while the ground was kept by a second company of Zouaves.

We had some time to wait for the arrival of the prisoners, and it was hard work to keep oneself warm at that hour in the morning. The sun had not yet risen, and the nights and early mornings in Mexico are desperately cold in the winter season. When at length the four culprits were brought on to the ground, escorted by a guard of Belgians, they seemed already more than half dead of fear and cold. As for the Belgians, they looked so warm and comfortable in their grey great-coats, that it was quite a pleasure to contemplate them. Nor was it difficult to read in their fresh complexions, which contrasted remarkably with the dusty worn looks of the Zouaves and Mexicans, that they had but recently arrived in the country.

The foremost prisoner—a poor shivering copper coloured creature, with his *scrape* wrapped round him like a blanket—was supported on to the ground between two priests, and made to kneel down in front of the file of soldiers. The three who followed were the exact counterpart of the first, and none of the four looked as if he could ever have had the courage to kill a mouse. At intervals of ten paces from each other, they were made to kneel down between the wall and their executioners.

The eyes of the prisoners having been blindfolded, and sentence of death read out, the word was given to fire, and the four prisoners collapsed at the same moment. Two fell stone dead, but the other two required an additional shot, which was administered by Zouaves at close quarters. Immediately after four plain deal coffins were brought forward, and the still quivering bodies placed in them and carried off the ground. The whole ceremony occupied less than ten minutes, and appeared to excite no kind of emotion among the spectators. The precaution of planting artillery on the ground seemed absolutely superfluous, as there was no crowd to overawe.

It wanted a quarter of seven, as I passed through the *garita* of San Lazaro, the same by which the Puebla road enters the city. That day week the diligence had been robbed in the most barefaced manner just outside the *garita*, for all I knew by the very brigands whom I had just seen shot. However, an armed traveller on horseback is a customer to whom Mexican brigands are not in general partial, preferring the tamer variety, which travels by diligence. For this reason I felt that I ran little chance of being robbed. In picturing to himself the Mexican brigand, I must caution the reader, once for all, against conceiving of an individual in any way resembling the traditional brigand of the stage, or even the less picturesque brigand of real life, as you find him in Italy or Spain. In those countries, if you are robbed or murdered, you have at any rate the satisfaction of feeling that the operation is being performed by fine-looking fellows; whereas in Mexico the chances are that your throat is cut by a miserable skulking ruffian, who is in a greater fright than you are all the time.

Four leagues of dusty road flanked by unsavoury ditches, beyond which extend unsightly expanses of bog and marsh, brought me to Santa Martha, the first post-station out of Mexico on the Puebla road. Shuddering at the dreariness of the deserted *hacienda*, with its ruined mud walls and dilapidated portico, to which a coating of plaster which had half peeled off gave a most leprous appearance, I passed on without stopping to the village of San Isidro—a noted robbers' nest—where the sandy track leading to Tezcuco branches to the left, bending round towards the lake.

At the point of junction of the two roads, I met the lumbering omnibus which plies daily between Mexico and Tezcuco, performing the distance of twenty-two miles in about four hours. In so thick a cloud of dust was the vehicle enveloped, that I could only just descry the dim figures of the passengers inside, who looked so miserable that I rejoiced that I had adopted a less painful method of travelling.

A little further on, I became aware of a figure in a black great-coat and wide-awake riding behind me. As the appearance of this individual was suggestive of anything rather than brigandage, I allowed him to overtake me, and wishing him "Good morning" in Spanish, made bold to ask if he was also bound for Tezcuco. To this question I got an answer in Spanish pronounced with such an unmistakeable English accent that I at at once tried English, and discovered, to my satisfaction, that I had fallen in with a fellow-countryman. He regretted that he was not bound for Tezcuco, having business in a village lying off the road on the borders of the lake; but, being well acquainted with the country, he was good-natured enough to insist on making a *détour*, which would enable him to accompany me several miles further on my road.

In the course of our conversation, my companion informed me that he was a Yorkshireman, and by trade a mechanic; that his present business was to repair some machinery in a factory in the village on the lake, for which he was bound. He expressed himself a good deal surprised to find a stranger like myself travelling quite alone, and proceeded to describe to me in detail his own frequent encounters with brigands, giving me to understand that he had been robbed so often that it was pretty well understood among the "caballeros de camino," or, in other words, highwaymen, that he was no longer worth robbing.

His case, indeed, seemed a very hard one, for it appeared that, when he was contemplating returning to England with several thousand dollars, which he had contrived to amass in the dozen years which he had passed in the country, he had been robbed, on separate occasions, of the whole of it, and was at the present time no better off than when he first set foot in Mexico. But what surprised me more than anything else was the extraordinary cheerfulness with which my companion spoke of his own losses. However, when I mentioned that I had that very morning witnessed the execution of four brigands, he seemed a good deal put out at having missed the spectacle, for he added with a grin, at the same time rubbing his hands, "I like to see the fellows rubbed off."

A little beyond the point at which my companion took leave of me, I espied a dilapidated *rancho* or farm-house, lying a little off the road, and, in despair of reaching any more promising halting-place, approached it with a view of taking some refreshment there. On reaching the place, I perceived smoke issuing from a mud hovel close to the entrance, and, on looking in at the gap which served for a doorway, discovered through the atmosphere of smoke a wrinkled old hag fanning a fire, over which some kind of a stew was brewing, gipsy-fashion.

On catching sight of me, the old woman seemed a good deal disturbed, evidently fearing that I had designs on the stew. It then occurred to me that my revolver and riding dress may have given me the air of a brigand, so I did my best to allay the alarm of the old lady by offering to pay handsomely for anything she might be pleased to give me. However, on her solemnly declaring that she had not even an egg on the premises, I was preparing to give the matter up as a bad job, when a young Indian girl appeared from within, and entered into conversation with the old woman. At the end of a few minutes the girl again disappeared into the recesses of the place.

Famished as I was, I could not resist the impulse to follow her, and presently found myself in a straggling farmyard, surrounded by sheds and stabling. Making for the furthest corner, the girl dived through a gap in a mud wall, and disappeared.

Leaving my horse in the stables, I continued the pursuit, and soon reached the portion of the tumble-down premises in which the family of the *ranchero*, the tenant of the *rancho*, resided. In a mud-floored chamber, with the usual arrangement of planks in the corner doing duty for a bed, I found the wife of the *ranchero* and four black-eyed children, the eldest a little girl with a very pretty face.

My appearance among them seemed to occasion no sort of alarm, for the good woman instantly begged me to make myself at home, and cheerfully set about getting me eggs and *tortillas*. Indeed, so pressing was my hostess that I should establish myself indoors, that when I requested to be permitted to take my meal in the open air, I am not sure that I did not inadvertently offend her.

Before long I had made great friends with the children, thanks to the medium of some sweet biscuits, which I had brought in my pocket from Mexico. The advances which I made to the children seemed quite to win the mother's heart, and when I took advantage of the favourable impression I had made to beg for some fodder for my horse, she dived with great alacrity under the bed, and, with some difficulty, scraped together a feed of barley from off the floor.

At the end of a couple of hours I took leave of my hospitable hostess and her family, from whose ragged, slovenly appearance, which was quite in keeping with the general air of the place, I should have augured a very different reception. Again passing the hovel of the old hag, who guarded the entrance like a Cerberus, I proceeded on my way to Tezcuco.

The country which I was now traversing appeared well-cultivated and fertile, in spite of the depth of sand in the road, which rendered fast riding impossible. On either side of me extended boundless fields of maize, which yields in that district, on an average, not less than two hundred-fold. The road itself was more or less shaded by the graceful Peru tree, which is almost the only tree which seems to flourish on the table-land in the environs of Mexico.

A ride of three hours brought me to Tezcuco, at the entrance of which place I found a more than usually numerous assemblage of half-caste women at the water-tanks around the public fountain, busily engaged in the double operation of gossiping and unmercifully belabouring linen. Passing down a long street, between a double row of elongated grated windows, behind the bars of which señoras with complexions the colour of old parchment, and tawdry dresses were drawn up in a row, in arm-chairs, as is the fashion all over Mexico, I at last emerged into the market-place, which now presents a most forlorn appearance, but was formerly the centre of what has been styled the Athens of the Western World. This market-place is probably identical with that mentioned by Prescott, as having formed the exterior portion of the huge inclosure, more than 1,000 yards square, which included the royal palace, public offices, judgment hall, &c.

This market-place was formerly inclosed, in much the same fashion, as the Place du Carrousel is now, since it has been built up within the wings, by which the Palace of the Tuileries is joined on to the Louvre. Indeed no modern group of buildings would furnish so apt an illustration of the stupendous inclosure which formerly existed at Tezcuco, both as to its general plan, and the varied purposes to which it was applied, as the twin palatial blocks of the Tuileries and Louvre since their union, effected by the present ruler of France.

With some difficulty I found my way to the Casa Grande, where I was hospitably entertained by Mr. Hay, the owner of the contiguous salt and soda factory, during my three days' stay in the place.

The Tezcuco of to-day, above ground, bears absolutely no traces of its former importance. Its population, which at the time of the conquest rivalled that of Mexico, has dwindled down to 5,000 in spite of the productiveness of its territory; and, but for Mr. Hay's factory and some glass works established by a Frenchman, where Mr. Hay finds a market for his soda, there would be absolutely no signs of life in the place.

But if the population of Tezcuco is small, it is at the same time select, and it is the boast of Colonel Feliciano Rodriguez, the energetic prefect, that you might search in vain among its 5,000 souls for a thief or a beggar. I understood, from a well-informed source, that this result has been attained by hanging or shooting all such persons as could not prove that they were in the habit of getting their living by honest means. I fear that if this course were universally pursued in Mexico, the country would very soon become depopulated.

Mr. Hay, better known in the neighbourhood where he is the solitary Englishman as Don Guliermo, sets a splendid example of British energy and enterprise. For the twelve years during which he has been in possession of the salt works, he has never once been at a greater distance from home than the mining district of Real del Monte, where he finds a ready market for all the salt he can produce, immense quantities of which are used, in conjunction with sulphurate of copper, in the so-called *patio amalgamation* process (to be explained hereafter).

From time immemorial the Indians on the shores of the lake of Tezcuco have been engaged in the laborious operation of extracting salt, not from the waters of the lake, but from the earth overflowed by it in the rainy season. When the waters retire, a white incrustation, called "tequesquite," is left on the surface of the soil; but, inasmuch as the water of the lake contains but one and a half per cent. of salt and soda combined, it follows that the earth overflowed by it will not be very richly impregnated with these ingredients.

In the villages about the lake, the traveller will observe great heaps of washed-out soil, similar to those mentioned in the last chapter, piled up among the mud hovels, which serve the Indians for dwellings. Their process of extracting the salt is as follows. A hollow, in the shape of a boiler, is excavated in the top of the heap, and filled with water, which, having taken up the salt as it trickles through, runs off into earthen jars placed below to catch it. At this stage of the process, the water is found to contain on an average 20 per cent. of salt. It is then transferred to a large flat pan, and condensed over a fire of dried manure, so scarce is fuel in the neighbourhood. In each village there is but a single pan, which is common property, and is passed round from family to family. This, such as it is, is the sole industry of the Indians on the shores of the lake, and Prescott tells us that when the Tlascalans went to war with the Tezcucans, they were obliged to get on without salt, of which Tezcuco enjoyed the monopoly.

When Mr. Bowring—Mr. Hay's predecessor—established the salt factory at Tezcuco, there was a great outcry among the Indians, who thought they were going to be ruined. But when they discovered that the factory concerned itself solely with the water, and left them in undisturbed possession of their precious "tequesquite," the Indians began to look upon the intruders with indifference, which gradually ripened into interest when they discovered that they could earn more money by working in the factory, than by extracting the salt on their own account, and taking their turn at the common pan.

Tezcuco, which, like the city of Mexico, at the time of the conquest, was washed by the waters of the lake, is now stranded high and dry at least four miles from its present level. Mr. Hay is therefore under the necessity of conveying the water in barrels from the lake to his factory in the town—not however in its state as it is found in the lake, containing but 1½ per cent. of salt and soda combined, but condensed by evaporation in a succession of extensive shallow tanks, till it contains at least 25 per cent. of these ingredients.

At some distance from the works, on the present border of the lake, Mr. Hay pointed out to me the head of the canal down which Cortes is said to have floated his brigantines into the lake.

In the rainy season, during which he is compelled to suspend his operations, Mr. Hay devotes himself to works of benevolence, and, thanks to the united efforts of Colonel Rodriguez and himself, a society has been formed at Tezcuco, having the double object on the one hand of assisting the muncipality in carrying out public improvements, and on the other of relieving sick and necessitous persons. Of the latter branch, Mr. Hay was unanimously elected president, and I had the unexpected pleasure of assisting at a *séance*, where various projects of poor-relief were discussed with considerable animation. The meeting was chiefly attended by ladies, and was concluded by a ceremony which I take the liberty of recommending to the notice of the secretary of the Social Science Association. At the conclusion of the debate, the president sent for a fiddle, and deliberately waltzed round the room with the lady who had taken the most active part in the proceedings. If it could be announced in the advertisements of the Social Science Association that Lord Brougham would at the close of the *séance* dance a polka, or waltz, with Miss Emily Faithful or Miss Bessie Parkes, I have little doubt that there would be a tremendous rush for tickets.

At the meeting, I had the honour of being introduced to the Prefect, of whose energy I had heard so much. On my communicating to him my intention of visiting the pyramidical ruins of the Teocalli of the Sun and Moon at San Juan Teotchuacan, Colonel Rodriguez at once placed his carriage at my disposal, and requested his secretary to accompany me. However, on my expressing my preference for proceeding to the pyramids on horseback, he was polite enough to direct his secretary to call for me on horseback at seven o'clock next morning.

Accordingly, on the following day, soon after the appointed hour, the secretary rode up to the Casa Grande attended by an escort of five lancers, whose red pennons waved gaily on the breeze. As we rode through the streets of Tezcuco, with the escort at our heels, our cavalcade seemed to excite no little interest, and I felt that the inhabitants were regarding me—the stranger whom the Prefect delighted to honour—with the same kind of admiration with which the population of the Persian capital is said to have looked upon Mordecai, when, with a gold chain hung about his neck, he made his triumphal progress through the city on the king's mule.

My companion, I am fully persuaded, did his utmost to make himself agreeable, but his information did not turn out to be extensive for a cicerone, for he did not even know the name of so conspicuous a feature in the landscape as the snow-capped volcano Iztaccihuatl, although he had been born and bred in the valley of Mexico.

The road from Tezcuco to the pyramids of San Juan Teotchuacan is as devoid of interest as roads only can be on the Mexican table-land, where one becomes tired to death of the crumbling thirsty soil, and the eternal cactus and maguey. About half way, we came upon the line of road which has been levelled for the railway, and cut through the extensive maguey plantations with which the plains of Appam are covered. The magueys are planted in rows, and at a distance are—at least, in the dry season suggestive of fields of Brobdignag turnips desperately in want of rain.

Some six miles before reaching them you catch sight of the pyramids, over a monotonous expanse of magueys, from among which the white walls of *haciendas* gleam out here and there. At first sight, the pyramids appear to be quite close, but as you advance seem rather to recede than to get nearer. When at last you do get up to them, after a steeple-chase over cactus hedges, deep sandy gullys, stone walls, &c. your first impression is to think yourself a great fool for having come so much out of your way to see a couple of very ordinary mounds.

In spite of assiduous investigation, and poking about among the loose stones and cactuses with which the teocalli are covered, I found absolutely no trace of regular stone work or masonry of any kind. On the platform, at the summit of the lesser of the two pyramids, is a kind of altar, composed of two very ordinary blocks of stone, to which the remains of a coating of white plaster, which they must have received at a comparatively recent date, give a blotchy appearance. In the centre of the upper stone is an aperture, supposed to have served to carry off the blood of the victim. This is the so-called " Stone of Sacrifice."

By a somewhat lively exercise of the imagination you can perceive the original plan of the whole, dimly shadowed forth. In front of the Pyramid of the Moon, you discover a number of little pyramids, ranged in the form of a quadrangle, which seems to have been approached by an avenue of more little pyramids communicating with the Pyramid of the Sun. Behind one of the little pyramids we discovered a massive stone column half buried in the ground. On the front of it, in the centre of the three squares into which it was divided, was carved a gigantic human face. With the exception of a piece of obsidian—a hard flint, which the Aztecs used as a substitute for iron—I did not succeed in finding any further objects of interest.

On descending from the pyramid we proceeded to the village of San Juan Teotehuacan, and joined a party at the *fonda*, whom we found sitting down to a miscellaneous meal, consisting of rice, soaked in grease and on fire with chilles, tortillas, stewed meat, poached eggs, and beans. To wash all this down, we were supplied with abundance of the *pulque* for which the district is so celebrated, served in washing jugs—an arrangement which struck me as being more practical than elegant.

In the course of the entertainment, I made the discovery that the leader of the party which we had joined, and at whose right hand I was sitting, was no less a personage than the Provost-marshal of the district, and the terror of all evil doers.

As this dreaded individual answered to the name of "Don Nestor," and was dressed in Mexican costume and surrounded by Spanish-talking lieutenants, I was somewhat surprised when he informed me that he was a German from Elbingerode in the Harz Mountains, a village with which I happened to be acquainted. This circumstance made us intimate at once, and we continued our conversation in German, Don Nestor—alias Herr Ernst Maymburg—declaring that it did him good to speak his native tongue. At the close of the meal, drawing his pocket-book out of his pocket, he produced a letter, which he told me he had lately received from his old mother, who was still living in their native village.

In spite of the hardening nature of his profession, it was very evident that Don Nestor had some tender cords still left in his heart, and as I listened to him talking of his old mother, I could hardly believe that his business in life consisted in hanging and shooting brigands. Referring to the last execution which he had been called upon to perform, Don Nestor related to me a somewhat touching episode which occurred at the end of it.

For many months the plains of Appam had been infested by a band of brigands, led by a desperate fellow called Juan Osorio, who was renowned for his audacious robberies and the cruelties practised on his victims. The most skilfully laid plans to entrap him had failed one after the other, till, not long previously, an accident had delivered him into the power of Don Nestor. To hope to keep such a slippery fellow in custody was not to be thought of, so there was no alternative but to shoot him on the instant.

As soon as the life was out of the body, Don Nestor, having seen to its being hung on a tree in a conspicuous place by the road side *pour encourager les autres*, went his way to get some refreshment in the nearest village.

On his return in the evening to the place of execution, he was surprised to find the body carefully laid out at the foot of the tree, in an extempore *chapelle ardente*, and an old woman sobbing her heart out over it. Observing Don Nestor approaching, the old woman pointed to the corpse, and gulped out through her sobs, "This was my son. I know he was a bad one, but he was still my son."

Having taken leave of Don Nestor we went out into the yard to mount our horses, and there found his band of rural *gendarmerie*, which consisted of some twenty doubtful-looking characters, who looked as if nature had rather marked them out for disturbers than preservers of order. They were armed with lances, and old-fashioned muskets with the

Tower mark upon them. With this pack of bloodhounds, Don Nestor and his two lieutenants, who seemed very decent fellows, were to start at nightfall on the track of some brigands, who were expected to be lurking in the neighbourhood.

Uninteresting, from the monotonous character of the scenery, as our ride to the pyramids had proved, it was still more or less enjoyable, as morning rides always are everywhere, especially in Mexico. Our ride back, however, was rendered perfect martyrdom by the blinding clouds of penetrating sand which continually swept past us, quite obscuring the landscape. It was a great relief to find oneself once more within the shelter of the Casa Grande, where we found a few of the local dignitaries, who had been invited to dinner, anxiously awaiting our arrival. On dismissing the escort, I was, as a matter of course, about to put some drink-money into the hand of the leader of the party, when the secretary detected me, and informed me that I was infringing regulations, and that he could not permit such a proceeding.

I have observed already that above-ground you can read no traces of the former importance of Tezcuco. I was informed, however, by my host, that he had never yet dug up a piece of ground, or made an excavation of any sort without coming upon some relics of its palmy days. In some cabinets in his own house he showed me an interesting collection of antiquities, all of which had been found on the premises.

But it is not in Tezcuco itself that the splendour of the court of Nezahualcoyotl, the Haroun-al-Raschid of Tezcucan history—can be best realised. The traveller who would conjure up the glory of the reign of this prince, of which the pages of his descendant Ixtlilxochitl are so full, should take his stand upon the hill of Tezcocingo—a rocky promontory protruding into the plain from the Rio Frio mountain range. What Chapultepec is to Mexico, that, in a milder way, is the hill of Tezcocingo to Tezcuco. Scattered pretty thickly about the summit and its rocky sides may be discovered traces of staircases, baths, and terraces, half concealed by a stunted growth of cactus and willow—at the best a miserable substitute for the grove of hoary-bearded *ahahuetes* which lends its chief glory to Chapultepec. And what makes it more provoking is, that only a few miles off, standing high and dry in the barren plain between Tezcuco and the lake, is a magnificent quadrilateral grove of these noble trees, doing no sort of good to anybody.

From his eyrie on the rock of Tezcocingo, Nezahualcoyotl, to whom, in the century before the conquest, even the Aztec emperor did homage, would delight to look out upon the wide expanse of plain, lake, and mountain, little thinking that upon the opposite shores of the lake was rising an empire which, even in the next generation, was destined to eclipse his own in renown. Had Cortes landed in Mexico half a century earlier, he would have found the land ringing with the fame of the wisdom of Nezahualcoyotl, instead of with the prowess of the Aztec emperor. To enable you to understand the superior degree of civilization which the Tezcucans had reached at a time when the Aztecs were struggling for bare existence, you have only to contrast the comparative fertility of their territory, with the unproductiveness of the lakes and marshy ground which lie about the city of Mexico.

In a *canada* or wooded glen, through which a mountain stream rushes, stands almost buried in trees the Molino de Flores—a beautiful oasis in the centre of the glaring treeless plain. But for the *cañadas* and *barrancas* which happily occur at not unfrequent intervals over many portions of the thirsty table-land, a journey across it would be altogether unbearable.

After a hot and dusty ride, it was enjoyable in the extreme to throw oneself down in the shade, and inhale the air, which was laden with the perfume of violets and roses, as one listened to the music of running water.

Having business on hand, the tenant of the flourmill—a Frenchman,—to whom I had a letter of introduction, left me to wander alone through the deserted gardens, a kindness for which I felt deeply grateful to him, for there was that about the air of the place, which inspired a wish to be alone—or at any rate not to have a chattering Frenchman at one's elbow.

At the extremity of the gardens, which were laid out on terraces cut in the face of the rock, I came upon a rustic wooden bridge, thrown across the torrent, which just above takes a leap of thirty feet down the sheer rock, moistening the air with spray. Crossing the bridge, I found that the path conducted me to the mausoleum of the Cervantes family, to whom the place belongs. The mausoleum was of the simplest description—being little else than a hollow in the natural rock, fitted up as a chapel. It would not be easy to imagine a more delicious spot to lie in, whether alive or dead.

On returning to the house and conversation of my host, I learnt that the vault had recently been opened to receive the remains of the old Marquis Cervantes, who had died universally lamented. It had been the old man's delight to gather the neighbourhood around him, and entertain them with dancing, music, and village sports in his favourite gardens, from which he could console himself, as his life drew to its close, that he would be hardly separated in death.

A Ride Round the Lake of Tezcuco.

Next day I was fortunate enough to make the acquaintance of his son, Don Pepe Cervantes, whose estate, called the Hacienda Grande, lies on the road from Tezcuco to Mexico, to one proceeding round the north end of the lake. In Count Cervantes, who was clothed in a complete suit of undressed leather ornamented with steel buttons, I found a real country gentleman—a class which is unhappily very limited in Mexico, where, partly from the constant risk which he runs of losing his life, partly from his preference of town life, it is exceedingly rare to find a landed proprietor resident on his estate.

In his own case, Count Cervantes informed me that, though a residence in the city was most painful to him, it was only since the arrival of the French troops in the city of Mexico, in June, 1863, that he had ventured to reside on his property; that in his absence the *hacienda* had been occupied by a band of Liberals, who made free with everything they could lay hands on, and at parting set fire to a portion of the farm buildings, which was still standing a blackened ruin.

Breakfast, for which the Count invited me to remain, was served at noon in a draughty apartment, with a brick floor, and windows innocent of glass. Of furniture there was not a trace, except plain wooden chairs and table. Along the walls stood several large empty jars, and in one corner of the room, a hen-coop. An open door, through which Indian women passed in and out with a constant supply of tortillas, hot and hot from the fire, which they pitched down on the table, afforded us a full view of what was going on in the kitchen.

At table were about a dozen persons :—the Count ; several of his younger children ; their governess, a French lady; the administrator ; the secretary, a clerk or two from the *tienda*—the shop attached to the *hacienda*; and several strangers.

Had I not already in a measure become used to the Mexican *cuisine*, I should hardly have been equal to the task of breakfasting off the dishes set before us, which were extravagantly national.

The conversation, which was chiefly kept up by the Count and the governess, was carried on in Spanish, for the Count rather prided himself on not speaking French, and I was a good deal amused to listen to a little friendly banter between them.

In his conversation the Count displayed a good deal of quiet humour, an exceedingly rare quality in Mexicans.

"Will you be good enough, Madame, since you tell me that your language is so remarkably rich, to inform me what is the French for *pulque*."

"We have no word, sir, in our language for *pulque*," replied the governess.

"Well then, how do you call *frijoles?*"—a bean peculiar to Mexico.

"*Frijoles*, sir, are not eaten in France, so we have no occasion to speak of them."

"At any rate you will have a word for *tortilla*, in your language?"

"I regret to say, sir, that we have not."

Upon this the Count seemed to think his triumph complete, and appealed to the company in general to inform him if that were a language fit for Christians to talk, in which there were no words for *pulque*, *frijoles*, or *tortilla*.

Although the apartment in which we had breakfasted was much inferior to most servants' halls in England, the rest of the house—of which the first floor alone was occupied by the family—was furnished comfortably enough. Over the line of arcades, which serve as shelter from the sun or rain, and which are invariably to be found in front of Mexican country houses, ran a shady verandah, communicating with the rooms on the first-floor. In this verandah, were ranged numerous garden chairs and ottomans, over which hung a wonderful collection of bird-cages. Altogether it seemed a very ideal kind of place for conversation over coffee and cigars.

But such pleasures were not for me, for I had a ride of twenty-five miles before me, and but four hours of daylight. Already, before I left the *hacienda*, the sky had become black and lowering, and I had not been half an hour *en route*, before a perfect hurricane began to blow, filling the air with whirlwinds of sand, which concealed even the outlines of the hills.

At this juncture, the road, which had been as indistinct as most Mexican roads are so far, completely lost itself in a labrynth of tracks, leading in all directions. Following one of these, I reached the shore of the lake, the waters of which were lashed by the wind into as great a pitch of fury as their shallowness admitted of. As I was traversing land which in the rainy season is overflowed by salt water, I was not surprised to find it absolutely destitute of vegetation. For two hours I did not come upon a trace of human habitations. At length I reached a deserted village, which I supposed to be quite uninhabited, until I caught sight of a couple of suspicious-looking characters lurking in a mud hovel. Observing that one of them was armed with a gun, which he seemed to be engaged in capping, I put my jaded horse into its best pace, thinking that, under the circumstances, discretion was the better part of valour, and was soon lost to sight in a cloud of dust.

Another half-hour brought me to La Villa de Guadalupe, whence I rode leisurely to Mexico, having accomplished the entire circuit of the lake of Tezcuco.

CHAPTER X.

MEXICO TO MORELIA.

Towards the end of my stay in the city of Mexico, I was fortunate enough to make the acquaintance of Mr. C. L—— well known in the country, where he is renowned for his remarkable courage and coolness in the face of danger, under the name of "Don Carlos."

This gentleman had lately made an agreement with a Mexican firm, Messrs. Ruiz and Erdozain, to take off their hands the remainder of the lease of an extensive *hacienda* called Guaracha, in the state of Michoachan, by the terms of which he was to enter into possession of the premises on February 1st. Now, as good luck would have it, Guaracha lay but a few leagues off the high road (?) to Guadalajara—to which city I was bound—to one taking the direct but dangerous route by way of Morelia, or Valladolid.

Situated as I was—about to lose my companion, who was to return to Europe by the February packet, and anxiously looking out among my acquaintances for one willing to face the dangers of an expedition into the interior—I felt truly grateful to Don Carlos for consenting to take me with him. Had I searched the country through, and had the pick of natives and foreigners, I am convinced that I should not have found a companion so eligible as chance had thus thrown in my way.

If, at the end of seven weeks, the traveller who has no other object but that of looking about him, does not get tired of life in the city of Mexico, of ringing the changes upon a ride in the eternal Paseo—which is only gay on Sunday—and lounging in the Calle de Plateros, where he will meet all his acquaintances about ten times a day, inasmuch as it is the only street in which anybody ever thinks of walking, he must be very peculiarly constituted.

But, before leaving the city of Mexico, the solemn ceremony of getting a passport at the Prefecture had to be performed. So imperative is this regulation, that an American gentleman, who had neglected to comply with it, on reaching Puebla on his way to Vera Cruz, was not allowed to proceed on his journey, and was compelled to return to Mexico. But not only is every respectable person who leaves the city required to obtain the permission of the civil authorities to run the risk of losing his life and property outside, but this permission must be endorsed by the French commandant. It being quite out of the power of the authorities to put obstacles in the way of persons who are bent on mischief leaving the city, they create employment for themselves by subjecting respectable travellers, who are nothing more nor less than food for brigands, to unnecessary annoyance. If the authorities could hope, by preventing harmless individuals from travelling in the country, to starve out the brigands by cutting off their supply of food, the policy of putting difficulties in the way of leaving the city would be intelligible. But, as they do not profess any object of this nature, they might as well let the victims depart in peace.

On the morning of January 27, our establishment in the Calle de Plateros broke up, and the occupants of the rooms at either extremity of the long *salon* left the capital on the same day, bound on very different errands—my companion with a delightful vision of the domestic hearth and English comforts before him — I with the prospect of adventures in the wilds of the interior; he whirled off towards Vera Cruz and the Atlantic —the side, which Mexico turns towards Europe —in a diligence drawn by eight horses, whereas eight mules seemed to be thought good enough for passengers bound for the Pacific.

On the eve of leaving the city we had the satisfaction of hearing that the diligence on the road we were about to take had been stopped at the Puerto de Medina—the mountain gate, which separated what was formerly the state of Mexico from the state of Michoachan—by the redoubtable Barragana—an Amazon guerilla, remembered by residents in the capital, as having ridden by the side of Juarez, on the occasion of his triumphal entry into the city in December, 1860.

The Casa de Diligencias being situated near the Alameda, at the western extremity of the city, we who had our faces turned towards the Pacific soon exchanged the painful jolting over the stony streets for the comparatively smooth motion of the Paseo, the dust of which, converted into mud by yesterday's watering, was still at seven in the morning in a transition stage, but by nine o'clock would be genuine dust again.

Passing out of the *garita*, which was held by a guard of Belgians, we turned to the right, and followed the aqueduct, which runs right down the centre of the road, as far as Chapultepec; then turning to the left we passed through Tacubaya, at the extremity of which village commences the ascent of the hills which separate the valley of Mexico from the valley of Toluca—the highest story in the Mexican tableland.

The landscape becomes dreary in the extreme, the road being cut through the *tepetate* rock—a sort of crumbling formation, upon which nothing but dwarf cactus and maguey will grow. Under the broiling sun the mules toiled painfully over the glaring rock, while our only amusement consisted in watching the movements of the *mozo* or imp attendant upon the coachman. Every quarter of an hour this individual would leap down and fill a bag with stones, with which he would climb up to his place again, and forthwith begin pelting the two leading mules, which were quite out of reach of the whip. Nor was this pelting confined to the *mozo* alone, for the coachman would constantly beg of passers-by to do him the favour of shying a stone at some particular mule, which happened to be refractory, while residents along the road would pelt the mules in general, without being asked.

Dreary as was the road, by which we were mounting, a sprinkling of fresh snow lent an unwonted beauty to the summit of Ajusco and the other hills before us, and we could not refrain from looking back continually to enjoy the grand spectacle of the snow-capped volcanos, whose glaciers flashed like plates of silver in the morning sun. Between them and us intervened the valley of Mexico, over which floated a milk-white sea of mist, out of which appeared the cathedral towers, and here and there the round back of an isolated "peñon."

By 10 A.M. we had reached Contadero, a small

village beyond Santa Fé, where the diligence halts for breakfast. As the real danger of the road is considered to commence at this spot, we took "on board," as the American expression is, an escort of a couple of the rural police force, as usual in their shirt sleeves, and armed with clumsy muskets, far more dangerous to friends than foes. This precaution of taking what they are pleased to call an escort is the merest farce in the world, for on the least appearance of danger your escort disappears, leaving the field clear for brigands. However, since it pleased the authorities to bestow an escort upon us, with our escort seated on the top of the diligence, we continued our journey after an excellent breakfast.

The more we mounted, the more attractive our road became. The glare of the bare *tepetate* rock, which forms the base of all the mountains which surround the valley of Mexico, was now exchanged for an abundant growth of dwarf oak, mixed with *escobilla* — a kind of broom — and other flowering shrubs, forming together a foreground most refreshing for the eye to rest upon. In the background a black pine forest mounted quite up to the summit of the hills. As our road wound by steep gradients up the wooded slope of the mountain, the overarching boughs almost brushing our faces, we were unpleasantly struck by the frequency of the roadside crosses, eloquent of past murders. The full meaning of the name, *Las Cruces* (The Crosses), which, from its unenviable reputation, has been given to the pass, came painfully home to us. It would not be easy to conceive of a spot more admirably adapted for deeds of blood, for without being seen themselves brigands might almost tickle their victims with the points of their rifles.

The view from the summit of the pass is less fine than that from a point some way down on the Toluca side, near which stands an obelisk, marking the highest tide of the victorious march towards the capital of Hidalgo, the priest-hero of the war of Mexican independence. The valley through which the road winds down the descent here opens out into a grassy amphitheatre, surrounded by wooded hills, broken by groups of jagged rocks. Just such a spot would Virgil have delighted to describe, and the " pius Æneas " would infallibly have selected it for those athletic games, which were to the Trojan youth as tough a bodily exercise as the description of them has been ever since a mental training to the youth of the British Isles.

As you approach the valley of Toluca, which lies more than 1,000 feet higher than that of Mexico, the scenery becomes less and less attractive, till you reach the town of Lerma, which is surrounded by a hopeless expanse of marshes, similar to those with which the traveller has become only too familiar in the valley of Mexico. In these marshes, which form the principal watershed in Central Mexico, the Rio de Lerma—the main river which drains the western slope of the Cordillera—takes its rise.

Called indifferently the "Rio de Lerma," or "Rio Grande," until it falls into the lake of Chapala, an inland sea, larger than the lake of Constanz—the largest of European lakes—the river on emerging from the lake assumes the name of Rio de Santiago for the remainder of its course. From its source, about the town of Lerma, 9,000 feet above the sea, to the point where it falls into the Pacific, near the port of San Blas, the length of the river, with its windings, is about 600 English miles.

At the foot of the hills which bound the valley on the west, lies the town of Toluca, 18 leagues, or 45 miles, distant from the capital. The place is approached by avenues of trees, which throw as inadequate an amount of shade as those which line the Paseo of the city of Mexico. But even for this shade one is deeply grateful in a country, where trees are so painfully scarce as on the Mexican table-land. As we rattled over the stones to the Casa de Diligencias, we had to cut ourselves a path through a swarthy sea of Indians, collected in the streets in great numbers.

Near the centre of the main street we came upon a

barricade, which at a distance appeared quite impassable, but which turned out to consist of two parallel lines of earth-work, overlapping each other. To pass this obstacle with a team of eight mules required all the driver's skill, for the space between the two mudbanks was very narrow, and it was necessary to describe one right angle to get in, and a second to get out. This feat, however, was safely accomplished, and in a few minutes we reached the inn, where we got a clean room, with a couple of iron bedsteads.

To help to kill the remainder of the afternoon, we proceeded to call upon the Prefect, for whom I had a letter of introduction from Señor Ramirez, Minister of Foreign Affairs. Passing the Belgian sentry on duty at the entrance of the Prefecture, and wondering at the strange chance which had brought Belgians to mount guard over a Mexican Prefect, we mounted the stairs, and were ushered into a long chamber, where the chief magistrate of the town was engaged in transacting business. After receiving us with that politeness, with which one invariably meets from Mexicans, the Prefect begged us to be seated, and proceeded to read the letter of introduction. As soon as he had read the document through, the good man, with some vehemence, declared himself absolutely at our disposal.

To have a Prefect at my absolute disposal was to me so novel a sensation, that I was utterly at a loss how to avail myself of the situation, and as the Prefect himself advanced no proposition, we sat regarding one another in the most hopeless perplexity. At length, to my great relief, some one suggested that we should adjourn to the *azotea*, the flat-terraced roof of the house, in order to get a good view of the town and surrounding country. We were well rewarded for our trouble.

The chief feature of the valley of Toluca is a magnificent snow-capped mountain, called after the town, from which it is seen to great advantage, Nevado de Toluca. The outline of this mountain is so surpassingly beautiful, that I do not hesitate to assign it the first place among Mexican mountains. Its slopes are clothed by a dense pine forest, which appeared to extend almost up to the snow line, which in Mexico begins at an elevation of about 12,000 feet above the sea. Take away its Nevado, and there would be as little left to admire in the valley of Toluca, as in the valley of Mexico stripped of its volcanos.

On our descent from the *azotea*, the Prefect, who was painfully anxious to make himself agreeable, at the same time that he had not the faintest idea how to set about it, showed us into a hall, round the walls of which hung portraits of former governors of the state of Mexico, of which Toluca was the capital. Leaving us there, he disappeared for a few minutes, at the end of which he returned with a huge map and a bulky volume of statistics in a paper cover, of both of which he begged me to accept. The gift, however, was accompanied by a few words of caution against putting too implicit faith in the figures, as the book, on examination, turned out to be a collection of state reports, drawn up for the use of the Central Government in 1849. I did not find it particularly serviceable otherwise than as a pad to protect the small of my back from an obnoxious iron rail on the top of the diligence, with which the tremendous jolting brought me into most unpleasant contact.

Being anxious to see something of Mexican family life in the provinces, I was disappointed that the excellent Prefect had not the sagacity to ask us to supper. However, I learnt afterwards that the poor man, on accepting the office of Prefect under the Empire, had been abandoned by his whole family, whose sympathies were strongly with Juarez.

Having returned to the inn for supper, we were served with a most sorry meal, in the middle of which I was surprised by the entrance of a German acquaintance, who had been a fellow-passenger from Europe. From this gentleman, who was a shareholder in some gold mines in the neighbourhood, I learnt that two days previously he had been robbed on the road which we were about to take on the morrow; that, in common with seven fellow-passengers, he had been compelled to submit to the indignity of lying flat on his stomach with his face to the ground, a ceremony called *boca abajo* or "mouth downwards," for the space of a whole hour, during which the brigands were engaged in rifling the baggage; that seven out of the eight had had watches with them, all hidden in their boots, and that, by a wonderful piece of good luck, the eighth alone, who had no watch, had been required to take his boots off; that as none of the passengers but himself were armed, he had taken the precaution to lock his own revolver up in his trunk, from which it was of course extracted by the brigand. Not much encouraged by this account, we went early to bed, as we had to make an early start.

Next morning, an hour before dawn, we were again rattling over the stones, the heavy rumbling of the diligence re-echoing through the silent streets, and rousing the drowsy inhabitants. At starting the stars overhead were shining brilliantly, but as we descended into the valley we found ourselves enveloped in a thick mist, which concealed everything from us. Of this mist we had been forewarned by the Prefect, who informed us it was of regular occurrence, but observed at the same time that, not being addicted to early rising, it was a natural phenomenon, which he rarely witnessed. And most heartily we wished ourselves out of it, for in a short time we were pretty well saturated with the penetrating moisture, which chilled one through and through. Indeed, I am convinced that it was only the excitement occasioned by the constant expectation of falling among thieves which kept our blood in any sort of circulation.

At a little before 7 A.M. we became aware that the sun was rising, and thought that the mist was about to disperse. In this hope, however, we were sorely disappointed; for, at the end of half an hour, it became thicker than ever, and the presence of the sun was only declared to us by a perfect white colourless rainbow, which accompanied us for half an hour without intermission. Shortly after the rainbow had disappeared, the sun got the better of the mist, and scorched us so unmercifully, that we would have given a good deal to have had the mist back again.

We were now traversing an arid, treeless plain, which extends almost without interruption from the town of Toluca to the *hacienda* of La Jordana, at the foot of the Puerto de Medina a distance of nearly sixty miles, which we accomplished in eight hours, from 5 A.M. to 1 P.M. In its whole length, the plain is utterly featureless, if I except occasional glimpses of the receding Nevado de Toluca, and the town of Ixlahuaca, picturesquely perched on some hills, through which the Rio de Lerma has forced itself a bed. Except about Ixlahuaca, the plain is quite uncultivated; but there it is dotted with Indian cottages, which enliven it a little. Each cottage stood in its own grounds, which consisted of a small garden plot immediately contiguous to the house, and enclosed by a wattled fence, and about an acre of land unenclosed.

Beyond La Jordana, the scenery completely changes. From a glaring expanse of plain, with scarcely a tree to be met with for leagues, we found ourselves transported into a delightful region abounding in forest trees; among which the oaks are especially conspicuous. Soon the road begins to mount, by a steep ascent, the pass called Puerto de Medina—the point where we were led to expect an encounter with the Barragana and her followers.

In the expression "puerto," applied to a mountain pass, one seemed to be furnished with a most apt illustration of those πύλαι mentioned in Xenophon's "Anabasis" as occuring on the road from Sardis to the Persian capital.

It is but a few years since this way was opened through the mountains by blasting away the rock. However, beyond the mere forcing an opening, no kind of steps have been taken towards forming a decent road; and the agony of the diligence, expressed in creaks and groans unutterable, as it came down with a great thud, each time the mules straining themselves to the utmost, succeeded in dragging its unwieldy body over some apparently insuperable block of stone, which lay in the road, seemed almost as intense, as our own became when, having reached the summit, we were whirled down the descent in a succession of wild bounds from rock to rock. About half-way down the descent, the drag gave way with a crash; but, by some lucky chance, our headlong course was arrested before the occurrence of the catastrophe which seemed inevitable.

While the *mozo* was proceeding to repair damages, we suddenly became aware of four armed horsemen barring the road a few hundred yards ahead of us. Making up our minds that at last we were to have a fight, we got our arms ready and prepared for action; but, as the supposed brigands approached, we were amused to discover them to be the advance guard of an escort of Mexican cavalry, sent forward to meet us from the *hacienda* of Tepetongo, which stands at the foot of the pass on the Michoachan side. By daylight, seen at a distance defiling through a mountain glade, or encountered anywhere by moonlight, a group of Mexican lancers presents an appearance so picturesque as to be an invaluable adjunct in a picture; but a nearer view of them is not to be recommended.

On reaching the *hacienda*, we found a body of government troops established there; who, in anticipation of being attacked by the Liberals, reported to be in considerable force in the neighbourhood, had hurriedly thrown up an earthen breastwork on the *azotea*, where a sentinel was posted to keep a look-out. In the courtyard below, the main body of the troops were scattered about in anything but picturesque confusion. A more ragged, filthy set of human beings I never saw collected together on any pretence whatsoever. Among them was a good sprinkling of slatternly women, of even more revolting appearance than the men.

The *hacienda* itself was a substantial building, and contained a suite of spacious scantily-furnished rooms, in which the proprietor informed me that the Emperor Maximilian had passed a couple of days, in the course of his journey to the interior. Owing to the abundance of water, the appearance of the surrounding country was exceedingly fertile, and the eye rested gratefully on bright green patches of young wheat.

From the *hacienda* of Tepetongo to the town of Maravatio, where the diligence halts for the night, setting out at 4 A.M. the following morning, the road traverses a well-wooded undulating country, inexpressibly refreshing to look upon after a lengthened sojourn in the valley of Mexico, from which the traveller escapes with a painful craving to look upon trees once more.

When we reached Maravatio, an hour after dark,

we found the market-place all a-blaze with wood
fires, around which groups of slenderly-clad Indians
were collected, discussing the exciting news which had
just reached the place. For it appeared that a fight
had lately taken place near the town of Zitacuaro,*
in the heart of the mountains, in which the Indians,
contrary to their wont, had taken a very decided
part; and, in conjunction with the Liberals, inflicted
an unexpected blow on the French, who considered
that they could certainly reckon on the neutrality
of the Indians. Luckily for the French, this rising
of the Indians did not spread.

At the Casa de Diligencias we got the usual decen
accommodation which one finds on roads traverse
by the diligences; and after a journey of fourteen
hours, during which we had accomplished ninety
miles, were glad, immediately after supper, to take
to our beds, which we were very loth to leave at
3 A.M. the following morning, at the summons of the
inexorable *mozo*.

It was little we saw of Maravatio; for we reached
it an hour after dark, and left it long before dawn;
but, from the glimpses we got of the place by torch-
light, we felt no sort of desire to become better
acquainted with it. As soon as we got out of the

---

* Of this town M. Chevalier inaccurately remarks (vol. ii. p. 40),
that it was treated like another Carthage, and has never risen from its
ruins.

town, we found our road blocked up by a French convoy, which detained us some time; and when we got clear at length, we made very slow progress, owing to the execrable state of the road, which was a repetition of that we had experienced in climbing the Puerto de Medina.

After a tedious drive of five hours, we reached the town of Acamboro, once a place of considerable importance, as evidenced by the ruins of its ecclesiastical edifices. The market-place, as usual, was swarming with Indians, but Indians of a very much higher type than those found in the valley of Mexico; who, although descended from the warlike Aztecs, are admitted on all hands to be the most degraded race in the country. On the stalls was exposed for sale an immense variety of fruits, vegetables, &c.— the produce of the three climates of the state of Michoachan, which is in itself the whole country in miniature. In its *Tierra Fria* and the higher portion of its *Tierra Templada* you find all the cereals and vegetables which flourish in England or France; while in the lower portion of its *Tierra Templada*, and its *Tierra Caliente*, the soil produces coffee, cotton, tobacco, rice, and sugar in great abundance.

At intervals of about six leagues, or fifteen miles, along the road, we found Mexican or French escorts awaiting the arrival of the diligence, so that we were well protected against the dangers of the road, if there were any, of which one began to entertain considerable doubts, in spite of all we had heard in Mexico to the contrary.

At the last post-station before Morelia, eight gallant greys were yoked to the diligence, so that it appeared that we were to enter the capital of Michoachan in style, in order to compensate us for the poor figure, which we had cut with our eight mules on leaving the city of Mexico.

At the swinging pace at which a Mexican diligence always starts, the greys whirled us along in a cloud of dust till we reached the foot of a steep hill, about a couple of miles ahead of us, and there came to a dead stop, refusing with one accord to drag us a yard further. Force and persuasion failing alike to make the animals think better of it, the passengers had nothing for it but to descend *en masse*, and walk up the hill, supposing the vehicle would follow.

As the evening was pleasantly cool, and no diligence appeared at the top, I walked on alone down the descent, over the next hill, and on, and on, till the short Mexican twilight had changed into night, and still there was no trace of the diligence. I had now accomplished several miles from the point at which I had left it, and began to think I should have to walk on to Morelia on foot, instead of making that triumphal entry I had been led to expect, when, to my considerable satisfaction, I caught the sound of approaching wheels, and I soon found myself seated once more behind the greys, who got over the remaining six miles of ground in a little over half an hour, and before 8 P.M. landed us in the courtyard of the Casa de Diligencias.

CHAPTER XI.

MORELIA

To the inquiries of the crowd of persons collected together in the courtyard of the Casa de Diligencias, anxious to learn particulars as to the state of the roads, and the latest news from the city of Mexico, we were enabled to give satisfactory answers; and, while the passengers, who had any friends to meet them were receiving their congratulations on their safe arrival, we made the best of our way into the inn, in the hopes of securing a room of some sort to ourselves. From the landlord, however, we learnt that every room in the house was already occupied, and in the end we had nothing for it but to put up with a share of an apartment, which served as a thoroughfare to two other bedrooms, and which was already tenanted by a Spaniard, whose presence was declared by heavy breathing proceeding from a bed in a corner of the room.

We had not been many minutes installed in this apartment when the door opened, and a young

Mexican dandy, wearing his mustaches twisted to a point, and dressed in an embroidered jacket and trousers ornamented by rows of steel buttons, burst into the room, and approaching my companion, proceeded to embrace him with a fervour with which only lovers meet in cold northern climes, but which characterises the greetings of ordinary acquaintances in regions nearer the sun.

This gentleman was introduced to me as Don Francisco Erdozain—one of the partners in the firm of Ruiz and Erdozain, off whose hands my companion, Don Carlos, was about to take the remainder of their lease of the *hacienda* of Guaracha. Don Francisco Erdozain, familiarly styled "Don Pancho," was to be our companion for the remaining portion of our journey, which was to be accomplished on horseback.

As soon as Don Pancho had withdrawn, Antonio, a body-servant of Don Carlos, who had been awaiting his master's arrival at Morelia, entered, and proceeded to make himself generally useful. Thanks to the exertions of this sagacious individual, we succeeded in procuring a basin and a jug of water,— articles of bedroom furniture considered quite superfluous by Mexicans *en voyage*, who defend their neglect of washing by maintaining that, as the bark saves the tree, so has the coating of dust contracted in travelling a tendency to preserve the wearer of it.

Having made as much of a toilet as the scantiness of our baggage admitted of, we left Antonio on guard at the door of our chamber, and descended to the *comedor*, or *salle-à-manger*, where we took our evening meal, during which we were waited upon by a French soldier, who did not think it derogatory to his high calling to eke out his meagre pay by letting himself out as a waiter during the hours which he had free from military service.

After supper, learning that the band was playing on the *plaza* in front of the cathedral, we strolled out, and passed a most enjoyable hour promenading by moonlight among the orange trees, which are almost invariably planted round Mexican market-places. A considerable number of persons were assembled, listening to the music, but there appeared to be very few ladies belonging to the upper classes, who seldom leave the house except for devotional purposes, or to take a carriage-airing just before sunset —so careful are they of their complexions. The cathedral, which occupied one side of the *plaza*, presented an imposing appearance by moonlight.

On returning to the Casa de Diligencias, our attention was attracted by some large handbills, conspicuously placarded on either side of the entrance, to the effect that Señor Rogers, the renowned chiropodist, would attend at the hotel between the hours of ten and four, for the purpose of relieving of their corns, at a moderate price, such persons as might stand in need of his services.

Soon after 10 P.M. we retired to our chamber, at the door of which the faithful Antonio was keeping guard. Within, the Spaniard was still snoring in the corner, but he had disappeared next morning before we were on the move.

It had been arranged overnight between Don Carlos and his friends, that we were to remove on the following morning to the house of the Licenciado Alvirez—the man of law, who being the intimate and trusted friend of both parties, was being employed by them in common to draw up the legal agreement, settling the terms of the sub-lease of the *hacienda* of Guaracha. A more ideally amicable method of transacting legal business can hardly have prevailed among the early Christians.

On repairing to the residence of the Licenciado next morning, Antonio bearing our very limited baggage before us, we found our host and his guest, Don Pancho Erdozain, about to sit down to breakfast in a small apartment facing the kitchen at the bottom of a narrow courtyard. As we had not yet breakfasted, we took our places at the table.

Through the open door we could observe all that was going on in the kitchen, where an old woman was busily engaged over the fire with a number of earthenware pots and pans, for metal utensils are quite unknown in the kitchens of the natives in Mexico. As for the old woman, whose complexion was of a rich copper colour, the Licenciado informed me that she had nursed him as a child, and was now his cook and housekeeper.

After breakfast we adjourned to the front room, the farther end of which was neatly furnished with sofa and arm-chairs, while the portion of the room nearest the entrance was fitted with writing-table, bookshelves, &c. and served the Licenciado as a place of consultation with his clients, who did not appear to be numerous. Two long windows, innocent of glass, but fitted with strong iron bars and wooden shutters, opened on to the street, along which barely half a dozen persons passed in the course of the morning.

Being provided with a letter of introduction to the Prefect, I waited upon him in the afternoon, and, I fear, disturbed him in the middle of the siesta, which is as fixed an institution with Mexicans as with Spaniards. For, as he requested me to be seated on the sofa, and declared himself to be at my disposition, the poor Prefect seemed so sleepy and helpless that I hardly had the heart to put him through a cross-examination as to the state of his department. And, indeed, as I poured in my questions thick upon him, hoping to get unattainable information about schools, Indian communes, state taxation, &c. I could see, from the impatient manner in which he chewed the end of an unlighted cigar, that I was inflicting cruel torture upon him. Had the excellent man had the good sense to avail himself of a diversion which occurred, and introduce to the inquisitive stranger his daughter—a very pretty girl of eighteen, who broke in upon the proceedings, apparently by accident, as she disappeared again immediately, receiving no encouragement from her father to remain—I should gladly have spared him any more of my questioning. But, as he did not choose to adopt so rational an expedient, I ruthlessly went on with my examination, and finally took leave, having succeeded in thoroughly boring the Prefect without learning anything worth mentioning from him, and vowing inwardly to get no more letters of introduction to prefects.

After a four o'clock dinner at the house of the Licenciado, we rode out in the cool of the evening to see something more of the city. Called Valladolid by the Spaniards, the name of the capital of Michoachan was changed to Morelia during the War of Independence, to commemorate the exploits and perpetuate the memory of Morelos, the successor of Hidalgo. Viewed from a distance, from the crest of the hills which surround it on all sides, the position of Morelia appears low and unhealthy, but as you approach it, you see that the city is raised well above the low ground which surrounds it, on a rocky platform, which must render it highly salubrious. Thanks to the fact that the ground falls away on all sides, the place is fairly well-drained—an exceedingly rare circumstance in Mexican cities and towns.

Taking it all in all, I should be inclined to pronounce Morelia the cleanest and best built of all the cities I visited in the course of my travels in Mexico. Small, as compared with the capital, Guadalajara, or Puebla, Morelia wears an air of substantial compactness, which distinguishes it from the above-mentioned cities, which straggle infinitely into suburbs, and lose themselves in nothingness long before their outer walls are reached. Even the private houses are, most of them, built of stone, and the massive simplicity of the numerous churches and convents is exceedingly imposing. Of these latter, at least two-thirds have been dismantled and given over to profane usage, several of them being occupied as barracks by the French troops.

Trade in Morelia there is none, and a most remarkable absence of any kind of life. Indeed, about the place there seemed to hang, in an exaggerated degree, that air of sleepy respectability which characterises our own cathedral cities, and which seemed to have worked so potently upon the French garrison as to have robbed them of their habitual gaiety and liveliness.

At the eastern extremity of the town lies the Alameda, a much shadier and pleasanter retreat than the more pretentious paved and dusty resort of the inhabitants of the city of Mexico. Skirting the Alameda runs the lofty and graceful aqueduct, which supplies Morelia with water.

In the evening, I accompanied Don Carlos to the house of Don Francisco Roman, one of the wealthiest citizens of Morelia. Unlike most Mexican ladies, our hostess, although a great invalid, was brimming over with intelligence and vivacity, and took a most lively interest in politics, which is exceedingly rare with Mexicans of either sex. She deplored deeply the degraded state into which her country had fallen, and spoke of her countrymen in terms, which showed that she thoroughly understood them.

Both she and her daughter, a pretty girl of sixteen, who spent the early part of the evening in cracking nuts with her lover, Don Pancho, complained bitterly of the want of any kind of society in Morelia, and bemoaned the evil fortune, which condemned them to live there. They were both longing to be off to Europe, to see what real life was like.

Having a couple of days to spare before setting out for Guaracha, I resolved to employ them in visiting the picturesque lake of Patzquaro, which lies some forty miles to the south-west of Morelia. The diligence, which runs three days a week, performs the distance in less than eight hours, which, considering the infamous state of some portions of the road, is very fair travelling.

For the most part the scenery is quite devoid of interest, consisting of wearisome expanses of monotonous undulating hills—either quite bare of vegetation, or scantily clothed with cactus, a leafless tree called "palo bobo," and a thorn bearing a yellow blossom called "ouasatche." Only at a single point, where the road traverses an oak forest much infested with brigands, does the traveller meet with anything in the way of beautiful scenery to reward him for the trouble of undertaking the journey.

Between Pontesuela, the second post-station from Morelia, and Patzquaro, we got a glimpse of the village which, standing close to the borders of the lake of Patzquaro, marks the site of Tzintzantzan, the former capital of the kingdom of Michoachan before its conquest by the Spaniards. Prescott has made us familiar with the melancholy fate of Montezuma, and the overthrow of the Aztec empire, but the English reader will probably hear for the first time of Caltzontzin, last monarch of the Tarascos or Otomis, as they are variously styled.

On receiving intelligence of the destruction of Tenochtitlan, the splendid capital of Montezuma— a step the necessity of which Cortes bewails so bitterly in his Letters—Caltzontzin lost no time in repairing in person to pay homage to the conquerors. Cortes, wishing to encourage other potentates in thus making voluntary submissions, received the monarch graciously, and dismissed him with the assurance that he would not be deposed from his throne, as long as he proved himself the true friend of the Spaniards.

For ten years after the fall of the Aztec empire, Caltzontzin was left unmolested, but his end was hardly less tragical than that of Montezuma. Taken prisoner by Don Nuñez de Guzman, Cortes' unscrupulous rival—who aimed at setting up on his own account in the provinces bordering on the Pacific—Caltzontzin was cruelly put to death, and his dominions taken possession of by his captor.

So absolutely uninteresting was the general appearance of Patzquaro, and so disgustingly dirty the Meson de San Augustin, in the yard of which we found ourselves landed, that had the diligence been returning that day, we should not have hesitated about turning our backs at once upon the place. However, as the vehicle was not to return till the morrow, we had no choice but to engage the only vacant corner on the premises—a dirty windowless den in the yard, something between a knife-house and a dog-kennel. However, before setting out from Morelia, we had taken the precaution to provide ourselves with a letter of introduction to the doctor of the place, and, leaving our baggage at the inn, repaired to his house, in the hopes of finding a better lodging.

On inquiring for the doctor, we learnt that he was at home, and were shown into his front room, a brick-floored chamber, scantily furnished with a long row of rush-bottomed chairs, a sofa, and one small table. On the sofa was reclining a woman, whose appearance was far more suggestive of a slatternly maid-of-all-work than of the mistress of the house. Nothing could be imagined less attractive in womankind than the Mexican females of the middle and poorer classes. It is a thousand pities that the harem system does not prevail in Mexico, for then a considerable proportion of the women would be shut up and kept decently out of sight. As it is, the music conveyed by the terms *señora* and *señorita* has hardly had time to die out of your ears, before the real woman appears in the flesh, and rudely dashes your ideal to the ground. In making these remarks, I would not be misunderstood to include the ladies of the upper classes, who are often as strikingly handsome as the women of Andalusia.

Presently the doctor appeared, and inquired in what way he could be of use to us. Thereupon we gave the excellent man a very broad hint that as we stood desperately in need of lodging and of food, he could not do a kinder act than supply our wants. Our remarks, however, fell quite flat, only eliciting the regret of our host that he had already dined, and the suggestion that we should adjourn to a neighbouring *fonda*, called 'La Sociedad,' and satisfy our immediate wants.

To this expedient we were fain to resort, and guided by our friend the doctor, who was good enough to offer to show us over the hospital *en route* — an offer which we declined on the spot, sick Mexicans being no very appetizing spectacle,—we made our way to the place of refreshment.

On entering the principal chamber, we found the tables covered with green baize instead of the expected white cloths, and a select party engaged at the interesting game of *monté*. So intent upon the game were the players, that our entrance excited no kind of attention, although the visit of foreigners to so out-of-the-way a spot as Patzquaro must be a very rare occurrence. But Mexicans at all times are a most incurious race, and play is their ruling passion.

After considerable delay, we succeeded in getting some excellent coffee, which was so invigorating, that on the strength of it we proceeded to climb to an eminence without the town, called Los Balcones, whence we obtained a magnificent view of the lake and mountains.

Were the state of Michoachan divided by a whole ocean from the state of Mexico, instead of by a mountain wall which may be passed in an hour or two, its configuration and scenery could hardly be more widely different. Whereas, for the most part, the state of Mexico presents a monotonous expanse of woodless, waterless, arid, table-land, the larger portion of Michoachan is delightfully diversified by lofty pine-clad mountains, rich valleys, and extensive lakes. So favourable, however, is this natural configuration to the operations of guerilla bands, that the state of Michoachan has in consequence given the French more trouble than any other in Mexico.

So lovely was the view over the lake at sunset, that we could not refrain from mounting to a higher point, in spite of the dark suspicious look of the woods which we had to traverse. After a tough climb of a quarter of an hour, we succeeded in reaching a clearance on the top of the ridge, whence we gazed across a yawning gulf of black pines, towards the still glowing western horizon, against which the outlines of the loftier trees cut clear and sharp. Diving again into the woods, we made our way to a point immediately overhanging the lake, from one end of which the sunlight had not yet died away, while the moon was reflected in the other.

Having gazed our fill on this scene of enchantment, we slowly retraced our steps to Patzquaro.
fonda, to which we repaired to get our supper, we were joined by the doctor, who not only insisted on

paying for all the refreshments, but informed us that beds had been prepared for us at his own house.

On returning to the Meson de San Augustin to fetch what few things we had with us, we found a company of Mexican infantry drawn up under the gate-way, having in their custody two French soldiers —probably deserters—whom they were conveying from Uruapan to Morelia, to be dealt with by the authorities.

Leaving Patzquaro before daylight next morning, we reached Morelia early in the afternoon.

CHAPTER XII.

MORELIA TO GUARACHA.

OUR preparations being finally completed, we left our pleasant quarters soon after sunrise on Friday, February 3. As our caravan, consisting of Don Carlos Don Pancho, myself, the faithful Antonio, and two other mounted servants, three pack mules, and a spare horse, moved through the streets of Morelia, our appearance created no little excitement, and some doubt seemed to prevail as to whether it would be more correct to class us with the preservers or disturbers of order. To satisfy the misgivings which the sight of our arms occasioned, an inquisitive Zouave approached me, and requested to be informed to what force we belonged, and did not know what to make of my reply, that we were English. On reaching the western *garita* we were stopped by the sentry on duty, who would not allow us to pass until we had satisfied him that we were provided with a permission to carry arms.

The *hacienda* of Guaracha, for which place we were bound, being some 50 leagues, or 125 miles, distant from Morelia, we proposed dividing the journey into three "*jornadas*" (day's journey), sleeping the first night at the *hacienda* of Zipimeo, a long *jornada* of 55 miles; the second night at the town of Zamora, and the third at Guaracha.

Having crossed the stone causeway, which is carried over the low marshy ground, which surrounds Morelia on three sides, we at once began to mount the shoulder of the bare rocky hills, which command the city to the westward. Carriage-road there was none, nor any track of wheels, only a narrow footpath, winding in and out among rocks and patches of stunted cactus and the *palo bobo*, sometimes losing itself altogether.

On our left, contrasting pleasantly with the nakedness of the lower hills, the Cerro de Chapula, densely clothed with pine to its very summit, reared its head high into the sky—the only striking feature in the landscape.

For the first ten miles out of Morelia we had hardly met a living soul, when, on turning a sharp corner, we suddenly found ourselves confronted with the head of the French column. It was very evident from his manner, that the officer in command had at first taken us for brigands, or a hostile Mexican force; nor was this mistake to be wondered at, for Don Carlos, who rode at the head of our party, in his broad-brimmed Mexican hat, jacket, and leopard's skin riding trousers, with his rifle slung at his side, and revolver sticking conspicuously out of his belt, looked so like a brigand, that his own mother would hardly have recognised him as her son. However, whether we owed it to our explanations, or not rather to the peaceable air shed over our caravan by the animal, which carried our bedding, proclaiming us to be effeminate, ease-loving mortals, we soon succeeded in divesting the French of their suspicions.

The officer in command then went on to inform us, that we were running a great risk in attempting to pass that way, for that a brigand chief called Ronda, whose videttes they had themselves plainly seen the day before, was scouring the Llano del Cuatro, a noted haunt of brigands, across which our road lay, with a band of 200 cavalry. At the same time he informed us, that if we pressed on the same night to the *hacienda* of Zipimeo, beyond the formidable Llano del Cuatro, we might perhaps get over the most dangerous part of the road before the rear-guard of the column, which was escorting General Niegre to Morelia, should have once more left the coast clear for the redoubtable Ronda.

In this hope we hastened on, but to no purpose, for we encountered and passed the rear-guard of the French more than an hour before we entered upon the ill-omened plain.

The Llano del Cuatro is a vast grassy plain, surrounded by low hills, and intersected by deep, muddy ditches, which are impassable in the rainy season, and in which your horse sinks up to his belly in the dry. Beyond the slopes which bound the Llano to the southward, stretches, as far as the eye can reach, a boundless expanse of pine-clad mountains, which form a most convenient shelter for robber bands, and whence they swoop down upon travellers passing over the plain.

In its longest diameter, along which our route lay, the length of the plain is little short of twenty English miles, and the sun had set before we were more than half way across. Just after sundown the servants, who were now riding a little in advance of ourselves, turned round and drew our attention to what, in the twilight, looked so exactly like a band of brigands, that neither they nor we doubted but what our passage would be disputed. So convinced was my companion, Don Carlos, in whose judgment I placed the most implicit confidence, that we really had a band of robbers before us, that he strongly advised that I should at once remove the white muslin curtain which I wore round my hat as a protection against the sun, and which is considered evidence of the wearer's being a Frenchman, in which case he is pretty sure of being put to death on the spot.

I was in the act of complying with this piece of advice, when, on drawing nearer, we discovered that we had been quite needlessly alarmed, for the supposed brigands turned out to be a party of harmless travellers, who, like ourselves, had probably hoped to get safely across the plain by taking advantage of the presence of the French force.

In the meanwhile, night had set in—cloudless, as is the wont of Mexican nights in the dry season ; and the bright moonlight enabled us to effect the passage of the above-mentioned mud ditches without any serious accident.

By eight P.M. we reached the further extremity of the plain, and struck the hills again with feelings of considerable relief. A little way up the slope we encountered a party of jolly *rancheros* (small farmers) evidently returning home from some merry-making, each supporting his wife in front of him on the saddle. From the crest of the hill we looked down upon a nameless stream of considerable breadth which flows by the *hacienda* of Zipimeo, whose white walls might be descried gleaming in the moonlight.

A descent of a few minutes brought us down to the banks of the river, the passage of which we effected by El Vado de Aguilar, a ford reported to be highly dangerous in the rainy season, but not by any means formidable in the dry. In a few minutes more we were safely landed in the courtyard of the *hacienda*, where, in the absence of his father, the son of the proprietor received us with no great show of hospitality.

Although the *hacienda* of Zipimeo must bring in

the proprietor an income of at least 25,000 dollars (5,000*l.*) a year, his son was living in a style of which a small farmer in England would have been ashamed. For the air of general neglect and discomfort which characterised the place, and for the miserable deficiency of its resources, our host apologised by explaining that, being constantly exposed to the visits of the "Chinacos"—one of the various names for Liberals or Juarists—who invariably made a clean sweep of everything found on the premises, it was not worth his while to surround himself by comforts, which would only serve to attract marauders. Neither bread, wine, milk, cheese, nor butter, were to be had, and a dish of beans eked out by a few lumps of hard stringy meat, and the never-failing tortillas, formed the meagre fare which was offered to appease appetites sharpened by a nine hours' fast.

Under the circumstances we did not scruple to produce some of the supply of provisions which we had taken the precaution to carry with us, being prepared to find little or nothing on a route so little frequented as that we were following. Nor was our host at all backward in sharing our viands; and, from the alacrity with which he accepted everything which was offered to him, it was easy to see that he did not often get the chance of a good meal.

After supper, which was served in a close, dirty little room, which seemed to serve the proprietor for office and sitting-room combined, we adjourned into a clean, airy apartment, to which the walls, which had been freshly painted with considerable taste, lent an appearance of elegance very rarely met with in Mexican country houses.

This apartment, which on our arrival was quite unfurnished, had in the meantime been converted into a bedroom by the ingenuity of Antonio. The appearance of our mattresses ranged invitingly along the clean brick floor was quite irresistible to mortals tired as we were, and in a very few minutes we were stretched on them at full length, and fast asleep.

It was past eight o'clock next morning before we effected our start from Zipimeo, whereas, with a long *jornada* of at least forty-five miles before us, we ought to have been off before sunrise. For this piece of imprudence we did not suffer as we deserved, for, luckily for us, the sky was overcast, and the sun never once pierced through the clouds. The temperature was quite perfect, and the scenery a great improvement upon yesterday's.

Leaving the wheel-track, called by courtesy a carriage-road, immediately beyond Zipimeo, we mounted the hills to the right of us by a steep zigzag path, and struck across country over the mountains, now skirting the woods, which consisted mostly of oak and pine, and now diving into the midst of them. From time to time we could not refrain from drawing rein to enjoy more fully the beautiful glens and wooded amphitheatres through which we passed in continual succession for some twenty miles. Although the sky was clouded overhead, a strip of blue was visible all round the horizon, but its tropical brightness was dimmed by a soft haze, pleasantly suggestive of a September morning in England. When, having descended from the hills again, we found ourselves riding by the side of the freshly reaped maize stubbles, it was difficult to believe that the season was mid-winter.

Not far from Tlasasalca, a miserable cluster of mud hovels, where we made the indispensable midday halt, the sight of five crosses, freshly erected by the roadside to mark some deed of blood, served to caution us against being lulled into too great security by the deceptive air of calm and tranquillity which reigned around.

On one of the crosses, which are stuck into heaps of stones to which every passing traveller is expected to contribute, was rudely inscribed in Spanish :—

> "Un padre nuestro y un Ave Maria por la alma del gefe Miguel Miranda."
> "A pater noster and an Ave Maria for the soul of the chief Miguel Miranda."

In the *fonda* in Tlasasalca, where we took some refreshment, we were astonished at finding the luxury of new and clean knives and forks, with patent India-rubber handles, on which was engraved conspicuously, "C. Puppenhausen's Patent, New York, March 31st, 1857." Opposite the *fonda*, and conspicuous through the open doorway, on the other side of the street, was an apothecary's shop, rejoicing in the sign of "Aurora Boreal," painted in huge letters of blue and gold, over the whole breadth of the house. Besides these flaming letters, and the shell of a handsome half-finished church, built of red sandstone, similar to that which imparts so much richness and warmth to the ruins of Heidelberg Castle, there seemed to be nothing whatever noticeable about the place.

Between Tlasasalca and Zamora—only eight leagues distant—there is a remarkable difference of climate evidenced by the respective productions of the two places. Whereas the soil about Tlasasalca produces maize, wheat, barley, oats, and the other cereals which are common in Europe, in the plain of Zamora you find yourself transplanted almost imperceptibly—so gradual is the descent—into the region of the sugar cane and plantain.

At least an hour and a half before we reached its walls, we caught sight of the towers and domes of Zamora, rising pleasantly out of the gardens, orchards, and orange groves in which the place lies embosomed. But as we advanced the town seemed to recede, and when at length we had passed the *garita*, we struck into a straight street, which seemed of interminable length. The appearance of the Plaza Mayor, when at length we reached it, was surprisingly gay and animated, for it was crowded with country-people, mostly Indians, and ornamented with orange and ash trees, planted alternately. Its eastern side is occupied by a huge unfinished church, similar in design and appearance to that we had remarked at Tlasasalca. Crossing the *Plaza*, we turned down a side street, and soon reached the *meson*, which bore the high-sounding name of "La Divina Providencia."

Turning into this filthy den, we left our beasts and servants there, and proceeded in search of more decent lodgings for ourselves. Unsuccessful in our first application for the rooms where Don Pancho was in the habit of putting up, we repaired to the store of a general dealer, who was an intimate friend of both my companions.

In provincial towns in Mexico a shopkeeper naturally enough enjoys a much higher position socially than in highly-civilized countries like England and France. The proprietor of the *tienda*, or store, is generally the wealthiest, and often the best-informed man in the place, and his return with his purchases from the capital, or from attending the great fairs which are held in various parts of the country, is anxiously looked for by his fellow-townsmen. The Mexicans are not yet sufficiently advanced in civilization to attach any kind of social disability to the calling of a tradesman. They still look upon him in the light of the public benefactor which he really is, and entertain towards him feelings of wonder and gratitude, analogous to that which children feel towards any one who, bringing curiosities and pretty things among them, makes a gratuitous display of them.

From this it results that the stores in Mexican towns are as much the resort of the idle and the curious, as of persons seriously bent upon purchasing the commodities there exposed for sale, and become centres where pleasure and business are blended together. On the present occasion, we found in the keeper of the store a good-looking young fellow, dressed in an embroidered jacket and trousers, and lounging about among persons, who had as much the air of being his guests, as his customers. He was of course smoking the cigarette, which is rarely out of the mouths of either sex in Mexico, when alone or in company.

The meeting between my companions and their friend was cordial in the extreme, and the warmest embraces were exchanged. A bottle of *vieux cognac* and glasses were at once produced, and we were regarded as little less than heroes, when it became generally known that we had taken the "dangerous and picturesque" route from Morelia. One of the company, who had lately arrived from the capital by way of Queretaro, Salamanca, and La Piedad—the point at which the road from Zamora to Queretaro crosses the Rio Grande—and who had made a very considerable *détour* in order to avoid the dangers of the Puerto de Medina and Llano del Cuatro, very materially increased the admiration of the company for us, by painting in vivid colours the dangers of the road from which we had just escaped. In the meantime, the shop was driving a brisk trade, for, apart from the fact of its being Saturday night, our presence operated as an additional attraction, and we had the satisfaction of seeing that we were drawing a full house. However, at the expiration of a couple of hours, we began to feel that there was satiety even in being admired, and it became an interesting question, whether we were likely to get supper on the premises, or should be driven to forage for it elsewhere.

Our doubts, however, on this head were soon set at rest by the announcement of our host that supper was served, accompanied by an invitation to follow him across the courtyard to the part of the house which served him as a private residence.

In the *comedor*—a good-sized room, with windows opening on to the courtyard, which was as usual ornamented with flowers, the effect of which was quite spoiled by the accumulated *débris* of packing cases—we found our hostess already seated at the table.

During the meal we were much entertained by the conversation of this lady, who was full of a journey which she had lately made to Mexico to see the Emperor and Empress.

Of course she had been perfectly charmed by their appearance, and, having never till then been more than a few leagues from her native town, she had been immensely struck with the grandeur and magnificence of the capital.

After supper our host conducted us to an elegantly furnished apartment, which was distinguished by the unusual luxury of a carpet, along which our mattresses were spread, and remarking that we must be fatigued after our long ride, wished us good-night, and left us to our own reflections.

In my own case, these reflections took the turn of wondering, in the first instance, at the existence of so good a room in so remote and out-of-the-way a place as Zamora, and in the second, at our own luck in finding ourselves the occupants of it. The profusion of elegant porcelain vases and jars scattered about the floor of the room was truly wonderful; and I lay awake, picturing to myself what awful havoc among the crockery and gashes to one's shins would result from walking in one's sleep. The night passed, however, without any catastrophe.

Next morning, it being Sunday, I strolled out before breakfast, with the double object of observing the people in the market-place, and looking into the church during the celebration of mass. In the market-place I found the usual throng of scantily-clad Indians, conversing and making their purchases for the week at well-stocked wooden booths, planted in the shade of the orange and ash trees.

Threading my way through the crowd of natives, I directed my steps towards the gaping portal of the huge unfinished church. On entering the building I found it empty, with the exception of a few women kneeling on planks scattered here and there about the muddy floor, to which, like shipwrecked mariners, they seemed to be clinging desperately.

In the course of my wanderings about the deserted edifice, I came upon the priest giving directions to the carpenters about the arrangement of some fittings in one of the transepts, and made bold to question him about his parish and the building of the church. The excellent ecclesiastic was, however, as I anticipated, quite unable to satisfy my curiosity, so I concluded our conversation by inquiring at what hour mass would commence. To this question the busy little man replied with great alacrity that, if I would only wait a "*tantito*," (a little bit), he was going to strike up. However, as the congregation was very slow of assembling, I slunk out by a side door before the performance commenced.

Soon after 10 A.M. we took leave of our entertainers, and, wending our way down the long streets, left Zamora by the western *garita*, having a short *jornada* of twelve leagues before us. The first portion of our route lay along a broad sandy road, flanked on either side by unsavory ditches, on the brink of which ran walls of mud bricks overtopped by orange trees laden with golden fruit. Nothing could have been more unsightly than the mud walls and the ditches, and nothing more lovely than the orange thickets beyond.

When we left the main road leading from Zamora through La Barca to Guadalajara, we struck into a foot track which pursued a winding course over hill and dale in a south-westerly direction.

In the course of our morning's ride we only met with two objects of any kind of interest, viz. a very pretty girl, with a remarkably fair complexion and modest downcast eyes, and a very fat priest, who, as he rode past us on his sleek ambling mule, looked the image of Friar Tuck.

About a league on the Zamora side of the *hacienda* of Guaracha, lies the little town or village of Guarachita, on the borders of a marsh which is occasionally converted into a lake by the overflowing of the waters of the great lake of Chapala. The place presented the usual battered appearance of Mexican towns, but the general ruin was partly concealed by the luxuriance of the vegetation which had sprung up, favoured by the moisture of the soil.

The church presented a most forlorn appearance, and I learnt that the priest having taken flight several years previously, no mass had been said nor religious service held there ever since.

Half-way between Guarachita and Guaracha we encountered Señor Guerrero—the *adminstrador* of the *hacienda*—and several attendants, who had ridden out to meet us, and almost at the same moment we caught sight of the *hacienda* itself.

CHAPTER XIII.

HACIENDA LIFE IN MEXICO.

CONSPICUOUS on the projecting shoulder of a conical hill, which rises to the height of a thousand feet behind it, and raised well above the confused cluster of farm buildings and Indian cottages which swarm at its base, the *hacienda* of Guaracha, with its white walls gleaming out in contrast to the sombre brown of the surrounding buildings, and its chapel turret at the north-west corner crowning the whole like a feather stuck jauntily in a cap, presents a decidedly attractive appearance to the approaching traveller. Planted with its back to the hill, and supported where the ground falls away in front by a lofty artificial terrace faced with stone, the hacienda looks as if it had chosen its position, and was prepared to make a fight of it. Indeed, there is a pugnacious air about the place, which invites attack, and seems to say, "Come on."

As we passed through the massive iron portal which forms the outer defence of the *hacienda*, and mounted, in single file, by a slanting narrow roadway cut through the terrace, and commanded by it, on either side I should have supposed that we were entering a fortress rather than a country house.

Having reached the level of the terrace, we found ourselves facing the gateway, which communicated immediately with the courtyard of the *hacienda*, into which we passed, and dismounting from our steeds were received with much show of welcome by the servants, and much wagging of tails on the part of half-a-dozen good-tempered dogs.

In the manner of our approach, and the picturesque grouping of horses, men, and dogs, an artist would have found a study for a picture of feudal times.

Like most country houses in Mexico, the residence at Guaracha is built in the form of a quadrangle, and consists solely of ground-floor rooms, opening on to a portico, which runs round the courtyard on the inside. The building itself seemed to be in an excellent state of repair, but the rooms were very scantily furnished, which gave the place a cold, comfortless appearance.

When my companions explained to me that out of a period of two months, which they had intended to pass in the autumn at the *hacienda*, they had only been left eleven days in peace and quiet, while the remainder of their time had been taken up in flying backwards and forwards from the Juarists, I was not surprised at the naked condition, in which we found the *hacienda*. Owing to the disturbed state of the country for the last few years, the wives and families of the landed proprietors have been entirely debarred from the pleasures, and healthy recreations, of a country life; and the proprietors themselves have in very few instances dared to expose themselves to the risk of being carried off to the mountains by remaining; so if they have visited their estates at all, they have done so stealthily, and remained a very short time. In the absence of the proprietor, the estate is managed by the administrador, who has a pretty hard time of it, being periodically carried off by the Chinacos, and dragged about, until he is ransomed. This vicarious suffering on the part of his administrador is a great saving to the proprietor; for where they would ask 10,000 dollars for the ransom of the owner, they will let the administrador free for 1,000.*

A long, airy, brick-floored room, with an iron bedstead in either corner—a luxury happily not appreciated by the Chinacos, and so not considered worth carrying off—was assigned as quarters to Don Carlos and myself; and, under the influence of Antonio's talent for arrangement, the apartment soon assumed quite a habitable appearance.

* After my departure, Don Carlos was carried off to the *Tierra Caliente*, and not released till he had paid a ransom of nearly 6,000 dollars.

Soon after four o'clock, dinner was served in the *comedor*. Furniture, other than a deal table and rush-bottomed chairs, there was none in the room, and the floor was, as usual, of brick. The fare set before us was not luxurious, but our meal turned out a very merry one; for Señor Guerrero, the administrador, proved excellent company, and a young gentleman—the owner of an estate in the neighbourhood—through which I fear he is running very fast—amused us excessively by his conversation. Referring to an excursion to Guadalajara, whence he had recently returned, he related to us in a very droll manner, how he had laid out the proceeds of the sale of his crop of Indian corn, which he had himself escorted to market. If the shadow of annoyance seemed to pass over his face, as he thought of his mis-spent crop, it passed away in an instant, and he added with great satisfaction, "I have got my wheat and *garvanza** coming on nicely, and I look to getting a good spree out of them." Here was almost a literal case of a young man sowing his wild oats.

From this reckless young spendthrift, who had himself proceeded to the spot immediately after the event to gratify his personal curiosity, I learnt the details of an engagement between the French and Mexicans, at a place called Jiquilpam, some five

---

* A vegetable about the size and shape of a large pea, of which large quantities are consumed on the western slopes of the Mexican table-land.

leagues distant from Guaracha. It appeared that a body of 300 Zouaves under Colonel Clinchant, detached from the main body under General Douay; the French commandant at Guadalajara, who had taken the field, as early in October as the cessation of the rains rendered military operations possible—had fallen in with and surprised, at 4 A.M. on the morning of November 23, 1864, the united forces of Arteaga and Echiaggaray, numbering at least 3,000 strong, and had completely routed them before sunrise, killing some 150, and wounding 80.

The immediate result of this victory was most disastrous to the neighbourhood. For thenceforth, instead of having an organized force to deal with, the peaceful inhabitants were preyed upon by the numerous smaller bands, into which the Juarist army was broken up.

After dinner we enjoyed, over our cigars, some of the excellent coffee, for which the state of Michoachan is so justly celebrated, and the bulk of which is bought up by German houses established at Colima, and exported to Europe *viâ* Manzanilla (on the Pacific coast).

Later on in the evening, we strolled out on to the terrace, and paced about in the moonlight. The night was surpassingly lovely, and so great a calm reigned around that we forgot for a moment, that we were in unquiet Mexico.

Next morning, the terrace presented an appearance

of life and animation, which contrasted strangely with the silence, which pervaded it the night before. For the half-castes and Indian population — the dwellers in the flimsy cabins which swarm at the base of the *hacienda*—had taken possession of it, and converted it into a market-place; having moved it up from below, within the walls of the *hacienda*, for the sake of greater security.

The whole terrace was carpeted with a variegated display of articles of food and dress, among which, piles of bright-coloured Manchester prints showed conspicuously.

The market at Guaracha is held once a week, on the Monday morning; but if the workpeople and villagers are in want of any commodities on other days, they have but to repair to the *tienda*, or general store, which is permanently established on every *hacienda*, and is a great source of profit to the proprietor. The clerk, who conducts the retail business, takes his meals at the table of the proprietor.

As a general rule, the spirit department of the *tienda* is the most lucrative part of the business; but at Guaracha this source of gain has been wisely sacrificed, and the sale of spirits abolished. For the proprietors, having carefully weighed the arguments on both sides, have arrived at the conclusion that the immediate profit realized from the sale of spirits is too dearly purchased at the price of the demoralization of the workpeople, who are utterly unable to resist the temptation of drink.

I understand that on some estates the *tienda* is employed by the proprietor as an instrument for holding his workpeople in bondage. For, by a law of the land, no dependent or workman who is indebted to the *hacienda* is permitted to move from the estate, and sell his labour elsewhere, until he has freed himself from debt. So that unscrupulous proprietors encourage their workpeople to run into debt, in order that they may retain their hold over them.

While the market was at its height, a report got about that the Chinacos were coming down upon the place, and a sudden panic seized the crowd. At the bare mention of the name " Chinacos " Señor Guerrero, the administrador, turned pale from fear, as he had lately received notice from them, that he was to be hung up whenever he should fall into their hands, for having once given intelligence of their movements to General Marquez, while in command of the Imperialist forces in the neighbourhood.

To test the truth of the report, a messenger was forthwith despatched in the direction from which the enemy was expected. At the end of a couple of hours he returned with the alarming intelligence that the advance-guard of a body of Chinacos, 500 strong, under a chief called Martinez, had already reached the village of Jaripo, less than three leagues from Guaracha, which was supposed to be their destination.

This was enough for Señor Guerrero, and, mounting his horse on the spot, he rode straight away into the mountains, and was heard of no more.

In the meanwhile a council of war was held, in which Don Carlos insisted on all who had no business there—myself among the number—quitting Guaracha at once. At the same time he announced his own intention of remaining, explaining that the only course open to him, now that he had decided to reside at Guaracha, was to stay, and make the best terms he could with the enemy.

Now, as I felt considerable curiosity to see something of these Chinacos, of whose doings I had heard so much, but as yet seen nothing, it was with great reluctance that I obeyed the general order, and joined the line of fugitives. On my expressing my inclination to remain, Don Carlos represented to me that it would be the height of folly to do so, for that he knew the Chinacos only too well, and that if they found me on the *hacienda*, where I confessedly had no business, they would certainly carry me off to the mountains and drag me about with them, if they did not despatch me on the spot for a Frenchman. So packing up my valise in haste, I took farewell of Don Carlos, and turned my back upon the danger.

About two leagues to the north of Guaracha, and lying well off any road, stands a small *hacienda*, called El Platanal, belonging to a retired lawyer from Guadalajara—a gentleman of large fortune but penurious habits, who considers it his greatest misfortune in life to be the uncle of the entertaining young spendthrift introduced to the reader above. Nothing but the information that the place had hitherto escaped the inroads of the Chinacos induced us to direct our steps thither. Following the main track by which we had arrived from Zamora as far as the village of Guarachita, we there struck into a narrow path to the left, which conducted us over low swampy fields of maize stubble to the foot of the brown arid hills which bound the view to the northward of Guaracha. A ride of less than an hour and a half brought us to our destination, and certainly the aspect of the place was not encouraging. At first sight the house appeared to be uninhabited, but on penetrating to the back of the premises we discovered a melancholy woman, who informed us that her master was out, but would probably soon be home. Accordingly we dismounted, and sat down on a bench to await his arrival.

After the lapse of half an hour, a slim town-bred little man of about fifty appeared upon the scene, and informed us that he had just returned from the daily walk which the doctor at Guadalajara had prescribed as necessary for the preservation of his health. Señor Ascencio, for such was his name, was evidently not best pleased at the invasion of his premises, and was at his wits' end to know where to stow us away.

A single brick-floored apartment, quite innocent of windows, light and air being only admitted by the door, served our host for bedroom and sitting-room, and there was no stranger's room; so there was nothing for it but to accept cheerfully the corner which was placed at my disposal. Our flight from Guaracha having taken place just before the dinner hour, we had arrived fasting, and made short work of a couple of skinny chickens, which were set before us late in the evening to appease our appetites. But for the *frijoles* which followed, and which come in at the conclusion of every meal—like " God save the Queen " at the end of a concert—we should have gone to bed famishing.

After supper a messenger arrived from Guaracha with the tidings that the Chinacos had not moved from Jaripo, and bringing us mattresses and a bottle of sherry, thoughtfully sent by Don Carlos. Both the news and the wine were most acceptable—for our host, who was himself a water-drinker, apparently did not think it incumbent on him to gratify the tastes of his friends for more generous liquor.

During the evening's conversation Señor Ascencio informed me that, although the Chinacos had hitherto abstained from quartering themselves upon him, Regules, their leader, had, only five weeks previously, sent him a polite message, requesting the loan of 500 dollars, with which exaction the *hacienda* had instantly complied, only too glad to get off so cheaply.

By noon next day we had received no further tidings from Guaracha, and began to think that the place must be in the hands of the Chinacos, which anticipations were soon confirmed by the news brought back by the messenger whom we had despatched to resolve our doubts. For the fellow very soon returned in a great state of alarm, and declared that he had himself seen the Chinacos arrive at the gates of Guaracha.

In consequence of this intelligence we were about to mount our horses and put a greater distance between ourselves and the danger, when a servant arrived from Guaracha with the welcome intelligence that the coast was clear for our return. It appeared that the Chinacos had not approached nearer than Jaripo, from which place they had broken up in the night, and made a raid upon the town of Jiquilpam, where they had pillaged the stores, and carried off with them to the mountains half a dozen of such of the citizens as they thought likely to be able to pay a good sum for their ransom.

This intelligence had been brought by a party of

fugitives from Jiquilpam, who had passed the night on the mountains, and who, as they approached Guaracha, riding in hot haste, were themselves taken for Chinacos, and created a panic among the Guarachenes. This at once explained the false report brought back by our messenger, who had reached Guaracha at the moment that the band of horsemen was seen approaching from the direction of Jiquilpam—an appearance which had even deceived Don Carlos.

So, the danger being overpassed, we retraced our steps to Guaracha, and congratulated Don Carlos on having escaped the expected visit of the Chinacos.

As the dinner hour approached, it was amusing to watch the fugitives dropping in from various directions, and to hear the adventures which each had to tell. Last of all, Señor Guerrero appeared upon the scene, having but just descended, with great caution, from his eyrie among the mountains.

After dinner, a letter arrived from a messenger who had been dispatched from Guaracha to treat with the enemy. For, in accordance with a not uncommon practice, the *hacienda* had made a bargain with the Chinacos, to pay them 1,000 dollars down, and 200 dollars per month, provided only that they kept clear of the premises. However, in consequence of the Chinacos having been lately dislodged from the quarters, where the money should have been paid, the *hacienda* was in their debt, to liquidate which the messenger had been dispatched.

The address on the cover,

> "To Señor Don José Maria Guerrero,
> "Wherever he may happen to be,"

showed that the writer was well acquainted with Señor Guerrero's habits.

The letter itself ran thus:—

"My very dear Sir and good Friend,

"As quickly as you can, and with the least delay possible, contrive to send me three thousand dollars. For, if the *hacienda* refuses to pay this sum for my ransom, I am to be shot, as I am informed by his Excellency Colonel Don Magdaleno Martinez. I pray you to do your utmost for me.

"Your affectionate friend, who kisses your hand,
"JUAN J. GONSALEZ."

To pay so exorbitant a sum was quite out of the question, and the threat would probably have been carried out, but for the intervention of a superior officer, who recognised the validity of a passport bearing the signature of Riva Palacio, the Juarist governor of the province, with which Gonsalez was luckily provided.

Accordingly, the prisoner was allowed to go about his business, and made the best of his way to

Guaracha, where he arrived in the middle of the night, throwing the *hacienda* into a state of alarm by his summons for admittance at that untimely hour, every one supposing that the Chinacos were at the gates. When the voice of Juan Gonsalez was recognised, the relief experienced was intense, and he was regarded as one raised from the dead. Although himself uninjured, the *mozo* belonging to the *hacienda*, who accompanied him, presented a deplorable spectacle, his head having been wantonly cut open by the Chinacos.

For the next few days we were kept in a state of constant uneasiness by alarming rumours of the approach of marauding bands, in consequence of which, the business of collecting together the horses, mules, and cattle, which, together with the agricultural implements, Don Carlos had agreed to take at a valuation, was postponed from day to day. For, with the Chinacos hovering about, it would have been in the highest degree imprudent to drive the animals together into one place, and thus expose them to the risk of being carried off *en masse*.

Dependent on the *hacienda* of Guaracha are several outlying ranchos or farms. To one of these, called San Antonio, it was thought, under the circumstances, advisable to retire and get through the business of branding the animals there, previously to commencing the operation at Guaracha.

So on the fifth day after our arrival, having packed up our bedding and set it upon mules, we mounted our horses, and left Guaracha a little before sunrise, reaching our destination, which was some four leagues distant, by eight A.M. Our ride was absolutely uneventful, and the scenery of an exceedingly monotonous description.

In front of the *rancho* or farm buildings we found a scene of wild confusion reigning, and the air was filled with the shouting of men, the neighing of horses, and the bellowing of cattle. In the *coráls*—the quadrangular enclosures, which are conspicuous features of every *hacienda*—were surging to and fro, like a troubled sea, herds of horses, cattle, and mules.

Upon our arrival we were conducted to seats of honour, which had been prepared for us under a wooden canopy, decorated with green, at one end of the *corál*. As we took our seats a band of rustic musicians—who played the same tune, with little intermission, for forty-eight hours consecutively—struck up, and the proceedings commenced.

The turn of the mules came first. These were let in, by tens at a time, into that portion of the great *corál* which was walled off for the branding. In this space about a dozen *mozos* were in waiting, and each man, selecting his mule as it passed, if he could, threw his lasso over its legs and so brought it to the ground, or if not, threw his arms about its neck, and wrestling with it, tried to throw it. As soon as the beast had been laid prostrate by either of these processes, a noose was passed over the four feet, which were thus firmly secured, while a *mozo* sat upon the head. Then the brander would approach with a red-hot iron, and, planting one foot firmly on the belly of the beast, would for the space of thirty seconds press the burning iron on to the hinder quarters of the prostrate animal. For the first fifteen seconds, the patient appeared not to feel any pain, but it would struggle so violently during the latter half, that the operator not unfrequently had to desist. Thus, in the space of three hours, some 200 young mules were branded.

At 11 o'clock we adjourned into the *rancho* to breakfast. The dwelling-house of Don Juan the *administrador*, which occupied but one corner of an extensive farm-yard, consisted of a suite of three rooms on the ground-floor with kitchen attached, in which a *zambo* with woolly hair, notorious for being the greatest rogue and best cook in the neighbourhood, was busy over his earthenware pots, getting ready our breakfast.

On the outside, the walls had lately received a fresh coating of plaster, but within, the mud-brick or *adobe*, of which the walls and flooring were alike constructed, was exposed in all its nakedness. However, in spite of the bareness of the walls, and an almost entire absence of furniture, there was an air of neatness about the place, for which it was difficult to account. The inmost of the three rooms was occupied by Don Juan as office and bedroom combined, and in that room the neatness culminated, proclaiming him to be the author of it. In one corner stood a clean iron bedstead covered with a red woollen wrapper, which seemed to shed its warmth and cheerfulness over the whole room. On the wall hung a little oil-painting of St. Anthony, the guardian saint of the rancho.

After breakfast the branding operations recommenced with renewed vigour, and continued until the evening, and all through the next day, the process of marking the calves and colts being precisely similar to that employed in the case of the young mules.

The operation of branding with a hot iron being only feasible in the case of the juvenile animals, the adults were simply driven into the enclosure, and counted as they passed out. Occasionally, the more active and refractory of these latter would jump clean over the wall into enclosures where they had no business, or try to escape altogether into the mountains. In this latter case horsemen in waiting would pursue them with the lasso over hill and dale, and the most exciting chases ensued, which invariably ended in the capture of the animal. In the case of young refractory bulls or oxen, it is the custom to bind them by the horns to steady old stagers, who drag the youngsters along with them everywhere, till their behaviour improves.

To the business of the second day an evening of pleasure succeeded. What remained of daylight was devoted to amateur bull-fighting—a sport from which the chief element of danger was eliminated by the precaution of sawing off the horns of the bull. When the amateur *picadores* had worried without injuring several bulls in succession, the sport was varied by one of the best riders getting on to the back of a bull, which tried in vain to dislodge him by a succession of wild bounds and plunges.

Last of all began the pastime of *colear*ing, literally, "tailing." This sport is the most severe test of horsemanship, and only the best riders escape severe falls. The thing to be done is to catch hold of the bull by the tail, while he is in full gallop, pass it between your right thigh and the saddle, and, by the sudden jerk of reining in your horse, hurl the bull to the ground. This exceedingly difficult operation was successfully performed both by Don Carlos and Don Pancho.

When darkness had set in, the company adjourned to the interior of the yard, where the band struck up the same monotonous tune which had been dinned into our ears all day. In their costume, which consisted of a shirt and trousers of coarse long cloth, a pair of sandals, and a broad-brimmed straw hat, the musicians were in no way distinguishable from the rest of the company.

Understanding that there was to be dancing by moonlight, we joined the motley throng of Indians and half-castes, but some time elapsed before the young men could overcome the bashfulness of the maidens. When at length the dancing was set going, only two couples could be got to stand up at a time—the rest of the company squatting round on the ground, and regarding the performers as persons who were making martyrs of themselves for the good of the public. It is only in countries, which have reached a higher degree of civilization than Mexico, that the inhabitants prefer dancing themselves, to getting others to dance for them.

The dancing itself was throughout exceedingly tame and monotonous, the artists merely attempting to beat time to the music by a shuffling motion of the feet, the men standing opposite to the women, and never approaching to close quarters. The performance, if not amusing, was at any rate highly decorous, and the audience seemed never weary of looking on, for the entertainment was kept up till the small hours of the night.

Next morning, we rode quietly back to Guaracha.

It was a Sunday, and something of a Sabbath stillness seemed to reign, but we listened in vain for the music of church bells.

Although churches are scattered plentifully all over the country, and the law provides that a chapel shall be attached to every *hacienda*, the priests have, in the disturbed districts, as a rule deserted their flocks, and left them without any kind of religious supervision. Yet so flagrantly immoral for the most part are the lives of the priests who remain, that the case of the communes which have been abandoned altogether is preferable to that of those, where the priest continues setting the people a vicious example. Of a truth the Mexicans are a people more to be pitied than blamed, for, if they are bad, it is really wonderful that they are not worse, when one considers fully the terrible disadvantages, under which they have hitherto laboured.

The Chinacos having left the coast clear, I devoted the remainder of my stay to making myself acquainted with a few facts relating to *Haciendas de Trigo*, literally "wheat farms," in general and Guaracha in particular.

In the first place, the farming operations are regulated by the seasons, which are but two—the dry and the rainy. The dry season, beginning in October, lasts till June, while the rains fall during our summer months, so that the Mexican year may be roughly divided into eight months of dry, and four of wet weather. In the course of the dry season rain falls about half a dozen times on the table-land, and rather more frequently on the slopes. Even in the rainy season the sky is unclouded till noon, when the clouds gradually begin to drift up from the horizon, and heavy rain sets in of an afternoon with remarkable regularity.

The crops best suited to the dry season are wheat, barley, and *garvanza*; and to the wet, maize, beans, and chili; but nothing will grow on the table-land in the dry season without artificial irrigation. The value of an estate on the table-land, of which two-thirds of the country consists, is mainly regulated by the available supply of water, and means for conducting it about the fields. The first point, to which the attention of a person about to purchase an estate on the table-land would be naturally directed, is the supply of water, for with water the Mexican soil will produce almost anything, and without it nothing. But unluckily the requisite supply of water is seldom forthcoming, and therefore wheat, which is a crop which can only be produced in the dry season, will always command a high price, and the consumption of wheaten bread will never be general in Mexico. While maize sells on an average at $4\frac{1}{2}$ dollars, or 18 shillings, the *carga* of 300 lbs. or (about) 5 bushels, wheat fetches $12\frac{1}{2}$ dollars, or 50 shillings the *carga* of

5 bushels—or 10 shillings the bushel, about twice as dear as it is in England. Sown in the month of December, the wheat is ready for cutting in May; and, immediately after the wheat harvest, maize is sown just before the rains set in. In the sowing of maize different methods prevail in different parts of the country. At Guaracha, where the return averages from two to three hundred-fold, it is customary to put the seed into the ground by three grains at a time, at intervals of four feet. Of these three grains, only one springs up, as a rule, but that one produces from two to three hundred-fold. In the most fertile districts—as for instance about Penjámon, in the celebrated Bajio—you may count as many as four to five hundred grains on a single ear.

If the maize is deprived by the unusual lateness of the rains of the soaking which it requires when at first put into the ground, the crop suffers irreparably, as was the case in the years 1863–1864, after which in the mining districts maize rose to famine prices.

After maize, *frijoles*, or beans, rank next in importance as an article of general consumption. These are usually sown with the maize, round the stalks of which they twine gracefully as they grow up.

The most remunerative crop of all is chili—an article in great demand among the Indians and lower orders in general, by whom it is chiefly used to give a flavour to the insipid tortillas which are to them the staff of life.

The arroba of 25 lbs. fetches on an average from 4 to $4\frac{1}{2}$ dollars in the Mexican market.

Planted in February, chili is ready for cutting in August, and is the only crop which can be got in during the rainy season.

CHAPTER XIV.

GUARACHA TO GUADALAJARA.

On St. Valentine's day I took leave of my kind host, and continued my journey towards Guadalajara, through which city I had to pass in order to reach San Blas, the port on the Pacific for which I was bound. Not content with having done his utmost to render my stay at Guaracha agreeable, Don Carlos directed his own body servant, the faithful Antonio, to accompany me on my way as far as I might stand in need of his services.

So, mounted on an excellent steed, which I had purchased of Señor Guerrero for the moderate sum of 8*l.* I sallied forth once more into the wilds, with Antonio following at my heels.

Of the two routes to Guadalajara, the one by crossing, the other by skirting, the great lake of Chapala, I had chosen the latter. For the passage of the lake is at all times a difficult one, and at that moment the Indians who dwell on an island, called Mescala, were reported to be in a state of open insurrection, and to have stopped all traffic on the lake.

Under ordinary circumstances, the farmers in the vicinity avail themselves of the lake of Chapala to transport their crops on their way to Guadalajara, thereby saving a considerable portion of the tedious land journey.

The great lake of Chalapa—the most extensive in Mexico, according to M. Chevalier *—extends over a surface of 750,000 acres, or nearly 1,200 square miles. This measurement would make it more than twice the size of the lake of Geneva.

It was already noon when I left Guaracha, so that night I did not attempt to get beyond the *hacienda* of San Estanzuelo, distant some ten leagues.

The scenery continued as monotonous as ever, ridges of bare hills, clothed with a scanty, burnt-up vegetation, succeeding each other in endless succession. In the valleys which intervened there was but little cultivation to speak of, although here and there crops were coming up, and from time to time we came upon a melancholy Indian or two scratching the surface of the soil with an antiquated kind of plough. In the only village through which we passed in the course of our ten league ride, we refreshed ourselves with pieces of fresh sugar cane, which I found exceedingly agreeable. Inasmuch as in Mexico your throat is

* "Mexico, Ancient and Modern," English Translation, vol. ii. p. 114.

always more or less dry, and your lips parched, from the combined effects of the rarification of the air and the amount of dust which it is impossible to avoid swallowing on the road, you feel intensely grateful for any means of moistening them.

Shortly before reaching our destination, I caught sight of a couple of *coyotes*, or jackals, slinking away into the bush. These were the first wild animals of any kind which I had seen in the country, with the exception of a couple of bluish speckled hares, with long ears like donkeys, which I started in a maize stubble near Puebla.

The almost entire absence of animal life in the higher portion of the Mexican table-land at the present day, is to be accounted for chiefly by the want of water. I say at the present day, for it is probable that in the period before the conquest, when the table-land is said to have been well wooded, the case was far otherwise.

After an exceedingly dull ride, it was a great consolation to come upon something attractive at the end of our journey. From the summit of the last of the innumerable ridges which we had surmounted during the long afternoon, we looked down upon a valley, through which meandered a broad, shallow river, whose course was marked by a serpentine line of verdure, which is sure to spring up in Mexico wherever there is water.

A short descent brought us to the *hacienda* of San Simon, the white portico of which, standing out against the leafy background, was very pleasant to look upon. The position of the *hacienda*, which is perched on high ground overhanging the river, is highly picturesque. Immediately *vis-à-vis* stands the lesser *hacienda* of Estanzuela, where I was to pass the night. The passage from one to the other is a somewhat precarious one, over a broken-down bridge, which, with its ruined arches, forms an exceedingly picturesque object in the landscape. Had the bridge been less rickety, I should gladly have paused a little to enjoy the view up and down stream.

On riding into the courtyard of the *hacienda*, Antonio advanced to the front, and explained to the wife of the *administrador*, who came out to learn our errand, that I was an Englishman just arrived from Guaracha, in want of a night's lodging. Upon this, the good woman gave us a ready welcome, and, showing the way, bade me follow her into the house. On entering the sitting-room, I was surprised to find there the extraordinary luxury of a carpet, which, combined with a piano, and two or three good engravings hanging on the walls, gave the place an air of unusual comfort and refinement.

Presently a dapper little Frenchman in a white jacket appeared upon the scene, and explained to me at once that he was not the husband of the lady before me, but only an *employé* of the proprietor, Don Diego Morreno, who was, as usual, an absentee, and resided in the city of Mexico. In the half hour which we passed together sitting on the sofa, awaiting the arrival of the *administrador*, the little Frenchman discoursed to me, with the volubility proverbial in his countrymen, on the state of things in general, and Mexico in particular, giving me plainly to understand that he felt himself, individually, quite thrown away in so abandoned a country. And, indeed, I did feel truly sorry for the little man, and heartily joined in the wish which he expressed, that the day was not far distant when he would again be treading his native *boulevard*.

Presently the *administrador* arrived, and renewed the welcome which we had originally received from his wife. The appearance of the master of the house was, at the same time, the signal for supper, which was served in an adjoining apartment.

The little Frenchman, who had long since given up the habit of trying in vain to masticate the hard, stringy meat of the country, supped off a basin of bread and milk.

Besides the little Frenchman and my Mexican host and hostess, there sat down to table with us a middle-aged young lady of very unprepossessing appearance, but unbounded good nature.

With this señora, in this absence of metal more attractive, the little Frenchman, as a matter of course, kept up a violent flirtation, and it was highly amusing to observe his gallantry during a round game of cards, at which we employed, as counters, *papiros*— little cigarettes, which are sold at about the rate of ten a penny throughout the length and breadth of the land.

These cigarettes are chiefly imported from the Havana, where I visited La Honradez—one of the principal factories where they are made. This factory turns out several millions of cigarettes daily, in the manufacture of which a large number of Chinamen, who engage themselves for a term of eight years, are employed. These Chinamen are boarded and lodged on the premises, and their dormitory is one of the drollest sights possible to witness. The ward in which they sleep is a perfect cube of beds reaching from the floor to within a few feet of the ceiling. In spite of so many beds being crowded into one room, the dormitory was excessively clean and airy —a thorough draught being kept up day and night by a system of perforated windows. In an adjoining compartment each man had his private locker, and on each locker the name of the owner was printed in large characters—not their real Chinese names, but adopted names, such as Pompey, Cæsar, Alcibiades, Socrates, Nero, Vespasian, Domitian, and a few modern heroes, as Napoleon, Wellington, &c. Besides the Chinese and others employed on the premises, a very large number of Spanish soldiers eke out their pay by what they earn in their leisure hours in folding up the cigarettes in their barracks.

In the factory of the Honradez, everything is made on the premises, even including the machinery; it is a most harmonious, self-contained whole. In the department for chromo-lithography, I was amused to notice a card of designs, on which among others I recognised portraits of the present Archbishop of York, the Prince and Princess Louis of Hesse, and Mr. Laird. On leaving, in accordance with the usage of the factory, I was presented with a packet of cigarettes, on which my own name was printed before my eyes.

After enduring a dull round game for the space of an hour, I pleaded fatigue, and retired to the carpeted sitting-room, where a bed had been extemporized for me.

Next morning, soon after sunrise, we were again on the road, bound for the *hacienda* of Buena Vista— the seat of General Vellarde, the most notorious personage in those parts. With the exception of the hot springs of Ixtla—a number of natural fountains, from which the boiling mineral water spouts up several feet into the air, and which would make the fortune of the place, were they anywhere but in Mexico — I observed nothing worthy of note until, after a three hours' ride, we came in sight of Buena Vista.

From the moment we entered upon the territory of General Vellarde, which is a kind of border-land between the states of Jalisco and Michoachan, I was struck with the neatness with which everything was kept. The fences, gates, farm buildings, &c. would have done credit to any civilized country in Europe.

Like Dumnorix in Cæsar's Commentaries, General Vellarde maintains a regiment of soldiers at his own cost, and I must do him the justice to admit, that his men present a more soldier-like appearance than the regular troops.

Having foreseen that a letter of introduction to this provincial potentate would be useful to me, I endeavoured, before I left the capital, to furnish myself with credentials of some sort. My efforts, however, all proved fruitless, for most of my influential acquaintances in Mexico were engaged in lawsuits with this eccentric personage, who is commonly known by the *soubriquet* of "el burro de oro" (the golden ass). In Zamora, however, thinking that any kind of introduction would be better than none, I had obtained a letter from the storekeeper, in whose house we were lodged. This letter was artfully couched in the most obsequious terms, and intended to flatter the vanity of the "golden ass."

On riding up to the main entrance of the *hacienda*, I learned that General Vellarde, who had lately been appointed by the Emperor, whose cause he had espoused, Prefect of the neighbouring town of La Barca, was at that time residing at his town house.

In his absence, the major domo received me so insolently, that I rode off to try if more hospitality was to be met with elsewhere. My next attempt however was even more unsuccessful, for, on entering a neighbouring house, I found it untenanted, except by a little child, which was prowling about by its bedside with its face covered by black plague-spots. Not encouraged by this spectacle, I beat a hasty retreat, and retraced my steps to the *hacienda*, determined this time to force an entrance at any price.

However, as I passed through the iron gateway leading into the court-yard, I encountered no opposition of any kind, and proceeded to establish myself quietly in the *comedor*—the walls of which were decorated with tawdry paintings of fruit and flowers.

Anticipating that I should find nothing to eat, I had purchased some *pan dolce* at the *tienda*, and being already provided with tea and teapot—my inseparable travelling companions—I only stood in need of boiling water.

But how to obtain boiling water in such inhospitable precincts? I would at any rate try, so I sallied forth from the *comedor*, and proceeded to make a thorough investigation of the premises.

Outside I found myself in a court-yard, the walls of which were covered with glaring frescos in the worst possible taste and style, representing mythological subjects. Into this court-yard most of the rooms opened, on the principle of a Roman or Pompeian villa, which the architect had evidently aimed at reproducing. Nor was the attempt by any means unsuccessful, for the whole house was characterized by an air of solidity and elegance, unsurpassed by any, with which I had yet met in town or country in Mexico. Indeed, but for the vile and profuse daubing on the walls, one could have imagined that one was wandering in some luxurious villa at Pompeii or Herculaneum.

In one of the recesses of the building, I discovered, over her earthenware pots, the old woman, upon whom you are sure to stumble, sooner or later, in Mexican houses, if you only persevere. As good luck would have it, this old crone was in the act of trying to blow into a sufficient glow to boil a jug of water, the bits of charcoal which, laid in a square receptacle sunk in the face of a solid brick counter, do the duty of a fire all over Mexico. From this old lady I obtained not only boiling water, but a couple of poached eggs, so that I fared sumptuously.

At noon I took my departure for La Barca, and in about an hour found myself standing on the banks of the Rio Grande de Lerma, waiting for the ferry to cross into the town, round the base of which the river sweeps. After considerable delay, the passage was safely effected, our horses swimming over, while we crossed in the ferry.

Immediately overhanging the river, on the opposite or Jalisco bank, stands the town house of his Excellency General Vellarde—a substantial well-built residence, which would be reckoned a sumptuous dwelling anywhere. About the entrance were buzzing, like bees at the entrance of a hive, some of those soldiers, whom the general keeps at his own expense. Demanding admission, I was at once shown into the presence of the potentate, who was taking his after-dinner cup of coffee in his office.

Reclining at full length on an elongated arm-chair, fitted with a rest for the feet, lay a flabby white-faced giant, dressed in a pair of bright red trousers, black jacket and waistcoat, and wearing a short highly-polished jet black wig, carefully plastered down over his forehead—reminding one irresistibly of a gigantic knave of spades. The great oval face wore an inane, self-satisfied expression, and was as innocent of hair as a woman's. The skin was perfectly white, and it was very evident that the general had been particularly careful of his complexion.

The conversation of the man—at any rate, that of it to which he treated me—was much of a piece with his appearance, and he had not even the civility to offer me a cigarette or cup of coffee. The office, in which our interview took place, was a most unpretending apartment, opening on to the street. What interested me most about the premises were some excellent maps of the various states into which the country was formerly divided—a division, which has since given place to departments on the French model, in order to facilitate centralization.

On my rising to take leave, the general was condescending enough to hold out a white flabby hand for me to shake, and I retain to this hour the sensation of inert clamminess, which it imparted to mine.

Leaving La Barca at about 2 P.M. I made for Ocotlan—a small town situated between two arms of the Rio Grande, a little below the point where that river issues from the great lake of Chapala. Unfortunately, owing to a misunderstanding, we had taken the inland road, which only afforded here and there an unsatisfactory glimpse of the great lake, which is said, with very little truth I suspect, to rival the Swiss lakes in beauty.

We had expected to reach Ocotlan, especially by the short cut we had taken, before sunset, but our short cut turned out a very long one, for an hour after nightfall we found ourselves still wandering about in the darkness, uncertain which way to turn. Antonio was quite at fault, and I of course utterly dependent upon him. Fortunately, however, in this extremity we stumbled upon some natives, who put us on the right road, and after a somewhat perilous ride over very uneven ground, we at length espied the lights of Ocotlan, and effected a safe passage across the long narrow bridge, looking fearfully down upon the black mysterious river. Crossing bridges in a country like Mexico, in the pitch dark, is an amusement exciting enough in its way, for you never feel sure that the bridge will not leave off in the middle, and you may reckon with tolerable certainty on finding more than one yawning gap.

Just outside the little town of Ocotlan, stands the huge establishment of the brothers Castellanos, the wealthiest people in the place, for whom I carried a letter of introduction. Riding into the spacious courtyard, I left Antonio in charge of the horses, and went in search of the brothers, and soon discovered one of them serving his customers in the *tienda*. This gentleman received me with great politeness, and had a room prepared for me at once.

After a somewhat restless night, during which my slumbers were much disturbed by the movements of a dog which had been accidentally shut into my room, I rose an hour before dawn to be in time for the diligence, which passed that way *en route* for Guadalajara. For I had arranged overnight with Don Pedro—one of the brothers Castellanos—to accompany him in the diligence to Guadalajara, while his servants were to lead my horse, along with several which their masters were sending to their own house in Guadalajara. In accordance with this arrangement, I had dismissed the faithful Antonio, with whose services I could now fairly dispense.

Soon after 6 A.M. a light covered van, drawn by six jingling mules, rolled up to the door, where Don Pedro and I stood awaiting its arrival. As the vehicle was quite empty, I supposed that we were destined to have the interior all to ourselves, until a lady, who turned out to be Don Pedro's sister, appeared upon the scene, and seated herself on the back seat.

Inasmuch as you can hardly travel in a Mexican diligence for five minutes together without coming into violent contact with some portion of your neighbour's person, the conversation begins of itself with apologies for these involuntary concussions. When you have given your neighbours several good digs in the ribs, and in return received their heads several times in your stomach, you seem already to know a good deal about your fellow-travellers, and conversation is thus rendered comparatively easy.

Between Ocotlan and Guadalajara—a distance of

about sixty miles—we saw nothing of interest except the *hacienda* of Atequiza, which is remarkable both for its size and the beauty of its situation. On our right we got occasional glimpses of the Rio de Santiago, while the view on our left was bounded by the bare mountains, which shut in the great lake of Chapala.

At the *hacienda* of Atequiza, we found stationed several companies of native infantry, which, like those in the pay of General Vellarde, had a less slovenly look than those you meet with in and about the city of Mexico. With this fact, the Emperor Maximilian appears to have been so much struck on his journey to the interior, that on his return to the capital he repeated more than once to those about him his conviction, that the provinces of the interior would eventually furnish him with excellent material for his army.

Shortly before getting involved in the intricacies of San Pedro, the straggling suburb of Guadalajara, we struck into the ordinary road leading from the city of Mexico to Guadalajara—the great highway from the capital to the interior.

From the suburb of San Pedro a long double avenue of respectable-sized trees leads into the city of Guadalajara. In this avenue we met, driving in her private carriage, the mother of my travelling companions, who had come out to meet us. The

equipage itself was not inelegant, but the old lady seated therein was so meanly dressed that, had you met her in England, you would have supposed her to be an inmate of the workhouse. Indeed, all over Mexico, nothing is more striking than the poverty-stricken, almost squalid, appearance of the persons you see reclining in vehicles, which you would have supposed quite beyond their reach. The consummation of beggars riding seems to be already realized in Mexico.

Confining themselves to saluting their parent, the brother and sister continued on their way in the diligence, till we reached the office in the city, where, after some delay, an individual turned up to receive our fares. This business over, we had our slender baggage transferred to a *fiacre*, in which we all three took our places, and drove to the Hotel Hidalgo, where I descended, declining the polite invitation of my fellow-travellers to take up my quarters at their house.

CHAPTER XV.

GUADALAJARA.

Of the excellence of the Hotel Hidalgo I had heard a good deal from various travellers, with whom I had fallen in on the road, and I found it at least as good as any of the more pretentious hotels of the capital.

As an hour of daylight yet remained, and my stay in Guadalajara was to be very short, after performing a hurried toilet, I set out on the evening of my arrival to call upon some of the citizens, to whose hospitality I had been recommended by friends in Mexico.

Within a few doors of my hotel lived Don Domingo Llamas, one of the wealthiest merchants in Guadalajara, and formerly chief magistrate of the city. On repairing to the residence of this influential personage I was shown into a very dingy office, at the foot of a handsome stone staircase, leading to the upper part of the house. In the office, several clerks were engaged at high desks, and I amused myself with watching their proceedings, while awaiting the arrival of Don Domingo.

Presently the great man, who had been fetched from the recesses of a *tienda* over the way, appeared, and, on reading the letter which I presented, declared himself, *more Mexicano*, at my absolute disposition. Nothing, however, came of this promising exordium, but an agreement to visit a cotton factory together on the morrow.

My next visit was to the Casa de J——, to which I had been accredited by my bankers in Mexico. The house of J——, like the firm of Graham, Greaves, and Company, in the capital, combines with their banking business speculating in dry goods in general, and so, besides replenishing my purse, I was enabled to supply myself at the same time with such indispensable articles of Mexican travel as tea, sugar, biscuits, &c. In addition to all this, at the last moment, the generosity of J—— threw in a bottle of brandy, without which no one should think of taking the road in Mexico. For it is highly imprudent to drink the water of the country pure and unadulterated, dysentery, cholic, and other ailments innumerable being apt to result therefrom.

From the Casa de J—— I proceeded to the house of Señor Gil Romero, a wealthy advocate in large practice, from whom I received an invitation to dine on the following evening.

On returning to the Hotel Hidalgo, I found there an intelligent young American, whose acquaintance I had already made in the city of Mexico, and I passed the rest of the evening in his company. This gentleman, who was a native of California, was, like myself, bound for Tepic, where he proposed trying his hand at growing cotton.

With daylight next morning I set about the task of "doing" the city. Guadalajara, the capital of Western Mexico, contains from ninety to a hundred thousand inhabitants, and straggles over at least as much ground as the city of Mexico, the population of which is said to be twice as large. The general appearance of the city is remarkably pleasing, and the private houses are, many of them, as elegant and substantial as the best in the capital. In the way of public buildings Guadalajara has not much to boast of, and a day and a half is amply sufficient to get through, what little sight-seeing there is to be done.

The Cathedral, the exterior of which is painted a light fawn colour, and the Foundling Hospital, are the only edifices of any architectural pretentions. The former, although by no means equal to the cathedrals of Puebla or Morelia, is rather a graceful building, and is set off to great advantage by the foreground of orange trees, with which the Plaza Mayor, on the north side of which it stands, is abundantly planted. The interior is very plain and unadorned.

La Cuna, or the Foundling Hospital, the centre of which is surmounted by a decorated dome, forms a very pretty termination to a vista of trees, which line the principal *boulevard* in the suburbs of the city.

As in all Mexican cities, arcades, under which the inhabitants find shelter from the sun, in the dry, and rain, in the wet seasons, are carried down most of the streets. Here a few hours may be whiled away pleasantly enough in studying the manners and customs of the people.

At eleven A.M., the hour appointed for our visit to the cotton factory, I repaired to the mansion of Don Domingo Llamas, and found him mounted on a strong chestnut cob awaiting my arrival.

As we rode through the streets towards the *garita*, Don Domingo was greeted everywhere with much show of respect, and, indeed, on his sleek ambling nag, looked the very picture of commercial prosperity.

Yet Don Domingo had had his reverses in his day. Indeed, he had but very recently recovered from them, for, in common with the majority of the men of substance in the country, he had unfortunately espoused the clerical or reactionary party, and had been compelled to fly to Europe, when Juarez and the Liberals came into power in December, 1860.

Availing himself of the French intervention, and

the comparative security of life and property consequent thereon, Don Domingo had returned to Mexico, about the time of the arrival of the Emperor Maximilian in the country, and, to judge from the position which he appeared to be enjoying, less than a year afterwards, in the estimation of his fellow-citizens, must have found his affairs in an unexpectedly flourishing condition, or have succeeded in setting them to rights unusually quickly.

As in the central parts of the city the houses are most of them comfortable and well-built, so there at least the streets are paved and fairly level; but, as you diverge more and more from the centre, you become aware of a gradual falling off in houses and streets alike, till in the extremities, where all regard for appearances vanishes, you find yourself traversing a waste of straggling mud hovels, intersected by broad sandy tracks.

When at length the traveller emerges into the open country from the outer *garita*, the prospect before him is not encouraging. An undulating expanse of bare table-land extends as far as the horizon, and hardly a tree is visible anywhere.

An hour's ride, along a bad dusty road, brought us to the calico factory, which is pleasantly situate at the foot of a slight elevation, by the side of a stream of water, which turns its machinery.

The factory itself is rather an imposing building,

and with the outhouses, offices, and the residence of the *administrador*, forms three sides of a quadrangle, the centre of which is almost filled up by a grove of spreading orange trees. This admixture of orange blossoms would, one would think, materially mitigate the dreariness of factory life.

A cotton factory is much the same thing all the world over, so I need not inflict a description of it upon the reader. It struck me, however, as a peculiar feature about this one in particular, that the Indian girls employed therein seemed to spend fully as much of their time in combing out each other's long, straight, jet-black hair, as in attending to the looms. They did not seem the least disconcerted at our finding them thus engaged, and coolly continued their combing, as if they were paid for that and nothing else.

The men, cut off from this source of distraction by the shortness of their hair, seemed to give more close attention to their business.

From the cotton factory, which seemed on the whole a well-conducted establishment, we proceeded to the paper factory, which may be regarded as its supplement, for there much of the cotton waste is utilized in the manufacture of paper.

In the paper factory very little else than the coarser descriptions of paper for wrapping, and all other purposes but writing, are manufactured. To watch the various processes, through which the mash passed, before it emerged on the wide rollers in the form of paper was interesting enough in its way, but it was exceedingly painful to observe the listlessness expressed on the faces of the women, whose duty it was to remove the sheets of paper from the rollers, and fold them.

From the paper factory we returned to the calico factory, and dismounted at the quarters of the *administrador*, who had invited us to call on our return, and take some refreshment.

Before we had been seated many minutes, an enormously stout woman in a dress of many colours appeared upon the scene, and was introduced to us by the *administrador* as his wife. As this lady on her entrance had not taken the trouble to close the door after her, it may be inferred that she was not averse to our catching a glimpse of her bedroom, which was remarkably neatly furnished.

Presently, wine, brandy, lemons, hot water, and sugar were produced, the latter articles at the especial request of Don Domingo, who conceived that nothing could be so grateful to an Englishman, under any circumstances, as to be furnished with the materials for concocting a glass of grog. His astonishment was unfeigned, when, neglecting the opportunity of indulging the national passion for hot and strong drinks, I addressed myself to the wine, which was of Californian growth. Its name "Benicarlos," sounded so attractive, that I hoped to have lighted upon an American "Monte Beni"—a wine which every reader of "Transformation," must long to taste once before he dies. In this hope, however, I was sadly disappointed, for the wine turned out most inethereal.

Upon my inquiring of the *administrador* whether a youth, who entered the room and took his seat at the table, was his son, he replied with much suavity, "Si, señor, y servidor de Vd." "Yes, sir, and your grace's servant."

After spending an hour over our cups, we remounted our steeds, and returned through the heat and dust to Guadalajara, where I arrived only just in time to keep an appointment which I had made with La Señora Castellano, who was bent upon conducting me over the Foundling Hospital.

On entering the family mansion, which is pleasantly situated on a *boulevard* lined with orange trees, I found my *señora* ready for business, so we set out at once for La Cuna, where we spent a couple of hours in inspecting the establishment.

The building, which is of enormous dimensions, is divided into a male and female department. Each department contains four *patios*, in three of which the foundlings are separated according to ages, while the fourth in each is used as a hospital for all the inmates in common.

T

In the female department, to which my attention was specially directed, the most interesting feature was the baby dormitory, down the whole length of which a double row of cradles was ranged.

As the girls grow up, they are instructed in sewing, washing, cooking, and such other useful accomplishments, as are likely to enable them to get an honest living. When old enough, situations are obtained for them in respectable families, and thus they are given a fair start in life.

To encourage the girls to be industrious, a show-room is kept, in which their needle and fancy work is exposed for sale at moderate prices, and the proceeds handed to the girls severally on leaving the establishment. Thus the visitor, who can hardly fail to be highly gratified at finding such a model and well-conducted institution in so disturbed a country as Mexico, is enabled at the same time to carry away an agreeable souvenir, and to help on the good work.

In one of the class-rooms, at the foot of a mountain of little girls, piled bench above bench, and reaching right up to the ceiling, stood, teaching them their letters, a diminutive Sister of Charity, whose face was beaming with goodness. Learning that she was French, I ventured to address her in that language, and found her very intelligent. She seemed hardly yet out of her teens, and all too young for the task she had undertaken.

In the boys' department, through which we passed hurriedly, the little fellows were engaged in mastering the rudiments of shoemaking, tailoring, and carpentering.

It was dark when we left the building, and I returned to my hotel highly interested with what I had seen.

At seven o'clock, the hour appointed for dinner, I repaired to the house of Señor Gil Romero, and found the family assembled in the saloon awaiting my arrival. Among the young ladies of the house were dispersed a few good-looking, well-dressed young men, who were introduced to me in turn. Shortly after my arrival dinner was announced, and we proceeded into the *comedor*, the lady of the house assigning me the place of honour on her right.

Having come direct from the capital, I was looked upon as an authority on the political and social questions of the day, and regarded in some measure as the exponent of the Imperial policy. In common with nine-tenths of the well-to-do people throughout Mexico, Señor Gil Romero and his friends were generally favourable to the Imperial cause, although the line of conduct which the Emperor was at that moment pursuing towards the clerical party had given them temporary umbrage. Hitherto—unhappily for the general well-being of the country—the landed and moneyed aristocracy has held itself almost entirely aloof from politics, which have been a monopoly of lawyers and unscrupulous adventurers. Consequently the wealthy merchants, manufacturers, and landowners do not by any means exercise that influence in the country, to which their position would seem to entitle them.

However, now that a respectable government has been established, it is to be hoped that they will come forward and lend it an active support. To bring about this desirable result the influence of their wives and daughters is sure to contribute largely. For, great as is their regard for the poor priests, whom they accuse the Emperor of treating so harshly, their love of gaiety and amusement is even more deeply-seated, and the glitter of a court, with its attendant festivities, has already proved an attraction, irresistible to all those who have come within its reach. As for Señor Gil Romero's daughters, several of whom had passed a few weeks of the season in the capital, they declared unanimously, that they could not conceive anything more delightful, than to pass a portion of each winter in that centre of elegance and civilization, the city of Mexico. Upon this one of the gentlemen, who had passed some time in Europe, cruelly remarked that you might live more in twenty-four hours in Paris than in as many months in Mexico.

Next day I left Guadalajara for Tepic, in charge of a grisly grumbling *arriero* called Catarino, who had agreed to take me there and back for the sum of thirty dollars and his expenses.

Before starting I had entered a grocer's store, attracted by some boxes of sardines exposed for sale. Having completed my purchase, I was about to leave when I espied a book-shelf at the farther end of the shop. Having by this time exhausted my meagre stock of literature, which originally consisted of a Mexican Itinerary, a " Life of General Santa Anna " (presented by himself) and an old number of the *Saturday Review*, I caught eagerly at the hope of finding there some mental food, but the titles of the first half dozen books, which I took up, were not encouraging. In Mexico there is very little demand for secular literature, and I was contemplating the purchase of " Meditations for Lent," " Prayers for every day in the year," or the " Life of San Isidro "— works which would at any rate have improved my Spanish—when I caught sight of a little volume, bound in whole calf, with " El Vicario de Wakefield " printed in golden letters outside. Fearing it might turn out a cheat, I opened it eagerly, and was overjoyed to find the very Vicar of Wakefield turned into good Castillano. Here was portability, entertainment, and the means of improving my Spanish all in one, price one dollar. With this treasure I went on my way rejoicing.

The distance from Guadalajara to Tepic is about

70 leagues, or 175 miles, which I accomplished on horseback in four days. The road is for the most part uninteresting, and the discomfort and fatigue so excessive, that had I not been above all things bent upon reaching Tepic and the Pacific, I should have been inclined to turn back half-way. By day you are exposed for ten hours to a tropical sun, and by night to the ravages of vermin innumerable in the damp mud-hovels where you cannot choose but put up. Under these circumstances it is not surprising that a journey from Guadalajara to Tepic is seldom undertaken for pleasure.

CHAPTER XVI.

TEPIC.

THE first aspect of Tepic is not promising, but no sooner do you find yourself within the hospitable precincts of the Casa de Barron than you perceive that you have got to the right sort of place at last. Everything is well-appointed around you, and you are aware of having passed from slipshod-dom to the domain of neatness and order. Had I not known it to be so, I should have at once guessed that the place was tenanted by an English family.

Mr. Price, the British Consul, who was then in occupation of Mr. Barron's house was, as I learned from one of the clerks, who was engaged in an office furnished with polished mahogany desks, at that moment absent on an excursion in the country. However, in anticipation of my arrival a room had been prepared for me, and the butler, who attended to my wants, informed me that his master would be back before nightfall. Mounting to my chamber, which opened on to the *azotea*, and drawing an arm-chair into a position so as to command a view of the mountains, which look down upon Tepic, I threw myself into it, and resigned myself to a delicious sensation of repose.

Of all the enjoyments incident to travel I know of none to compare with that of finding yourself suddenly transported from the extreme of discomfort to the delightfulness of a house, which combines English comfort and cleanliness with the ease and sunniness of a residence in a southern clime. Such was now my lot, and I felt duly grateful for it.

When I had come to the end of my reflections, as if to crown my happiness, I discovered a novel, and was already deep in it, when a good-looking young fellow in riding costume—embroidered jacket, chapereros (leopard-skin leggings) and jingling spurs—dashed into the room, and, introducing himself as Don Diego, proceeded to give me a boisterous welcome. Of this Don Diego, who was half English, I had heard from various quarters, and so I was less taken aback, than I otherwise should have been, by his somewhat headlong behaviour. Without more ado, Don Diego proposed that we should ride out and meet Mr. Price and his party returning from the country. Not knowing how to decline the proposition I rose and followed him, although I would have given a great deal to have been left in the enjoyment of my arm-chair. As I had already been ten hours on horseback that day, I was not best pleased to find myself again in the saddle, and mounted on a pulling mare, at least seventeen hands high, which had not been out of the stable for a fortnight. However, there was no getting out of the bargain, so off we set at a fast canter, not to say gallop, through the back streets of Tepic, out of the town and past the great cotton-factory, getting a glimpse of the rushing stream, which turns the machinery, and its beautiful flower-garden. The hour of evening prayer or "oracion" having sounded, the workpeople were streaming out of the building, and opened their ranks in dismay to let us pass through them. By this time my suspicions that my companion had taken a little too much, became confirmed, and I was agreeably surprised to find that, as darkness came on, he had sufficient self-possession left to suggest that we might as well turn back, as we must have missed the returning carriages. On reaching home we found that the party had arrived some time before us.

In the hot and temperate regions of Mexico an agreeable custom prevails of ranging lounging chairs in a row in the portico, which runs round the *patio*. Here many delightful hours of the day and evening are passed in the enjoyment of the air which we, in our northern clime, spend boxed-up in close rooms. Here the family assembles before dinner, and here returns when the meal is over, and the time has arrived for coffee, cigars, and conversation. Here the traveller, to be off again on the morrow, may dream away the sultry noonday hours, which yesterday found him toiling along dusty tracks, and will feel inclined to exclaim with the followers of Ulysses, when they reached the land of the Lotus-eaters, "We will no longer roam." The climate of Tepic, which is situate at an elevation of about 3,000 feet above the sea, much resembles that of Orizaba, and the temperature, in the shade is said to be agreeable throughout the year. Under one of these porticos, I found Mr. Price, his wife, and sister-in-law.

A remarkable feature in the dinner which followed, was a dish of oysters from the Pacific. The flavour of the salt water was to me positively delicious, and only thoroughly to be appreciated by one, who has had his palate dried up by a three months' residence in the rarified atmosphere of the table-land, not to speak of the constant doses of dust and sand, which you cannot but swallow, every time you go abroad.

Having for the last month stammered through up-hill conversation in Spanish, I was in a condition fully to appreciate the luxury of talking English to a couple of agreeable and intelligent ladies, who, if they maliciously would not admit that they were English, at any rate spoke English as well as I did. Under the circumstances, I could not regret that there were no other guests at the table, nor even that the place of the gay Don Diego on my left was vacant. That youth had prudently withdrawn to his own room.

After dinner we retired to the portico, where we remained enjoying the bright moonlight till we were summoned to tea and music in an elegantly furnished English drawing-room, where Mrs. Price holds receptions every night in the week, Sundays included, and to which all the notabilities of Tepic drop in, as they please. But for the Casa de Barron, Tepic, albeit it numbers ten thousand inhabitants, is a place of which, in all probability, no one would ever have heard—much less taken the trouble to visit. On my return to the capital and elsewhere I was often asked, "How did you like Tepic?" Now no human being, I imagine, could like Tepic for its own sake, but to this question I invariably answered that I liked it very much, meaning, of course, that I liked the Casa de Barron and its inmates very much. Without the Casa de Barron, Tepic would be a body without a soul.

When blood is shedding in its streets—a not uncommon phenomenon in Tepic—the Casa de Barron is converted into a fortress, and the principal families flock in for protection. Many a siege has the Casa stood and not yet been stormed. Like most Mexican houses the Casa de Barron is admirably adapted for defence, and a raking fire may be kept up on the mob without from a breastwork thrown up on the *azotea*, and from the windows on the ground-floor, which are carefully barred and grated. On one occasion the siege lasted so many days that the inmates were well-nigh reduced to starvation, and the floor-matting had to be given to the animals for fodder.

The morning after my arrival at Tepic I awoke, almost for the first time for nearly three months, without feeling my mouth parched. This I attributed to the agreeable moisture of the air of Tepic, which, as the crow flies, is distant less than thirty miles from the Pacific ocean. Several times during my stay the town was invaded by sea fogs, which distressed most of the inhabitants, but which I gulped down with avidity.

After breakfast I set out, under the guidance of Don Diego, who was many degrees more sober than the previous evening, to lionize the place. In the first place our steps were directed to the new Penitentiary, an elegant building now erecting from the designs of Señor San Roman, a citizen of Tepic.

The prison is constructed in the shape of a wheel —the cells occupying the wedge-shaped spaces between the spokes—each cell opening on to a circular courtyard, in the centre of which a fountain was constructing.

Inspecting the building like ourselves, we encountered Don Manuel Rivas, the worthy Prefect of Tepic, with whom I was already acquainted, and a certain learned Doctor Narvaez, who placed himself at once at my disposition, and volunteered to conduct me over the principal school. This offer I gladly accepted, and quitting the Penitentiary, in a few minutes reached a building, over the door of which was written, "El Seminario de Tepic." Here we found two rooms filled with benches occupied by about 100 boys of all ages. Having first introduced me to the schoolmaster, Dr. Narvaez called his own son up to him, and bade him show me his writing, which was excellent. After this the lad, who was but twelve years of age, went through his Latin and arithmetic very creditably. The appearance of the boy—which was difficult to reconcile with his Mexican extraction, for his complexion was very fair, his hair almost flaxen, and his eyes light blue—was very prepossessing, and there was a dreamy look of genius about his eyes.

On examining several other specimens of writing, Latin, and arithmetic taken at random, I was astonished at their general excellence, and on leaving could not refrain from congratulating the master on the proficiency of his pupils. During Juarez's tenure of office this school, like many others throughout the country, was closed.

At one of the desks a son of Lozada, the celebrated Indian general, to whom I was subsequently introduced, was pointed out to me, and my cicerone informed me that the father had only recently taught himself to write—having probably availed himself of the copies brought home by his son. If true, this fact seemed to me to speak volumes in his favour.

From the school we proceeded to the church, and the doctor pointed out the font, in which he had been baptized sixty years ago. Mounting the bell tower, we reached the roof, and looked down over the earthen breastwork into the *Plaza*, to which its fringe of orange and ash trees, and a display of many-coloured stuffs, exposed for sale on booths, imparted an attractive and cheerful appearance.

The earthen breastwork, on which we were leaning had been thrown up some time previously by order of Lozada, who, on the last occasion of an attack, had defended Tepic successfully against the murderous Rojas—formerly the great upholder of the cause of Juarez in Western Mexico. It is impossible to state exactly how often Tepic has been sacked by one or other of the contending factions, but it was painfully evident, from the lamentable state of ruin which extended on every side, that the town had come in for more than its share of destruction.

From the church Dr. Narvaez conducted me to his own residence, and introduced me to several of his daughters, the youngest of whom—a pretty girl of fourteen, but already a woman—was the exact image of her brother. Before leaving, the Doctor showed me over his library, which was in great disorder, and served him and his son for bedroom. The collection of books was not large but well selected. Among them I found Humboldt's "Essai politique sur la nouvelle Espagne," a work in five octavo volumes, and of which I had been long in search. This work, strange to say, is exceedingly scarce in Mexico.

Observing my satisfaction at the discovery, the excellent doctor at once begged me to accept of it as a souvenir of Tepic and his family, but to this of course I could not consent. Those who are acquainted with the Mexican custom of declaring everything which is admired at the disposition of the admirer, will perhaps be inclined to smile at my taking the offer for a moment as a serious one, but I am inclined to believe that Doctor Narvaez was in earnest.

Returning to the Casa de Barron early in the afternoon I rested until the hour of the evening promenade, when a pawing of steeds in the courtyard below announced that the riding cavalcade was about to start. Our party consisted of Mr. and Mrs. Price (of whose riding prowess I had heard much), her sister, Don Diego, and myself. We were all well-mounted on horses belonging to the house, and the ladies of the party at any rate, from the elegance of their riding habits and their remarkably good seats on horseback, would have put in a very creditable appearance in Rotten Row.

In the course of the evening entertainment which followed, and at which his Excellency the Prefect,

Señor San Roman, and several other distinguished citizens were the guests of Mr. Price, a good deal of amusement was occasioned by the arrival of a letter, which was found to contain a copy of verses dedicated "To the amiable wife of the British Consul by one Diego, at present confined in the town prison."

CHAPTER XVII.

TO THE PACIFIC AND BACK.

HAVING been informed on the day after my arrival at Tepic, that the diligence for San Blas would start on the morrow and return on the following day, I resolved on availing myself of that mode of conveyance, in preference to performing the distance (fifty miles) on horseback. Accordingly I sent overnight to secure a place. Next morning at three A M. such is the consideration enjoyed by the "house," I was startled out of my sleep by the porter, who was the bearer of a polite message from the diligence office, to know at what time I should like the vehicle to call for me.

While deeply touched by this delicate attention, I should have appreciated it more if it had come rather later; but, now that I was once fairly awake, I thought it better to have it round at once.

By four A.M. we were rattling over the stones, and when day broke had left Tepic several leagues behind us. As the light increased, it was amusing to watch the features and study the forms of my fellow-travellers emerging from the obscurity. From their conversation in the darkness I had already gathered that they were not best pleased at the undue attention shown to the distinguished stranger from the "house." But we soon became very good friends. Only on one occasion did the conversation wax somewhat warm, in the course of a discussion relating to the territorial extent of Mexico, which at the date of the establishment of the independence, according to a table drawn up by M. Lucas Alaman, amounted to 216,012 square leagues, and has now dwindled down to 106,067. Now one of my fellow-passengers, who was conspicuous for his patriotic ardour, had been for some time bewailing, as a great national misfortune, the wholesale absorption of Mexican territory by the United States. With this view of the case I ventured to differ, and I fear sadly wounded the feelings of the patriot, by giving it as my deliberate opinion that, by curtailing the Mexican territory, the Americans had in fact rendered a great service to Mexico.

For reduced, as it now is, to about half of its former extent, the country, which is even now nearly four times the size of France, is still far too big to admit of any government, established in the capital, making its power sufficiently felt at the extremities; and the remote provinces of Yucatan and Chiapas in the south, Cohahuila and Chihuahua in the north, are still rather a source of weakness than of strength to the central government.

My opponent, however, would not for a moment admit the force of this reasoning, and warmly maintained his original position, that the Mexican territory could not be too big, and that his countrymen had already had sufficient experience of the Yankees to make them desirous of any fate rather than that of being incorporated with the United States.

The vehicle, in which we were performing our journey, was a light covered van drawn by six mules. In the space of four hours, during which we pursued a zig-zag course over and among hills covered by a dense matted vegetation, we had accomplished half of the distance, and the whole of the descent of 3000 feet, the remainder of our road to the Pacific being quite level, or only slightly undulating.

. About half-way between Tepic and the second post-station, which is established at the foot of the hills, where the *Tierra Caliente* begins, our road suddenly dived down into a deep *barranca*, at the bottom of which we could see growing plantains and other crops which require tropical heat for their production.

Having scaled the opposite bank of the *barranca* by means of very steep zig-zags, we found ourselves perched on the crest of a ridge, from which we caught sight for the first time of the distant blue line, which marked the Pacific, and for which I was eagerly on the look-out.

After a brief halt at the second post-station for breakfast, which was served in a bamboo cottage by a buxom landlady, whose face shone like polished mahogany, we continued our journey to San Blas. So far, owing to the hilly nature of the road, the diligence had been drawn by a team of mules, but these were now exchanged for horses, which set off at full gallop, as Mexican horses always do.

For some distance, the road continued fairly good, and, for the first time, I found diligence travelling in Mexico enjoyable. For although the sun was burning fiercely overhead, the overarching boughs almost sheltered us completely from his rays, which only here and there penetrated through the dense foliage beautifully lighting up the spreading, fan-shaped palms, which filled up the interstices between the gigantic forest trees. It was as if a carriage road had been conducted for miles through some huge conservatory.

In about a couple of hours, during which we accomplished six leagues, or fifteen miles, our road continued through woods of great beauty, but as we approached the coast there was a gradual falling off in the size of the forest trees, which finally disappeared almost entirely, giving place to a dense jungle. The road, too, became outrageously bad, the mules—we were only treated to one stage of horse-power—sinking up to their knees in slush. In accomplishing the last stage, we occupied fully as much time, as we had done in getting over the two preceding ones. At one point, in a clearance in the woods, we drove straight across a field of rank grass, so tall that the mules disappeared altogether in it.

The swampy region, which the road traverses for several leagues before reaching San Blas, is intersected at intervals by sluggish streams, which widen out into lagoons, as they approach the ocean. High and dry on the muddy banks of one of these streams I caught sight for the first time of an alligator, basking in the sun. In colour he was barely distinguishable from the surrounding mud. For the rest of the way, looking out for alligators lent a little excitement to the tedium of the journey.

At about four P.M.—two hours before sunset—we emerged from the jungle on to the narrow slip of *terra firma* on which San Blas is built, and which is slightly elevated above the surrounding lagoons.

Immediately in front of us rose up to the height of some 300 feet the huge isolated rock, about a mile in circumference, on which old San Blas was built, and the ruins of which extend over its whole surface. The slopes and summit of this enormous block of rock, which may compare with Gibraltar in strength, are covered with a tangled vegetation, which render climbing it a work of time and trouble, and I regret to say that I left San Blas without mounting to the top.

Passing along the base of this eminence, we soon entered upon the precincts of the modern town of San Blas, which is a poor bankrupt-looking place, consisting of a single street of miserable tenements, with their backs turned to the sea, the view of which is intercepted by an intervening ridge of shingle. To reach the diligence office, we had to pass down the entire length of the straggling street, but although I had all my eyes about me, I failed to get a glimpse of the open sea.

Fronting the diligence office stands the hotel of San Blas—an establishment the exterior of which was so unpromising that, leaving my fellow-passengers to what I deemed their wretched fate, I turned my back upon it with thankfulness that I was well provided with letters of introduction to Señor Ascona—the agent of Barron, Forbes, and Company, and as such the principal personage in San Blas.

Retracing my steps up the street, which consisted of half a dozen *tiendas*, two or three lodging-houses, of most uninviting appearance, a few public offices, the most conspicuous of which was the custom-house, and a sprinkling of private houses, I shortly found myself in front of Señor Ascona's office, a very poor place, which I naturally supposed to be merely his place of business.

While Señor Ascona was examining my credentials, I waited in the confident expectation that he would offer to put me up at his own house. I was, therefore, a good deal taken aback when, turning to his *mozo*, he gave him directions to take me to the hotel, and see that a room and dinner were prepared for me.

Now, from what I had seen of the hotel, I was so averse to falling in with this arrangement, that I gave Señor Ascona a broad hint, that I should much prefer remaining where I was. However, when I became aware of the style in which the Don was living, I felt less disinclined to give the hotel a tria

At either end of the miserable brick-floored apartment, which served him for bedroom and sitting-room, stood a wooden bedstead, covered with a greasy counterpane, and hung with dirty mosquito curtains. The remaining furniture of the room consisted of a couple of rush-bottomed chairs, a wooden bench, and a common deal table, on which stood a quart and a pint bottle of spirits, half a cheese with the centre eaten out, a cheese grater, and a bowl of tobacco. The windows, which looked on to a filthy back yard, were without glass, and fitted with unpainted Venetian blinds.

At the sight of Señor Ascona's quarters my heart sank within me, and I asked myself, "What must the dwellings of the rest of the inhabitants be like, if Señor Ascona, plenipotentiary of the great house lives in such a den as this?" Full of dismal anticipations, I followed the *mozo* who carried my valise to the hotel.

When the landlord, who was a Yankee, appeared, he inspected me from head to foot, and, having settled in his own mind what rank he should give me, replied to my question, if I could have a room,—

"Well, captain, I'll do my best for you, but for to-night I have only got a single bed, in a four-bedded room, free."

Upon this he showed me into a room about fifteen feet square, with no other furniture than a bed in each of the four corners. Then, pointing to the only disengaged bed, he observed:

"For to-night, captain, you must put up with that. You will share the room with three American gentlemen."

Now I had not expected much of San Blas; but I had cherished a vision of a clean room, with a view over the Pacific, in which I could have been alone at any rate for a few hours in the day or night; and I confess that I felt cruelly disappointed, as this dream vanished before the stern reality.

However, I resolved sooner to sleep upon the beach

than share a room with three strangers, and Yankees into the bargain; so leaving the hotel, I prowled disconsolately up and down the street looking out for a room. Not one was to be had anywhere, and I know not what would have become of me had not one of my fellow-passengers—Señor Torres, the proprietor of a *tienda*—had compassion on me, and placed the second bed in the storehouse, in which he slept himself, at my disposal.

As there appeared no chance of getting a meal elsewhere, I returned to the hotel for five o'clock *table d'hote*, and was agreeably surprised with the behaviour of the company, and the manner in which the dinner was served.

Immediately after dinner, I strolled out on to the beach, in order to inspect the harbour, the mouth of which appeared most dangerously narrow: once you are over the bar, it widens out inconsiderably, but is nowhere commodious. The greatest depth of water is said not to exceed seventeen feet. A single small craft was unlading its cargo, which was conveyed ashore on the backs of Indians.

The schooner bound for Mazatlan, in which most of my fellow-passengers were to embark on the morrow, was lying at anchor in the offing. No other vessels were in sight.

In selecting San Blas at all for their principal establishment on that portion of the coast of the Pacific, the Spaniards were probably more influenced by the advantages it held out as an impregnable military position than by any other considerations.

As long as they held Mexico, the Spaniards attached great importance to San Blas, and from this post was kept up their chief communication with the Californias; indeed, in the old Spanish mercantile charts, San Blas is commonly styled, "San Blas de las Californias."

When the Spaniards were expelled from Mexico, the old town was abandoned, and the ruins of its churches, magazines, barracks, and storehouses now lie buried deep in a rank vegetation of half a century's growth.

Simultaneously with the abandonment of the old town, a modern settlement sprang up along the seashore at its base; but, owing to the unhealthiness of its position, and the growing fortunes of its rival, Mazatlan, San Blas rapidly declined from its former importance.

The inconvenience of transporting heavy goods from the ships, which discharged their cargoes in the harbour up to the magazines in the old town, where alone they were safe from the ravages of the white ant (*jejen*), which is the bane of San Blas, had long been felt as a great drawback; and San Blas, with a harbour of acknowledged inferiority to that of Mazatlan, was probably only clung to by the Spaniards because of its great strength.

Turning my back upon the harbour, I walked for

some distance along the deserted shore to the southward, and sat down upon the beach. In the meantime the brief tropical twilight had changed into night, and the darkness became so thick that I could scarcely distinguish the sea-line; for the sky was completely overcast, and only the faintest streaks of light, which soon vanished altogether, were at first visible on the western horizon; not a star was to be seen, and a darkness that might be felt seemed to brood over the face of the waters, while the heaving of the ocean only made itself heard in the gentlest of ripples. Then I was struck by the propriety of the name "Pacific," which Magellan, its discoverer, gave to this ocean in grateful commemoration of the calm weather, which lasted during the whole of his voyage, and to which alone he owed his preservation.

Along this portion of the coast, the jungle comes down so close to high-water mark, that only a narrow belt of sand is left between it and the sea. By the aid of the faint light reflected by the light sand, between the dark line of jungle and the scarcely less dark sea-line, I groped my way back with some difficulty towards the harbour. There should by rights have been fire-flies; but San Blas, which abounds with noxious flies and gnats of all kinds, is unblest by whatever is bright and luminous in insect life.

Groping my way back to the detached warehouse,

where a lodging for the night had been assigned to me, I found the door open, but the room empty. Lighting a candle, I proceeded to reconnoitre the premises, and was agreeably surprised to find two comfortable beds, spread with clean linen, and hung with mosquito curtains. In other respects the apartment was as unlike a bedroom as a room well could be, for sacks of flour, beans, sewing machines, scales, &c. were scattered about the floor in picturesque confusion.

Presently Señor Torres, a wrinkled, dirty, leathery half-caste, of about fifty years of age, and suffering from asthma and jaundice combined, made his appearance, and, keeping up a running commentary on the weak state of his health, proceeded to undress, an operation which was very soon over. As he got into bed, and his form disappeared behind the mosquito curtains, I could not help thinking that he was cruelly profaning clean linen in presuming to bring his yellow body into contact with the fair white sheets.

Having nothing else to do but to follow the example set me by my host, I too undressed, and, blowing out the candle, crept warily under the mosquito curtains. As the heads of our beds almost touched, I could hear every movement of my companion, and did not altogether relish the prospect of passing the night in the proximity of such an invalid. It was in vain that I tried to get to sleep, for what with the noise of the rats chasing each other about the room, the boisterous revelry in the next house, a band of music in the streets, and the heavy breathing of my host, it was little rest I got that night, and I was thankful when, at three A.M., the *mozo* from the diligence office knocked at the door.

Getting up at once, I struck a light, made a hurried toilet, and cramming what few things I had with me into my valise, was about to blow out the candle and creep out of the room, when a sepulchral voice made itself heard from the recesses of the bed, enjoining me not to omit to mention, when I got back to Tepic, that I had passed the night beneath the roof of him, Señor Torres.

Having set the mind of the invalid at rest by giving the required promise, I left him to slumber on, and made the best of my way in the dark to the diligence office. Here, seated at a long wooden table, and making their *desayuno* off black coffee, I discovered the three Americans, with whom I was to have shared a room at the hotel. Besides the Americans, there were two Mexican women, one of them prodigiously stout, a little girl, and two men.

It was not yet four A.M. when the diligence got under weigh, and as we rolled down the now silent and deserted street, not a light was visible in any window.

The Yankees, who were styled respectively colonel, captain, and doctor, by no means improved upon acquaintance, and the general tenor of their conversation was of such a nature, as to make me thank my stars that I had declined sharing a room with them. However, I could not but envy them the satisfaction which they appeared to derive from reflecting, how admirably adapted for the production of cotton was the swampy jungle, through which we were ploughing our way. For myself, I was very far from sharing the desire which they expressed unanimously, of owning several thousand acres of it.

Before we had been an hour upon the road, "liquoring up" commenced. When first called upon, the doctor, to whom, as the least thirsty soul of the trio, the liquor had been entrusted, made some difficulty about producing it. The colonel, however, insisted, ejaculating impatiently—

"Darn it, doctor, I must wet my lips with that whisky."

Upon this the doctor gave in, and handed a black bottle to the colonel, who took a long pull at its contents, remarking, as he removed the bottle from his lips, and handed it to the captain—

"I'll be blamed if that's the same liquor we had last night."

On this point, the captain and doctor both agreed with him, and coming to the conclusion that they had been done, proceeded to curse the landlord of the hotel, who had supplied it.

All this time we had been getting over the ground at the rate of about three miles an hour, and, as there appeared no prospect of our pace improving, as soon as it got light I took advantage of a stoppage—occasioned by our vehicle sticking in the mud—to get out and walk. For while the road was almost impassable for carriages, it was more practicable for travelling on foot or on horseback, inasmuch as a narrow track, trodden hard by the *arrieros* and their droves of mules, meandered through the sea of slush.

Glad to escape from the uninviting society of my travelling companions, I pressed on alone on foot, and for several miles encountered no other living objects than a party of black bald-headed vultures breakfasting off the carcase of a dead horse—a spectacle horribly suggestive of a party of mutes regaling themselves after a funeral. A creeping silence reigned in the woods, and the boughs were so completely interlaced overhead, that I felt more as if I was following the run of some wild animal than a highway. Soon, however, the road became much frequented, and long strings of heavily-laden pack-mules defiled passed me in continual succession. In less than two hours I counted 500 of them.

Presently the stream of mules ceased to flow, and I had encountered none for some time, when I met a disconsolate individual, like Saul, looking for his mules, which had gone astray. I was, of course, unable to assist him in the matter, although he seemed to expect it of me.

About half-way between San Blas and the first post-station, which I reached on foot at least half an hour in advance of the diligence, I picked up an interesting companion in the shape of an Indian courier, who was the bearer of despatches from the authorities at Mazatlan to General Lozada at Tepic. The Indian was in the lightest possible marching order, carrying a thick stick in his hand and a bundle on his back, and having nothing on but a pair of drawers and sandals. When first I caught sight of his dusky athletic form gliding through the trees in advance of me, I could have believed that he had walked straight out of one of Cooper's tales. Doubtless just such a messenger had carried to Montezuma the tidings of the landing of the Spaniards on the coast.

Readers of Prescott will remember that he relates how by means of a system of running couriers fish were served at Montezuma's table in the capital, which the day before were swimming in the Gulf of Mexico. Indeed, nothing appears to have struck the Spaniards more, than the remarkable rapidity and regularity, with which communications were kept up between the Aztec capital and distant parts of the empire. For this service the wiry frame of the Indian is still admirably adapted.

A glass of milk, a small quantity of which we were lucky enough to find at the first post-station, was all the sustenance which the Indian required to support him during his fifty-mile walk. He assured me, when I took leave of him and continued my journey in the diligence, that he should reach Tepic soon after sunset.

CHAPTER XVIII.

A TRIP TO A COTTON PLANTATION ON THE RIO SANTIAGO.

AFTER resting a day in Tepic, I set out once more towards the Pacific for the purpose of visiting a cotton plantation on the banks of the great Rio de Santiago, which flows into the sea some fifteen miles to the north of San Blas. In this expedition, which could only be accomplished on horseback, I had for my companion and guide one Rodriguez—the administrator of a *hacienda*, farmed by the "house" in the district, for which I was bound. During my absence at San Blas, Señor Rodriguez had arrived at Tepic for the purpose of settling his accounts, and, having transacted his business, was now returning to the town of Santiago, where he had resided, as he informed me, ever since the liberals had burned down his dwelling-house on the estate.

Taking the San Blas road, which was now quite familiar to me, we followed it as far as the second post-station at the foot of the hills, where I had already twice breakfasted. On the present occasion, we shared the slender accommodation which the place afforded, with two strangers—a Mexican lady and her husband, an American, who uttered an angry growl, as I accidentally disturbed the *siesta*, which he was taking in the hammock, which was swung across the entrance of the bamboo cottage, as if on purpose to trip up unwary travellers. However, on my apologizing, we became excellent friends, and he was soon pressing me to partake of the contents of his black bottle.

Like many of his countrymen *en voyage*, this American was dressed in a suit of black—of all costumes, the most unsuitable for travelling in Mexico, where you are alternately in a cloud of dust, or likely to be submerged in mud, and constantly exposed to a burning sun.

In the course of conversation, my friend informed me, that he had formerly been employed in making a survey of that portion of the Pacific coast, but I had not had time to discover the nature of the business, on which he was at that moment engaged, before he turned to his wife, and suggested that it was time to be off. Had not our roads unfortunately diverged at that point, I should have gladly continued my journey in the company of an individual, who was so able and willing to give me information about the country, and was evidently not too polite to set me right in my ideas.

For Señor Rodriguez combined in a remarkable degree the two Mexican virtues of politeness and reticence, and never once during the whole course of our ride together advanced an opinion of his own, or ventured to differ from any which I advanced.

The first and last principle inculcated on Mexican youth is, that it is, under any circumstances, an unpardonable breach of good manners to disagree openly with your interlocutor. Consequently, discussions are carriedon under considerable difficulties, and the truth is not easily arrived at. But then, truth is a thing which does not exist, even in idea, in Mexico, and may not even be found at the bottom of a well. A Mexican of good education, and accustomed to the usages of polite society, will not only appear to agree with any opinion you choose to express, but may be made to say just anything you please. Even if you should happen to say anything particularly wounding to his feelings, he will appear to agree with you cordially at the time. From caring absolutely about nothing —in fact, from having none—Mexicans are exempted from the infirmity of losing their tempers.

While the Yankee took the carriage road to San Blas, Rodriguez and I struck off to the right, and, following a narrow mule-track, dived into the wood, which at that point was very thick. Presently, however, the dense jungle was exchanged for open glades, ornamented by the graceful cocoa-nut palm, which, at first scattered in groups, became more and more numerous as we went on, finally forming a grove, which extended almost without interruption to the banks of the Santiago.

About half-way between the post-station we had just quitted and the town of Santiago, for which we were bound, we came upon an Indian village called Souta, situated on the banks of a sluggish stream, which was almost concealed by the overhanging foliage. Near this village, an enterprising citizen of T⋯ had made a clearance in the woods, and conv⋯d some twenty acres of jungle into a flourishing cotton plantation, to visit which we made a slight *détour*.

At first sight the appearance of a cotton plantation is suggestive of a field of over-grown potatoes, each plant being about the size of a full-grown gooseberry bush. I had arrived precisely at the right moment to see the crop, which appeared a very flourishing one, to perfection; for the pods, or "bolas," of which I counted on an average seventy to each plant or "mata," were just ripe, and in a more or less advanced stage of bursting.

The pod or *bola*, which contains the cotton, is about the size and shape of a bantam's egg, and, when the shell bursts, the cotton is hatched. The little cotton chickens, if I may so call them, were just pushing their soft milk-white nozzles out of the brown pods, and seemed to be looking about them to see what kind of a world they had been born into.

Having viewed the plantation, we retraced our steps to the south, and again struck into the main track leading to Santiago, which we followed for several miles without encountering a human being. At last, however, we met a party of Indians carrying a wounded man in a litter. This group was scarcely out of sight, when we became aware of the approach of a gang of half-naked Indians, streaming through the woods in the greatest possible disorder. That these fellows were soldiers was suggested only by the fact, that most of them were armed with muskets. Their dress, which consisted of a broad-brimmed straw hat, a calico shirt, drawers, and sandals, differed in nothing from that of the ordinary Indian field-labourer. From the worn and battered appearance of the men, it was evident, that they had recently been engaged in some hard service.

In the centre of the column rode a couple of officers, wearing some pretence of an uniform; but in their general appearance hardly less soldierlike than the men. Happening to be acquainted with one of them, my companion reined in his horse, and inquired the news.

The officers of course had a victory to report, for Mexicans, according to themselves, come out of every affair with flying colours; but I must say that it required a very lively exercise of the imagination to conceive of the kind of enemy, which would have run away from such fellows.

From the following remarks, which I overheard accidentally, it was evident that these gallant fellows had formed a very low estimate of the French troops, with which they had been associated in their recent operations. About their worthlessness for the purposes of guerilla warfare both officers were agreed, affirming emphatically, "*No valen nada los Franceses.*" But, while the first speaker attributed this want of success to their ignorance of the *terrain*, the second put it entirely upon their want of pluck, observing, with a knowing glance, "*Tienen miedo los Franceses.*"

The sun was just setting as we reached the banks of the Santiago, and the rosy tints of the evening sky were beautifully reflected in the broad shallow stream. On the opposite bank of the river, and overhanging its abrupt sandy banks, stood the town of Santiago, or rather the ruins of what once was a town, for all that remained seemed to be a church tower, and a confused cluster of tumbledown tenements picturesquely grouped about it.

There was however considerable stir on either bank,

and canoes full of people were plying backwards and forwards, while horses and mules, with ropes attached to prevent them from being carried down stream, were fording the river alongside the canoes.

While waiting for the ferry, I had time to examine a green crop of Indian corn—a thing very rarely met with in Mexico during the dry or winter season. For in Mexico, where the young crop is exposed, directly it springs up, to the scorching rays of a tropical sun, only such a tremendous soaking, as it gets for twelve hours out of the twenty-four in the rainy season, will keep any life in the young plant.

In the present instance the facility of artificial irrigation afforded by the proximity of the river had enabled the grower to produce in the dry season the crop, which, except in such exceptional cases, can only be raised during the rains.

Observing, at a short distance, from where I was standing, an individual, who seemed to regard the crop with considerable interest, I went up to him, and addressing him in Spanish, asked if he were the owner.

To my astonishment the man answered me in English, which he pronounced with an Irish accent, that such was the case. To find one fellow-countryman at such a remote spot would in itself have been sufficient surprise, but I had not done wondering what strange chance could have induced an Irishman to settle in such an out-of-the-way corner, when another Briton appeared upon the scene in the person of Mr. Joshua Mellor—a very great man in those parts, as the Irishman informed me, and as I very soon found out for myself.

At this juncture, Rodriguez approached with the announcement that he had secured a canoe, which was in readiness to convey us across the river; so leaving the Irishman to enjoy the comfortable reflections with which the flourishing state of his crop seemed to inspire him, I followed Rodriguez to the canoe, Mr. Joshua Mellor giving us the benefit of his company during the passage.

The canoe, in which we were ferried over, was about fifty feet long, and consisted simply of the trunk of a cedar tree, hollowed out in the centre. The horses, which forded the stream alongside of us, were never once out of their depth, though in several places the water reached up to their backs. This fact seemed to throw considerable light on the disputed question of the navigability of the Rio Santiago. Even bearing in mind that we were then in the middle of the dry season, and that hardly a drop of rain had fallen for five months, I should have expected greater things of *the* one river, which drains the western slope of the Mexican table-land, than that it should yield such a poor result, as a depth of five feet of water within fifteen miles of its mouth. Just four weeks before I had passed by its source in the dreary marshes about the town of Lerma, in the mountain basin of Toluca; had followed it under the name of Rio de Lerma, as far as the lake of Chapala, touching its stream at Ixtlahuaca, Acambaro, La Barca; taken up the lost thread at Ocotlan, where the river emerges from the lake baptized with the new name of Rio de Santiago; sighted the bluff porphyry rocks, through which it forces a channel some fifteen miles to the northward of Guadalajara, and finally fallen in with it again near the ocean, the goal for which it had been painfully making all through its career.

In a note to the passage in his "Sinai and Palestine," where Dean Stanley dwells upon the extraordinary fall of the Jordan, he remarks that the Rio Sacramento in California is the only known river, the fall of which, in proportion to its length, is greater. I would venture to submit to his consideration the claims of the Rio de Lerma-Santiago, which in a course not exceeding 600 miles falls nearly 9,000 feet.

By the time we had reached the opposite shore, and clambered to the top of the precipitous banks, it was quite dark, and I know not how we should have found our way to the market-place in which Rodriguez's dwelling was situated, had not the lurid glare of many fires served to guide us. For it was Saturday evening, and the Indians, who had flocked in from the surrounding villages, were as usual protracting their marketing into the night.

Conducting me into a dismal tenement, suggestive of one of those dens in Bethnal Green or Shoreditch, where coals, potatoes, cabbages, and bundles of firewood are sold in small quantities to the squalid inhabitants of the surrounding courts, Rodriguez intimated to me, in the politest manner possible, that we had reached his abode.

The bare thought of passing the night in such a place was enough to make one shudder, and shudder I did to some purpose. For Mr. Joshua Mellor, who had followed us thus far, was so much struck with the expression of horror and disgust, with which I regarded the hovel, which Rodriguez called his residence that, moved by pity, he then and there retired to consult with his wife about the feasibility of lodging me in their own house. In the meantime, I, who had no inkling of Mr. Mellor's charitable intentions, proceeded to look about me for the least objectionable corner of the premises, and finally decided in favour of a small granary, which opened on to the backyard. Presently, however, Mr. Joshua Mellor re-appeared with the announcement that Mrs. Joshua hoped I would repair to their house at once. Obeying this summons with alacrity, I followed my guide down a narrow street leading out of the extremity of the market-place. Passing between a double row of ruined tenements, we soon reached a house of some pretensions—almost the only one still standing upright in that quarter of the town.

This was the residence of Mr. Joshua Mellor, which, as I subsequently learned, had been spared by the express order of the infamous Rojas, between whom and Mr. Joshua Mellor so excellent an understanding had existed, that they stood to each other in the relation of *copadrree*, than which no more sacred tie is known in Mexico. If by consenting to be joint sponsor with a reputed murderer, Mr. Joshua Mellor —*alias* Don José—had preserved his life and property from destruction, who shall blame him?

Passing through the courtyard, which was carefully laid out as a garden, and neatly planted with shrubs, we entered an airy apartment, furnished with a couple of arm-chairs, and a four-poster hung with mosquito curtains.

Although Mrs. Joshua had not yet made her appearance, the presence of a good housewife made itself felt the instant I crossed her threshold, in the cleanliness and neatness of all the household arrangements. When that lady came into the room, she was so exactly the kind of person I was prepared for, that my host might have spared himself the trouble of introducing her as his wife. In her face you could read at once, that she was the sworn enemy of dirt, and that her ruling passion was for the unlimited use of soap and scrubbing brushes. A few hundreds of such women as Mrs. Joshua Mellor would go a long way towards regenerating Mexico.

The following day was Sunday, but Santiago had long since been deserted by its priest, so the inhabitants had to do without a religious service of any kind. In default of mass, I set off with Mr. Joshua Mellor to inspect his cotton plantation, which is situated on the opposite bank of the river.

In the whole of the Santiago district, there were, in the month of February, 1865, at the highest computation, 1,500 acres under cotton. To this total the plantation, which we saw stretched out before us, contributed very largely, for on measuring it, we found it to be upwards of 900 yards square, which gives a superficial measurement of about 350 acres. Besides this large plot, Mr. Mellor informed me that he had several smaller plantations, all reclaimed within the last twelve months from the surrounding waste, and already bearing flourishing crops, so that he had a right to hold his head high among the inhabitants of Santiago.

A mechanic, and like his wife a native of Stockport, Joshua Mellor had emigrated to America, and, after a variety of adventures, settled down at Santiago, where he was evidently rapidly making his fortune. Had he remained at home, he would have been lost in the crowd, and painfully earning thirty shillings a week.

In Mexico, from the mere fact of being an Englishman, and possessed of an ordinary amount of industry and enterprise, Mr. Joshua Mellor was looked upon by the limp and indolent natives in the light of a demigod.

The cotton harvest had just commenced, and Sunday being his pay-day, I had an opportunity of watching the labourers receiving their hire. While Mr. Joshua Mellor sat at the table in his office—a wooden shed on the edge of the plantation—with little heaps of silver dollars, *reals*, *medio-reals*, and copper *tlkakos*, spread out before him, the overseer read out the names, and the amount due to each.

As each name was read out, the owner of it stepped forward from the crowd of men and boys collected at the entrance, and received his wages from the hands of the master himself—he who got most receiving about five dollars, or twenty shillings, for six days' work.

For light work, like cotton-picking, women and boys may earn almost as much as able-bodied men. It is reckoned a fair day's work to pick 100 lbs. of cotton *per diem*, for which the labourer receives six *reals* or three shillings, so that, during the brief period, over which the cotton harvest extends, a family of five persons might earn nearly five pounds per week.

In compliance with a requisition on the part of the

British Government, Mr. Glennie, the Consul-General in Mexico, lately sent round to all his Vice-Consuls printed forms of questions having reference to the amount of cotton grown, land available for growth, &c. in their respective districts, with the request that they would get them filled up to the best of their ability. Up to April, 1865, such is the difficulty of getting accurate information on any subject in Mexico, only a single one of these forms had been returned filled up. It is signed by Consul Woolrych, British Vice-Consul at Mazatlan, and has reference to the district of Sinaloa—

	1863.	1864.
Land under Cotton . .	1,300 acres.	10,500 acres.
Produce	500,000 lbs.	4,200,000 lbs.
Amount sown per acre .	10 lbs.	10 lbs.
Price per lb.	12 cents or 6*d*.	12 cents or 6*d*.
Produce per acre . . .	4 quintals of 100 lbs.	4 quintals of 100 lbs.
Consumed by Factories in Sinaloa		1,000,000 lbs.
———— ———— in Jalisco .	————	5,000,000 lbs.

From this return, it will be seen that there was more than eight times as much land under cotton in that district in the year 1864, as in 1863. This increase is, no doubt, mainly to be attributed to the increased feeling of security occasioned throughout the country by the establishment of what the Americans speak of as "the so-called Empire."

It is evident, however, that so far from any of this cotton being available for exportation, the factories in the neighbouring state of Jalisco, where, a year ago, as far as I am aware, cotton growing was confined to the district of Santiago, would consume more than the 3,200,000 lbs. which would remain after deducting a million pounds for consumption in Sinaloa. There is, however, little doubt that the produce, both in the states of Jalisco and Sinaloa, as well as in other states throughout the country, will be found to have increased largely in the year 1865, while the home consumption will have remained stationary, or nearly so. The first result, however, of this increased production will not be to set any large amount of cotton free for exportation to Europe, but merely to stop the importation into Mexico from Texas, which has hitherto been very considerable.

After viewing the cotton plantation, I mounted my horse, and set off on my return to Tepic, attended by a *mozo* thoughtfully sent to take care of me by Rodriguez. However, being much better mounted than the *mozo*, I soon left him behind, and saw nothing more of him, till he made his appearance an hour after my arrival at the breakfasting place at the foot of the hills, where the Santiago track runs into the San Blas road. During my solitary ride, I encountered no other living things than two Indians and one jackal, which trotted quietly ahead of me for upwards of a mile, taking care to keep well out of pistol shot. The heat throughout was intense, and the sun scorched me so fiercely that I felt, on reaching the shelter of the post-station, as if I had escaped from a furnace.

Throwing myself into the hammock, which was swinging in the shade, I was enjoying some quiet reading, when a tramping of steeds, and a clattering of scabbards, suddenly made itself heard, and a party of armed horseman emerged from the woods.

Now a stranger would certainly have taken these fellows for brigands, and might have felt inclined to hide himself in a tree, as Ali Baba did on the approach of the forty thieves (would that thieves could be counted even by forties in Mexico!); but I was by this time sufficiently acquainted with the people to recognise in these worthies gallant defenders of their country.

The get-up of the leader, who introduced himself to me as Don Antonio Mendez, *sub-prefecto y commandante militar de Acaponeta,** *gefe de la linea, y servidor de Vd.*" was so remarkable, that I jotted down the items on the spot. It consisted of the usual broad-brimmed felt hat with silver

---

* A town half way between San Blas and Mazatlan.

embroidery, a dirty washed-out French grey Garibaldi shirt, a dark blue scarf across the breast, a black and lavender tie, a black lace watch-chain, a cartridge belt round his waist made of leopard skin, marked with the letters A. M. worked in silver on it, a double-barrelled rifle slung across his back, an iron ramrod swinging at one side, a big sword on the other, a pair of leopard-skin overalls drawn over a pair of leathern breeches, from the pocket of which the neck of a quart bottle of brandy protruded conspicuously, and a pair of spurs about three inches in diameter.

Dismounting from his steed, which was no bigger than a pony, and so covered with sweat that it looked exactly like a drowned rat, he gave it to an orderly, and entered the breakfasting compartment followed by his two aides-de-camp.

At the conclusion of their meal, during which I derived infinite entertainment from watching Don Antonio's comical behaviour, I requested permission to avail myself of his escort for the rest of my journey to Tepic.

Before we had been many minutes on the road, Don Antonio became perfectly frantic, and, drawing his sword, suddenly turned his horse round, and charged headlong at his aides-de camp, who were riding quietly behind us. Having routed them ignominiously, he was pursuing them down hill, when he was pulled up by observing that, in the act of drawing his sword, he had cut through the abovementioned black lace watch-guard. Supposing that his watch had fallen to the ground, he ordered his aides-de-camp to ride back and look for it, while he proceeded quietly with me.

Hardly, however, had the aides-de-camp got out of sight, when Don Antonio, somewhat subdued by his supposed loss, discovered the watch sticking in his fob, and riding rapidly back, soon overtook the aides-de-camp, who were searching for it.

After this we rode on quietly for several leagues, and no further outbreak occurred, until we met an old woman riding a donkey, and wearing a broad-brimmed straw hat. The instant Don Antonio caught sight of her—apparently unable to control his feelings any longer—he put spurs to his steed, and drawing his sword, rode at her at full gallop. The donkey, startled by such a proceeding, suddenly swerved round, and the old woman must have been unseated, had not Don Antonio, reining his horse in on the instant, supported her with his left hand. This done, his next proceeding was to bonnet her.

Having recovered her senses a little, the old lady raised the hat from over her eyes, and regarded her assailant with such a comical expression that I almost fell off my horse for laughing. Then followed a little mutual bantering, and it soon became evident that they were old acquaintances. At the conclusion of their interview, which ended most amicably, Don Antonio rejoined me, remarking, "The people about here like me, because I protect them from the Chinacos. I am always fighting with the Chinacos."

Some way further on, we encountered a suspicious looking character prowling about with a musket on his shoulder. Here was Don Antonio's opportunity of showing that he was a person in authority; so, putting on for the occasion his severest manner, he rode up to him, and demanded in a stern voice, what his business might be.

Not considering the first reply satisfactory, Don Antonio went on to subject the poor fellow to a most severe cross-examination, and, as he was by this time well-primed with liquor, it would hardly have surprised me had he proceeded to shoot the fellow on the spot. However, perhaps out of deference to me, the culprit was presently allowed to go about his business.

Then Don Antonio, riding close up to me, with a knowing look, remarked, almost in a whisper, "Come now, I will be frank with you, and confess that we Mexicans understand one thing to perfection, and that is robbing;" adding abruptly, "Not I, mind you, but my fellow-countrymen."

Presently we arrived at the brink of the great *barranca*, the passage of which we had so painfully accomplished in the diligence going down to San

Blas, and saw stretched out a thousand feet below us flourishing plantations of the bright-green broad-leaved banana—the unmistakable ensign of the *Tierra Caliente*.

As we were slowly descending the steep zigzags, Don Antonio surprised me by remarking that he had once held a farm at the bottom of this very *barranca*, adding, "Rather a curious story attaches to my farming. I will relate it to you. Whenever I had occasion to pass this way, I could not fail to remark the richness of the soil at the bottom of this *barranca*, and it occurred to me that it would be pleasant to turn farmer, if one could get hold of land like that.

"So, when the lease of the former occupant had expired I offered myself as a tenant, and was accepted. Scarcely, however, had I entered into possession, when the Chinacos became so troublesome that, before I had had time to sow my fields, I was summoned by my chief Lozada to follow him to the wars.

"At the expiration of about a year, I returned home, and to my astonishment found flourishing crops growing on the land which I had left unsown. Inquiring the meaning of it, I learned that while I was away, fighting for my country, an unauthorised person had taken possession of my land, and sown it with banana and maize in the hopes of getting a crop off it before my return. In this, however, the rascal was disappointed, for I ejected him immediately, and reaped crops that I had never sown."

In turning farmer, in the short intervals between his military expeditions, Don Antonio had only followed the example of Lozada, his chief.

To my companion, the whole road we were following was classic ground, and he took delight in pointing out to me the various spots, where he had been engaged in desperate encounters with the Chinacos.

When we had accomplished our last climb, and saw Tepic spread out before us, my companion inquired where I lodged, and thought me in great luck to have quarters at the Casa di Barron. "For my own part," he went on to say, "I have no idea, where I shall put up. All I know is that I have a wife and family, whom I have not seen these two years, somewhere in Tepic, and I shall go and search for them." And so we parted.

CHAPTER XIX.

THE CARNIVAL AT TEPIC.

I HAD hurried back to Tepic in order to be in time for the ball, with which the carnival festities were to open, for far-distant Tepic has its carnival, as well as Rome. Indeed, it is their carnival, and nothing else, which keeps the inhabitants of Tepic alive from year to year, and saves them from dying of utter inanition. For the three days preceding Ash Wednesday, all Tepic agrees with one accord to go mad, and for the remaining 362 days of the year ruminates over its madness. During the six summer months, Tepic looks back to its last carnival, and during the six winter, looks forward to the next.

The expenses of the festivities are defrayed by public subscription, and a committee, consisting of the Prefect, the President of the Board of Works, Señor San Roman, and the British Consul, had been appointed to arrange the programme, the carrying out of which had been left to Señor San Roman.

whose taste and talent for arrangement were truly remarkable.

On a previous occasion, this functionary, being rather pressed for time and workmen, had, with a fine irony, resorted to the expedient of setting the prisoners in the town gaol to work at the preparations for the carnival ball. At a critical period, however, when the Señor San Roman was especially relying on this forced labour, he received the alarming intelligence, that all the prisoners had suddenly escaped, and it subsequently transpired that, for the consideration of a dollar per man, the Prefect had given secret orders to have them all let out.

On the present occasion the ballroom to which we repaired at 9 P.M. was a *chef d'œuvre*. The "patio" of one of the best houses in Tepic had been neatly floored with smooth planks, and roofed over in the shape of a tent — alternate breadths of red and white calico stretching downwards in graceful curves to the capitals of the columns, which ran round the cloistered quadrangle. While white and red were thus the prevailing colours of the roof, the pole in the centre and the columns themselves were gaily decked out with green festoons, adding the colour which was wanting to complete the Mexican national colours. When all this—set off by innumerable candles, stuck everywhere where they would stick, and their light enhanced by a skilful arrangement of mirrors and reflectors — burst upon us suddenly as we came in from the dark street, the transition was so dazzling, that we seemed to have been transported into fairyland.

About the general appearance of the company there was nothing particular to remark, as the people were dressed much as they would have been at a second-rate ball in England.

Inside, most of the well-to-do families in Tepic were represented by the younger members; while outside, a curious crowd of Indians and half-castes was struggling round the doorway to get a peep at the scene of enchantment within—the foremost male or female ragamuffins being from time to time pushed right into the room.

Of the company inside, the most conspicuous personage by far was General Don Carlos Rivas, brother of the Prefect. This distinguished individual appeared in the full-dress uniform of a general officer, and was of course the lion of the evening.

But in the crowd outside was one greater than he — the Indian general Lozada, whose influence over the Indians in the states of Jalisco and Sinaloa is so extraordinary, that the lives of the inhabitants may almost be said to depend upon his sole will. Being recognised by the authorities, who of course cultivate him assiduously, Lozada was prevailed upon, much against his will, to show himself in the ballroom, where he seemed as much out of place as her Arab husband's spear, which I once saw standing in a lady's boudoir at Damascus—a lady, the daughter of one English peer, and former wife of another.

Having heard so much of this terrible Lozada, I was prepared to be introduced to a very monster, and so my astonishment was unfeigned, when I saw before me a slim beardless individual, of rather youthful appearance and not unpleasing countenance. His dress was excessively unpretending, and consisted of a black cloth jacket, brown stuff trousers and waistcoat, and plain cloth cap. In manner he was extremely reserved, but courteous, and, I could with difficulty bring myself to believe that his hands were so deeply dyed with blood, as I was assured that they were.

To most conspicuous valour, Lozada adds an extraordinary amount of firmness and resolution, and is known to have shot with his own hand his brother and uncle, whom he observed flinching in the presence of the enemy. His whole existence—Lozada is really many years older than he looks—has been one prolonged life-and-death struggle with his rival Rojas, who is painted in the blackest colours by the Imperialists, while the Liberals, for their part, teach their children to execrate Lozada as a monster of cruelty. To whichever the palm for blood-thirstiness be assigned, one thing is certain, that, between them, these two have laid one half of the towns and villages along that portion of the Pacific coast in ruin, and caused the streets to flow with blood. At the present time Lozada, who at once espoused the Imperial cause, reigns triumphant, his rival Rojas having lately been captured and shot by the French. In spite, however, of their having put him under a great obligation by thus ridding him of his rival, Lozada is extremely jealous of the French; and, whenever he is called upon to co-operate with them, holds himself as much aloof as possible from all personal communication with the French officers.

In times of peace, which hitherto have been with him rare intervals, arranged, if possible, to release his followers at harvest and seed time—so much method have Mexicans in their madness—Lozada, like Cincinnatus of old, may be found following the plough on the estate which has been called in honour of him, San Louis de Lozada. It is said that, at his call, from six to ten thousand Indians will flock at any moment to his standard.

The Monday following the Sunday ball, there was a lull in the festivities, and what few entertainments took place were of a private nature. Tepic was gathering up its strength for its great outburst on the morrow—our Shrove Tuesday, their *Festividad del*

Divino Rostro—as I find it in an almanac which I purchased at Guadalajara.

At about noon on the great day, on which the Roman Catholic religion encourages its votaries to take a surfeit of pleasure, in order to be able to do without any for the space of forty days, Don Diego, dressed from head to foot in white, and with a bag of flour slung over his shoulders, burst into my room, and announced that it was high time to go a visiting.

Knowing that resistance would be quite unavailing I surrendered unconditionally, and allowed myself to be rigged out in a similar suit of white. However, when the question of head-gear came to be considered, I had nothing for it but to put up with an old battered straw hat, which contrasted miserably with the elegant cap with a red tassel, which was jauntily stuck on Don Diego's head.

As we passed out of the Casa we encountered my *arriero*—the wretched Catarino—crouching as usual in the doorway, and I was amused at finding him already freely besprinkled with flour. Our first visit was a complimentary one to the house of the Prefect, whose daughter Don Diego anointed in due ceremony with flour on both cheeks, forehead, and hair. This done, he proceeded to break an egg filled with bits of coloured paper, chopped up fine, over the crown of her head. This ceremony was repeated wherever we went, and the demure gravity with which the *senoritas* put up their faces to be smeared, hardly once smiling, was very remarkable.

At first, being quite unused to the thing, I prudently confined myself to watching my companion's proceedings, with a view to beginning on my own account, when I should have mastered the rudiments of the science. However, I could see at a glance the hopelessness of aspiring to attain to anything like his perfection, which was evidently the result of long practice, combined with great natural aptitude. Besides, as compared with Don Diego, I laboured under the disadvantage of not being provided with a flour bag, and I felt how awkward it would look, to be obliged to plunge one's hands continually into one's pockets to get at the ammunition, with which they were stuffed.

However, in spite of this drawback, I summoned up courage, and proceeded with great diffidence to try my maiden hand on the youngest daughter of Dr. Narvaez, into whose house we broke at an early stage of the proceedings. The excellent doctor himself was nowhere to be found, and we learned from his daughters, who submitted like lambs to the operation, that their father had locked himself in his own room, where he intended remaining all day, in order to escape from incursions.

After about an hour of this amusement, I suggested to Don Diego, that it might be prudent to retire and take a little rest before the main proceedings of the afternoon should commence; but he would not hear of desisting for an instant, so I withdrew alone.

Soon after four P.M. attracted by the beating of a drum, and the sound of boisterous merriment in the street below, I looked forth from my eyrie on the azotea, and beheld a great company of revellers, clad from head to foot in white, streaming past the house. Descending at once into the street, I joined this Bacchanalian procession, which was appropriately headed by an imp mounted on a donkey, both alike liberally besprinkled with flour, the donkey looking as if he did not at all know what to make of it. Behind the donkey followed the band, or rather the big drum, which completely drowned the other instruments, if there were any.

After the band followed the notabilities of Tepic, amongst whom I recognised, with some difficulty, the portly figures of His Excellency the Prefect and the British Consul, both freely besprinkled with flour, and looking, in their short jackets, like a couple of jolly millers out for a holiday.

On this, the great day of their year, Tepic expects of every man to lay aside his dignity, and to do his duty by joining in the general festivities. Should any citizen refuse, and his absence be noticed, as it is sure to be, intimation of it is given to the imp on the donkey, who forthwith leads the whole band to the house of the defaulter. Should the doors and windows be closed, the more agile members of the avenging crowd will clamber up the pipes on to the *azotea*, or by some means force an entrance, and then a double measure of wrath, in the harmless form of showers of flour, will be poured upon the devoted head of the victim and his family discovered skulking within.

Now that they are covered with flour, these last will no longer refuse to join the throng, and so, ever swelling, the crowd passes on to the residence of the next defaulter.

While we were crossing the market-place, on the way to pay one of these domiciliary visits, the church doors were suddenly thrown open, and the priest passed out with the " Viaticum."

In the presence of the host, the whole company instantly dropped upon their knees, and remained kneeling till the procession had passed. The next moment the merriment was as boisterous as ever.

The flour ball, which took place in the evening, was a very curious spectacle, for the ladies and gentlemen alike were clad in white, and armed with bags of flour and coloured eggs. Not a speck of black was visible anywhere, except on my own boots, of which I felt much ashamed, and on Don Diego's face, for, in order to make himself conspicuous, Don Diego had blackened his face, and in his white dress looked, for all the world, like a figure emerging from the collodion in that dark chamber, into which photographers dive after taking one's likeness.

For conversation on this evening there was happily little occasion, for whenever one was in difficulties— and that was very often—one had only to pay the lady the compliment of breaking an egg over the crown of her head, or anointing her cheeks with flour. My only partner who volunteered a remark throughout the whole evening, informed me that she had stood sponsor to upwards of a hundred children!

When the revelry had raged for six full hours—from nine P.M. to three A.M.—I could stand no more of it, and retiring unobserved, snatched a little sleep before leaving Tepic on my return to Guadalajara. To comb the flour out of my hair, and wash myself clean from the stains contracted on the day before— an operation on which all Tepic is engaged on the morning of Ash Wednesday preparatory to putting on sackcloth and ashes—was a work of so much time and trouble that we did not get under weigh till eight A.M. a very late start for Mexico.

Leaving Tepic on Ash Wednesday, March 1st, I reached Guadalajara on Saturday, 4th, having run my money so fine, that I had not even the requisite coppers left, to pay the toll demanded of all travellers on entering the city. In my anxiety not to be worth robbing, and in my desire to experience something of the hilarity which, according to Juvenal's famous line—

Cantabit vacuus coram latrone viator—

results from travelling with a light purse, I had quite overreached myself, and was reduced to living on dry bread during the latter part of the journey.

CHAPTER XX.

A VOYAGE OF SIX DAYS IN A DILIGENCE—GUADALAJARA TO MEXICO.

THE distance from Guadalajara, the capital of the west, to the city of Mexico, by the great natural highway leading through the populous towns of Lagos, Leon, Guanajuato, and Queretaro, is estimated in the Mexican itineraries at 184 leagues; or 460 miles—about 60 miles greater than that from London to Edinburgh, which is accomplished in ten hours. To have performed the journey on horseback would have required at least twelve days, whereas the diligence gets over the same ground in six; so, being pressed for time, I decided in favour of the diligence.

In spite of his having fallen with me seven times in the space of three weeks—a fact which I attributed to his having been shod for the first time in his life, and the clumsiness of his shoeing—I had already formed an attachment to my horse, and it was painful to me to have to part with him at the last moment to Catarino for the modest sum of 2*l*. 17*s*. 6*d*.

The diligence ticket cost me sixty dollars, or twelve pounds sterling, and I don't suppose that any investment would bring you in more pain for your money. The wrench of having your tooth pulled out costs you a guinea, and lasts but a few seconds; but here the agony—in the worst parts of the road scarcely less acute—lasts six whole days, and the charge is only twelve pounds!

Under the circumstances I was not in the least surprised to find that I was the only passenger who had paid the fare for the whole journey. The diligence which I had seen entering the city of Guadalajara from Mexico a fortnight previously was absolutely empty. On the present occasion there were two passengers besides myself; but they soon got out, and I should have had the whole conveyance to myself had not the conductor, for decency's sake I suppose, got inside to keep me company.

Did the Atlantic roll between Guadalajara and Mexico communication would be kept up between the two places at infinitely less cost and trouble than are required to overcome the land journey. The jolting, which is really terrific, would certainly kill a delicate lady or an invalid.

From this state of things it results, that families living at Guadalajara are not unfrequently quite unacquainted with their own relations living in the city of Mexico or Puebla, from whom they are separated by a barrier, as impassable, as any gulf could be.

We had started from Guadalajara at four A.M. and reached Puente de Tololotlan, where the high road crosses our old acquaintance the Rio Santiago, at about sunrise. At that point the river presents a very attractive appearance. Its surface is dotted with numerous green islets; and, as it frets over its rocky bed, the stream from its shallowness is broken into innumerable ripples, making most melodious music.

A few leagues farther on, we came to the brink of a steep descent, leading to the Puente de Calderon, a bridge which spans the Rio de Calderon, a tributary of the Santiago, and famous in the annals of Mexico for the defeat of Hidalgo, the famous soldier-priest, and foremost ringleader of the insurgents, by General Calleja, on whom the title of Conde de Calderon was conferred in honour of the victory.

From the Puente de Calderon to the Venta de Pegueros, where we halted for the night, the country is absolutely featureless, and the monotony of the landscape unutterably dreary.

For the whole of the next day, there was no improvement in the scenery, and we passed through no place of interest except San Juan de los Lagos, remarkable for its December fair.

At Lagos, where the diligence halts for the second night, the great northern road from Chihuahua, Mapimi, Durango, and Zacatecas joins the great western road, leading from Guadalajara to Mexico. Should the Mexican table-land ever be traversed by a railway, Lagos, which is already a considerable town, would become a place of great importance.

Starting from Lagos at five A.M. next day, we had to support some four hours more of the barren featureless plateau, which extends for 200 miles almost without a break, from Guadalajara to the ridge above Leon, where the ground suddenly falls away, and gives place to the plain which, under the name of El Bajio, is celebrated throughout Mexico for its extraordinary fertility.

From the brink of this ridge, down which the diligence was compelled to proceed with great caution, we beheld stretched out at our feet a bright carpeting of green, inexpressibly refreshing to look upon after so much unbroken sterility.

The direction of this plain, which runs from northwest to south-east, is mainly determined by that of the famous silver-producing range, whose base it skirts, on which are situated the world-renowned mines of Zacatecas and Guanajuato. For its whole extent this mountain range is absolutely treeless, and its outward appearance hopelessly unattractive and sterile. But for the happy juxta-position of this plain, which is so to speak its complement, it would have been quite impossible to work the silver mines with any profit in a country like Mexico, where mining is absolutely dependent on agriculture. For in the absence of steam or water-power, the number of horses and mules employed in turning the machinery, and conveying the ores from the mouth of the mine to the Haciendas de Beneficio, is so enormous, that mines can only be profitably worked where fodder is cheap.

As it is, the mining settlements in the mountains are abundantly supplied by the plain with maize, which commonly yields from three to five hundredfold. Now inasmuch as maize is the one thing needful to keep men and brutes alive in Mexico, being consumed in the form of tortillas by the men, and eaten raw by the brutes—a circumstance which may perhaps help to account for the slender difference perceptible between men and brutes in Mexico—the failure of the maize crops is the greatest calamity which can happen. This event unhappily occurred in 1864, owing to the extraordinary dryness of the season; and, when the Emperor Maximilian visited Guanajuato in the autumn of that year, maize had reached a famine price, and was selling at 9 dollars the *fanega* (150 lbs.), instead of at $2\frac{1}{4}$ dollars —at 36s. instead of at 9s. In the district of Zacatecas maize was not to be bought at any price, and women were seen fighting in the market-place over what little was exposed for sale. As the whole plain may be said to be the complement of the mountain range, so is a farm in the plain a necessary adjunct to individual mines in the mountains.

The plain of El Bajio is emphatically the garden of Mexico, and might become the granary of the whole country, but for the absence of roads, which renders the transport of grain in large quantities an impossibility.

As it is, the great towns can only be supplied from their own immediate environs, which is a bad look out for the city of Mexico, surrounded as it is by unproductive marshes. In consequence of this lamentable state of things, which railway communication alone can remedy, famine may be raging in the capital, while the farmers of the Bajio—less than 200 miles distant—are at their wits' end to know how to dispose of their superabundant harvest.

To the imagination of the inhabitants of a large portion of the thirsty barren table-land, El Bajio is a kind of land of Egypt, from which they are cut off by a desert, which is to all intents and purposes impassable. In bad times, a few well-to-do landowners—like the patriarch of old—may send their sons down into the land of Egypt to buy corn, but these will not bring back more than enough for themselves, and the mass of the people must starve.

El Bajio has naturally become a great centre of population, and the towns of Leon, Silao, Irapuato, Salamanca, Celaya, and Queretaro contain between them nearly a quarter of a million inhabitants. To this total Leon alone contributes 100,000.

In most of these towns are at least two or three factories of some kind—cotton and paper being the most common; so that the manufacturing interest of the towns fully keeps pace with the progress of agriculture.

Happily for Mexico, the open plains of El Bajio are so ill adapted for guerilla warfare that its prosperity has been comparatively little affected by the revolutions, which have ravaged less favoured portions of the country. Of course, forced loans have been levied upon the wealthy miners, manufacturers, and agriculturists of this district by the unscrupulous partisan chieftains, who have passed from time to time through the towns, but the industry of the district has continued throughout without any considerable interruption. The habit of work may be read in the appearance of the inhabitants, who are several degrees less degraded than the generality of Mexicans.

Seeing the importance of winning over the inhabitants of the Bajio to his side, the Emperor Maximilian, within a few months of his arrival in the country, during the season of the rains, undertook a painful journey, which nearly cost him his life, in order to bid for the suffrages of the population, and make himself personally acquainted with that portion of the country. Having myself passed through all the principal places visited by the Emperor, and enjoyed constant opportunities of sounding the opinions of the principal inhabitants, I can vouch for it that this journey was by no means thrown away. Wherever he went, the Emperor won himself golden opinions, and the inhabitants of the Bajio are now decidedly in favour of being taxed by the Imperial Government, rather than of submitting to the arbitrary exactions of forced loans.

The city of Guanajuato, to pass through which the diligence makes a painful *détour* to the northeast, lies up in the mountains, off the direct road to the capital. To reach it you must climb a mountain staircase, up which eight mules, straining every nerve, can hardly drag the huge unwieldy diligence, which lurches and groans incessantly. The climb would at any time be painful in a wheeled carriage, but on this occasion, to make the matter worse, we were full inside, for the passenger traffic, like everything else, is comparatively lively in the Bajio, and the heat was intense.

Down the centre of the narrow rocky gorge, up which we were threading our way, trickles a muddy silver-laden streamlet, the waters of which are washed—

and much they look to need it—for silver by the natives. This gorge, the sides of which are lined by the Haciendas de Beneficio (establishments where the ores are reduced) ends in a *cul de sac*. As you mount, the valley opens out by degrees, till, on approaching the end of it, you see in front of you the city of Guanajuato picturesquely straggling up the rocky mountain sides in a manner truly refreshing to look upon, after the rectangular cities of the plain. The city looks as if it might have owed its origin to an eruption from some neighbouring crater, which had belched forth a stream of hot human dwellings, a portion of which, as they cooled down, had stuck to the face of the rocks, while the main stream had flowed on and filled up the valley.

According to Mr. John Bowring and Mr. Fitzherbert, to whose hospitality I was much indebted during my stay there, Guanajuato, in spite of its attractive and picturesque appearance, is a most undesirable place of residence, inasmuch as you can neither walk, ride, nor drive in its streets with any kind of comfort.

Towering conspicuously above the surrounding buildings, and almost choking up the valley, stands a huge massive quadrangular building called the Alhondiga—a public granary, prison, and general store-house all in one. To this building a bloody history attaches, for it was here that the undisciplined horde of Indians and half-castes, led on by the warrior-priest Hidalgo, the curé of the neighbouring village of Dolores, got their first taste of blood. Here burst forth, with terrible fury, the storm, which had been brewing during well-nigh three centuries of misrule and oppression. It was an evil day for the Spaniards when they roused the anger of the village curé by plucking up the vines and olives, to the culture of which he was so devoted. The sacking of Guanajuato, and the massacre of the Spaniards and wealthier Creoles who fled to the Alhondiga for refuge, took place in the month of September, 1810. It was the opening episode of the revolution, which has been raging with little intermission ever since.

Of all the English companies, which have embarked capital from time to time in mining adventures in Mexico, the United Mexican Mining Company, which has its head-quarters at Guanajuato, has I believe alone survived the general wreck. Under the management of the present director, Mr. Fitzherbert, the position of this company has so far improved as to be now yielding its shareholders a yearly dividend at the rate of five per cent. For the information of any person interested in this company, who may consider five per cent. an unsatisfactory return, I may add that, to the best of my belief, no other mining concern in Guanajuato is at this moment paying so well. In the whole place not a bit of machinery is moved by steam or water-power.

In consequence of the great falling off in the amount of silver produced by the mines about Guanajuato in the year 1864–1865, as compared with the preceding years—a falling-off chiefly attributable to two causes, first, the failure of the maize crops, which in some cases caused the entire, in others, the partial, stoppage of the works, and secondly, to the poorer nature of the ore extracted—the shareholders in the Anglo-Mexican Mint have probably had less reason to be satisfied with their dividends. For whereas the mint of Guanajuato, which is farmed by the Anglo-Mexican Mint Company, for the last fifteen years has coined on an average upwards of 5,000,000 dollars per annum, the director assured me that there was no probability of the total exceeding 3,000,000 for the year 1865. At the period of my visit in the March of that year, the mint was reduced to working half time, and it was an exception when any silver remained to be coined after twelve P.M.

After a stay of two days at Guanajuato, I left at three A.M. on the morning of Saturday, March 11th, for Queretaro, and accomplished the distance—just 100 miles—in fourteen hours, including a halt of one hour at the flourishing manufacturing town of Celaya.

At Queretaro the diligence, with praiseworthy

propriety, halts for the Sunday, and the traveller feels truly grateful for an interval in the jolting. To me this day's repose was rendered doubly enjoyable by the agreeable society of an English family, consisting of a newly-married couple, and the mother of the bride, whom I met at the Casa de Diligencias. These ladies—such is life in Mexico— were both armed with revolvers, and spent their Sunday morning in practising at a mark! In the afternoon we took a drive into the country to see an Indian dancing party, which was advertised to take place in the cock-pit on an adjoining *hacienda*.

In the month of September, 1789, a new volcano, that of Jorullo, which gives out flame to this day, sprang up in the southern portion of the state of Michoachan. In the agonies of its birth the mountain belched forth showers of ashes with such violence as to cover the roofs of the houses of Queretaro (125 miles distant.)*

Beyond Queretaro, where the Bajio may be said to terminate, the barren monotony of the table-land recommences, and extends—with the interruption of an occasional patch of bright green at the bottom of the *barrancas*, into which the road dips from time to time—as far as the city of Mexico.

With a feeling of relief scarcely less intense than that I had felt on turning my back on them six

* Chevalier, English Translation, vol. ii. p. 112.

weeks before, so weary had I then become of lounging away the day in the city—did I catch sight once more of the snow-capped summits of the volcanos, which have the valley of Mexico in their keeping.

As for the volcanos, they became visible while we were yet a great way off; but it was not till we had painfully surmounted the mountain wall, which shuts in the basin of Mexico to the northward, that we caught sight once more of the familiar towers and domes of the city itself.

For some leagues before reaching the capital, the road passes through a succession of straggling populous hamlets, of which Cuautitlan and Tlalnepantla —the former lying without, the latter just within, the valley of Mexico—are the most considerable.

As we approached the city of Mexico, it was impossible not to be painfully struck with the extraordinary change for the worse in the aspect of the population, which we encountered in the villages and along the roads.

As if to keep pace with the constantly deteriorating appearance of the inhabitants, the aspect of the country becomes more and more loathsome as you approach the capital. Foul pestilential marshes, only broken by ghastly heaps of leprous *tequesquite* and the ruins of abandoned mud villages, extend on every side, as far as the eye can reach, and the northern entrance to the capital is quite of a piece with the rest of the picture. At the *garita* the road, which is carried along a causeway so far, suddenly leaves off altogether, leaving you to thread your way, as best you may, among the ruins of churches and convents standing forlorn in waste sandy deserts.

CHAPTER XXI.

REAL DEL MONTE.

On my return to the city of Mexico, after an absence of rather more than six weeks, I found things going on much as I had left them, and after a stay of four days, on the morning of March 14th, set off in the diligence to visit the great mining settlement of Real del Monte, with the intention of proceeding thence direct to Tampico in the hope of catching the English packet, due there on the 28th. The road from the city of Mexico to Pachuca, a considerable town which lies at the base of the argentiferous range, in which the mines of Real del Monte are situate, is about the best in all the country. Leaving the capital by the northern *garita*, it is carried on a causeway across the marshes, as far as La Villa de Guadalupe, where dry land begins again. Thence it skirts the base of the bare mountain range, on a spur of which La Villa stands out conspicuously, till it reaches a second causeway, which is carried along a raised dam, separating the lake of San Christobal, on the north-west, from that of Tezcuco, on the south-east. Here, for the first time in my experience of the lakes in the valley of Mexico, I had genuine water to deal with, and after the unsightly bog land, across which every other causeway is conducted, it was highly refreshing to see the waves dashing up against the masonry, and actually to feel the spray in one's face. For the wind was very boisterous, and the lake of San Christobal, which was brimming to overflowing, seemed trying hard to overleap the barrier, which prevented it from inundating its sluggish and shrunken neighbour of Tezcuco. Whenever this restless lake clears the causeway, and finds the outlet for its superfluous waters, for which it is continually longing, in the bed of the lake of Tezcuco, the lower parts of the city of Mexico are laid several feet under water. This event, which occasions terrible distress to the inhabitants of the capital, occurred in the summer of last year.

The village of San Christobal, which gives its name to the lake, lies just off the road to the left, and is remarkable, in the annals of Mexico, as the scene of the execution of Morelos, after Hidalgo the most prominent of the batch of heroes who figure in the history of the War of Independence.

At Tisajuca, a small town about half way between the city of Mexico and Pachuca, I found the *mozo*, whom I had sent on the day before, to await me there with the sturdy cob, which we had purchased three months previously at the *hacienda* of El Carmen near Puebla. During my absence from the capital, I had lent this animal to my excellent friend Herr Ober-Garten—Director Grube, who used it for the purpose of accompanying the Emperor on the morning rides, during which the two would indulge in fond dreams of laying-out gardens everywhere.

In return for the loan of my horse, Herr Grube had kindly lent me his *mozo*, for the purpose of conducting my steed to Tisajuca, whence he returned to the capital by diligence, while I performed the remainder of my journey—about twenty-five miles—on horseback, reaching Pachucha an hour after the diligence. For at least two-thirds of its whole length, the road from the city of Mexico to Pachucha traverses a parched-up, featureless plain, of that monotonous hue, which so torments the unhappy traveller in search of the picturesque.

At Pachucha, the gale of wind, which is said to spring up every afternoon, was blowing hard when I arrived, and I made my way to the palatial residence of Mr. A., the director of the Real del Monte Mining Company, through whirlwinds of dust and sand. To gain the shelter of the *porte cochère* was an immense relief, but I was not best pleased to learn from the porter that Mr. A., to whom I had been specially recommended by Don Antonio Escandon, one of the largest shareholders in the Real del Monte concern, was then residing at his country seat at Velasco, twelve miles beyond Pachucha.

While I was considering what was best to be done under the circumstances, an English gentleman, who introduced himself to me as the medical officer of the company, came forward, and very kindly offered to put me up for the night, adding that he would see to my being sent on to Velasco next morning. With this offer I was only too happy to close.

From the outside, the doctor's house was not imposing, consisting in fact of some back premises attached to the director's palace; but within it was furnished with every English comfort. In the sitting room it was pleasant to see a bright fire burning, for Pachucha lies upwards of 8,000 feet above the sea, and the air was decidedly chilly. Here, listening to the entertaining conversation of the doctor and his father, who resided with him, I passed the evening so pleasantly, that I felt grateful for the accident which had thrown me on their hospitality.

Next day was Sunday, and learning from Dr. F., that Mr. A. was in the habit of repairing on that day to Real del Monte, half way between Pachucha and Velasco, for the purpose of reading prayers to the English miners settled there, I set off immediately after breakfast in the hope of arriving in time for the service, leaving the doctor busily engaged in attending to the wants of a crowd of sick and emaciated Indians, who had been besieging his doors since daybreak.

When once you have emerged from the tortuous, ill-paved streets of Pachucha, you strike into the excellent carriage-road, which has been carried up the bare face of the mountain to Real del Monte, on the summit of the pass, and down the opposite slope, as far as the *hacienda* of Regla. This road was cut at an enormous expense by the company for the transport of their ores, and an annual outlay of not less than 12,000 dollars is required to keep it in good repair. So costly a luxury is a decent carriage-road in Mexico!

Having heard so much of the beauty of the scenery about Real del Monte, it was a great disappointment to find the southern slopes of the silver-producing range, *i.e.* the side turned towards the capital, as bald and treeless as the mountains are, for the most part, which bound the valley of Mexico. However, no sooner do you reach the summit of the pass, than the scene suddenly changes, and you find yourself overlooking a well-wooded region. While the nearer and lower hills, immediately in front of you, are gracefully crowned with groves of oak, the slopes of the loftier and more distant mountains are clothed with dense pine forests, out of which the bare rock crops up freely, while above all jagged masses of precipitous crags tower into the sky, forming in stone shapes, hardly less fantastic, than those shadowed forth in the cloudy sculpture-gallery beyond.

Under the shadow of a wooded eminence, round which a public promenade has been conducted, lies the village of Real del Monte, straggling over the face of half-a-dozen hills, the highest of which is crowned by its picturesque and airy cemetery—the sleeping-place of many Cornishmen. If you happen to be blessed with a sunshiny day, as I was, you will infallibly fall in love with the place at first sight, especially if that day be a Sunday, when all the machinery is at rest, and the great tall chimneys are not belching forth volumes of black smoke into the liquid air.

I had arrived just in time for the morning service, and having delivered my letter to Mr. A., whom I found standing at the bottom of the stairs, was conducted by him to the upper chamber, where a congregation of about sixty English men and women with clean bright shining faces, inexpressibly refreshing to look upon after the dirty yellow complexions of the natives, was already assembled.

After the service, at which Mr. A. officiated himself, I was introduced to Mrs. A. and several ladies resident at Real del Monte, to whom I expressed myself highly delighted with the general aspect of the place. These ladies, however, were not prepared to admit that they were to be envied for living at Real del Monte, and seemed to be of opinion that had I been condemned to pass the whole winter there in the clouds—for Real del Monte stands upwards of 9,000 feet above the sea—instead of visiting it on a spring day, I should have retained as little liking for the place as they had themselves.

On my way down the hill to the building where the service was held, I had been so much struck with the picturesque grouping of some tumble-down wooden tenements, that I could not resist the temptation of remaining to sketch them, while Mr. A. returned in his carriage at once to Velasco, to which place it was agreed that I should follow on horseback later in the afternoon.

So intricate and rambling a place is Real del Monte that, in attempting to get to my sketching ground by a short cut, I completely lost my way; and, after wandering about for some time in a network of ravines, stumbled upon a shrine in which stood an image of our Saviour, wearing a crown of thorns, great drops of blood trickling down His agonized countenance.

While I was regarding this figure, an Indian, whose skin was marked with alternate blotches of white and brown—the first specimen I had seen of the race known as *Pintos*—made his appearance on the scene, and in piteous accents begged me not to depart from the shrine without leaving a gratuity behind me to be invested in candles in honour of *Nuestro Señor de la Salud.* In the person of the strange being before me, the Ethiopian trying to change his skin seemed to have met the leopard half way in its attempt to change its spots

So importunate was this *pinto* in his begging for "candles," his delicate way of expressing that he should like to drink my health, that I resolved to take him literally at his word, and told him to lead the way to the "shop," where I would buy him some candles. Not a little taken aback by this manœuvre, the Indian, throwing his *scrape* around him, preceded me in silence along a narrow footpath, which presently struck the high road at the very point from which I had determined to take my sketch. A hundred yards farther down the road stood the *tienda* for which the Indian was making.

Following my spotted guide into the shop, I gave him a *real* (6*d.*), and told him to call for candles, thinking that he would make a better bargain than I should. The keeper of the store, however, turned out to be a Cornishman, who appeared to find shop-keeping more profitable than mining. Having served him with three pennyworth of candles, the Cornishman handed his spotted customer a *medio* as his change, which the Indian eyed so wistfully, that I told him he might keep it for himself. Upon this his gratitude knew no bounds, and he declared repeatedly, "That I was a very excellent Christian."

While I was engaged at my sketching, an English miner sauntered up to me, and entered into conversation. From him I learnt that part of the group of buildings I was sketching, did duty as a prison, and that yonder fine-looking fellow with a bushy beard was an Englishman, named Chawner, confined there for the murder of several Mexicans.

Having finished my sketch, I presented myself at the door of the prison, and was allowed to pass unquestioned to the presence of my dangerous countrymen, the slipshod sentry on duty seeming to consider it no business of his to stop persons from going in or out. As I entered Chawner's chamber, and met his honest gaze, I could not help thinking that I had never seen any one less like a murderer in my life, and have no doubt that he told me the truth when, in confessing to having caused the death of Mexicans, he declared that he had merely acted on the defensive. The poor fellow went on to tell me that, in making a journey to the capital several years back with his wife, the diligence in which they were travelling had been attacked by brigands, and his wife shot dead in his arms.

In the same prison were confined 150 able-bodied malefactors, who are lent by the government to the company for the purpose of working in the mines, the company undertaking to feed and clothe them while so employed.

At about four P.M. I got upon my horse and took the road to Velasco, which is carried by zigzags down a rocky ravine, shut in on both sides by lofty pine-clad mountains. At several points along the road we passed Haciendas de Beneficio—extensive establishments, where the silver is extracted from the ores by various processes. These *haciendas* are stationed at distinct stages of the descent, in order that their water-wheels may be successively turned by the slender artificial stream of water which, having been originally pumped up from the bottom of the mines at Real del Monte, where it does unmitigated harm, is thence carried down the ravine in a leaky wooden aqueduct, and ingeniously made to do the work of a friendly agent on its way.

At the foot of the ravine lies the little town of Omitlan, and, in the plain beyond, the mining community of Velasco, with its tall chimney, surmounted by a little smoke-blackened cross, proclaiming it to be the most Christian of chimneys. At the northern extremity of the village, pleasantly nestling among trees, stands the delightful summer residence of the director of the Real del Monte Company, a rambling overgrown summer-house, as enticing to behold from without, as it is comfortable within.

Were the duties of this official ever so arduous his post would still be an enviable one, for you would hardly find in either hemisphere a spot better calculated to make labour delightful, or more soothing to the troubled mind. In point of fact, as far as I could judge during my brief visit, the director is very far from being overworked, for his duties seemed mainly to consist in riding about from one *hacienda* to another, through scenery which is often strikingly beautiful. He is thus enabled to combine work with pleasure, in a manner which can hardly be less agreeable to himself than to his guests. These rounds of inspection, however, are not always unattended with danger, for the director is occasionally kidnapped by the various partisan leaders, who visit Real del Monte for the purpose of exacting forced loans.

Mr. A. informed me that he had himself been twice seized in this manner, and once forced to remain by the side of his captor during a sanguinary engagement, which took place on the Pachucha road.

On the morning after my arrival we made a delightful excursion to the *hacienda* of Regla, celebrated for its cascade and basaltic columns, which are both utilized by the company. For the water is made to turn their wheels, and the columns are ruthlessly sliced up into millstones, and pressed into the service of grinding the ores into powder.

Half way between Velasco and Regla, embowered in woods of the most tender green, and by the side of a limpid stream, stands the *hacienda* of San Miguel, where the poorer and more refractory ores, containing on an average less than a quarter per cent. of pure silver, are reduced by the barrel amalgamation process, imported into Mexico from Germany. Regla, on the other hand, is the head-quarters of the "patio," or purely Mexican process, which can only be applied with advantage to the so-called richer ores, which contain above one per cent. of pure silver. The *patio* amalgamation process is a very singular one. For the space of about twenty-eight days several yokes of mules or horses are incessantly driven about in round mashes of mud about twenty feet in diameter and a foot deep, several of which are spread out in the same *patio* or courtyard. These mud mashes consist of the good docile ores, ground into a powder, and mixed with water, and require to be stirred up in this strange fashion to enable them to reap the full benefit of atmospheric action.

A worse fate is reserved for the refractory ores, which are put into a barrel and well shaken for twenty-four hours. After this ordeal they no longer refuse to yield up their silver.

The Real del Monte Company, as all the world knows, has, since its formation in 1824, been a most fluctuating concern, and there are probably Englishmen still living upon whom the bare mention of the name will act like waving a red flag before a bull. As the concern is at this moment in a most flourishing condition, it may be worth while briefly to epitomize its history from the beginning, from which it will be seen that there is plenty to exasperate the former English shareholders.

So much encouragement does the Mexican law hold out to mining adventurers, that it compels the owner of the soil to sell or lease his land to any person who *denounces* it, as the term is, for the purpose of working a mine under it. In fact, in Mexico miners enjoy the same kind privilege of giving people notice to quit, which is now-a-days so freely exercised by railway companies in England.

Taking advantage of this singular provision of the Mexican law, a certain Don Pedro Terreros, of Queretaro—known later as El Conde de Regla—a title which he may be said to have dug out of the earth, for it was purchased of the King of Spain with the silver extracted from these mines—in the year 1749 associated himself with one Bustamente in making a general *denuncio* of the Real del Monte district.

However, before the expiration of the ten years' siege, which they laid to the mountain, and during which they were occupied in pushing their approaches, of which the main work consisted of a tunnel or adit, 3,000 yards long, at a depth of 200 yards from the surface, Bustamente died, leaving Terreros to reap the fruit of their joint labours.

This fruit took a very substantial form, for during the period of twenty-two years, from 1759 to 1781, over which Terreros, first Conde Regla, lived after the completion of the adit, he extracted no less than 15,000,000 dollars from the Biscayna and Santa Brigida veins alone. The second Conde was less successful, for in the twenty-eight years from 1781 to 1809, he only got 8,400,000 dollars out of the mine. The third Conde, who succeeded his father in 1809, had a very bad time of it, for he had scarcely been a year in possession, when the War of Independence broke out, bringing general ruin in its train.

So severely did the outbreak of the civil war tell upon the yield of the mines of Real del Monte, that the total produce of the next ten years amounted only to 1,600,000 dollars' worth of silver.

For the next five years the mines went so completely to decay, that on his arrival in 1824, Captain Veitch —the first director of the ill-fated company which had been got up in England in the meanwhile—found the whole district overgrown by dense underwood, the roof of the great adit fallen in, and the mouths of the shafts choked up. In consequence of this state of things, a very heavy outlay was required to put the mines into a proper state of repair, and a large quantity of costly machinery was sent out from England for the purpose.

When the English company was first formed, there was a general rush for shares, so favourable was the report of the mining engineer—Mr. John Taylor—who had been sent out to survey the Real del Monte district. That there was plenty of silver to be had was enough for the English public, who plunged headlong into the concern without considering the enormous difficulties in the way of getting at it.

So unsatisfactory however did the speculation turn out that, at the expiration of twenty-three years, the books of the company showed a dead loss of nearly 5,000,000 dollars. In this period the mines had produced 10,481,475 dollars' worth of silver, in return for an outlay of 15,381,633 dollars.

By this time the patience of the shareholders was completely worn out, and the directors would have been only too glad to dissolve the company, had this course been open to them. But so heavy were its liabilities, that it was found impossible to wind up the concern, and the company might have lingered on indefinitely, had not Mr. J. H. Buchan—who is at this crisis brought upon the scene like a *Deus ex machina*—induced a couple of spirited Mexicans—Don Manuel Escandon and Don Nicanor Beistegui—

to take over the concern with all its liabilities. The dissolution of the English company, for which shareholders and directors alike had been so ardently longing, was thus unexpectedly brought about in October, 1848.

The English company having now ceased to exist, a Mexican company was formed under the auspices of Don Manuel Escandon and Don Nicanor Beistegui, who appointed Mr. J. H. Buchan director-in-chief. This gentleman, in whose judgment his employers appear to have placed the utmost reliance, began by introducing a radical reform in the system of working the mines. Hitherto, in consequence of their refusal to yield up the silver they contained under the ordinary *patio* amalgamation process, the poorer ores had been entirely neglected, and the exclusive attention of the company had been directed to the richer veins.

By introducing on a large scale the barrel amalgamation process, Mr. Buchan was enabled to utilize these poorer and more refractory ores, large heaps of which had already accumulated at the mouths of the mines. The result of this simple expedient, and of his general management, was so remarkably successful, that when he resigned his office in 1856, Mr. Buchan had not only refunded to the proprietors all the additional capital which they had invested, but left the concern in so flourishing a condition that the shareholders have ever since received, on an average, a yearly dividend of 2,850 dollars (£570), upon each of the shares, which they originally obtained for a mere song. The Company is at present divided into 232 shares, of which all but a few are held by Mexicans, the bulk being in the hands of the families Escandon, Beistegui, and Barron.

CHAPTER XXII.

REAL DEL MONTE TO ZACUALTIPAN.

HAVING heard so much from friends on whose judgment I could rely, of the beauty of the region called the Huasteca, which extends from Zacualtipan northwards to Tampico, I resolved at all hazards to give it a trial.

According to the last accounts which had reached Mexico from the Huasteca previous to my departure, the moment was not an unfavourable one for attempting to pass that way to Tampico. For Ugalde, the chief of the Liberals and arch-disturber of order in that region, was reported to be on his way to the capital, with a view of coming to terms with the Imperial authorities, and a kind of armistice—if that term may be applied to a suspension of robbing and throat-cutting—was said to have been proclaimed in the Huasteca, while the negotiations were pending.

Accordingly, at seven A.M. on Wednesday, March 22d, I tore myself away, not without a pang, from the comforts and elegancies of Velasco, and took a six-days' plunge into the wilds.

My little caravan consisted altogether of four animals—a horse and mule for my own riding, a mule for my *mozo*, and a baggage mule. All four animals were in excellent condition, and thoroughly reliable, which was of the utmost importance, as only by travelling at the rate of forty miles a day for six days consecutively could I make sure of catching the steamer due at Tampico on the 28th of the month. The whole distance from Real del Monte to Tampico is rather less than 100 leagues, or 250 miles. By starting from Velasco, I reduced the distance by a few miles.

No start was ever effected under more favourable circumstances than mine from Velasco, for the sky was overclouded—an inestimable boon in the tropics —the temperature was perfect, and the road, or rather mule-track, so smooth and elastic that it was impossible to resist the temptation to break into a canter. If anything was wanting to enhance the enjoyment of this ideal state of things, it was supplied by the sense of the precarious nature of such happiness in a country like Mexico, where a good bit of road is sure, sooner or later, to be atoned for by a bit unusually bad. The longer the retribution is in coming, the more severe will it be, when it comes.

In the present instance my tenure of enjoyment

was unusually protracted, for the road continued fairly level for nearly twenty miles, until it brought us abruptly to the brink of the great *barranca* of Mextitlan. So far all had been plain sailing, but now the tug of war was to begin. Looking over the edge of the barranca, I beheld in the deep bottom, 3,000 feet below me, the whitewashed walls of the *hacienda* of Guadalupe gleaming out from the midst of bright green patches of young wheat. Within those walls we were to make our mid-day halt, but the place seemed quite unreachable.

By this time I had had some experience in descending steep places on horseback, but I had not yet learned to ride down a perpendicular wall of rock, with nothing to hold on by, and little short of that seemed to be expected of one here. However, the header had to be taken, and the less time spent in shivering on the bank the better. Only stopping to shift my saddle from horse to mule—a beautiful sleek iron-grey about fourteen hands high, than which I never saw a finer specimen in any country—I took the inevitable plunge, leaving my *mozo* to follow as best he might with the other animals.

Having the utmost confidence in my mule, I thought it more advisable to let the animal take its own course, rather than assume the responsibility of directing its steps; so I confined my efforts to rendering it whatever assistance I could with the bit towards keeping its legs. When, after a succession of slippings and slidings, varied by more or less successful goat-like bounds from rock to rock, we had accomplished about half the descent in safety, to my unfeigned astonishment, we came upon a party of Indians engaged in mending the road. On watching their proceedings, however, I observed that these swarthy navvies restricted their exertions entirely to removing the larger boulders, which obstructed the narrow mule-track. They had, apparently, only commenced operations a few days before, for the track was only comparatively cleared of the more formidable obstacles for a very short distance, when it became so bad again, that there was nothing for it but to dismount, and scramble down the rest of the way on foot. When at length we reached the bottom, and looked up at the mountain wall, down which we had ridden, it seemed incomprehensible how we had got down such a place without breaking our necks.

The worst of it was, that we had but climbed down to climb up again the other side; for the *barranca*, which must have been fully 3,000 feet deep, was less than a quarter of a mile broad. The princess, flying from the giant in the German fairy tale, would have cleared it easily, and the giant would have just missed it, and have been dashed to pieces in his fall, as such monsters deserve. Would that we could have taken the leap with the princess, instead of wasting weary hours in painful climbing up and down.

From the *barranca* of Mextitlan to the town of Zacualtipan, which is said to stand even higher than Real del Monte, is an almost unbroken climb. Both at Real del Monte and at Zacualtipan the cold in winter is very severe, and the inhabitants complain of being constantly enveloped in fog and mist. You may get from the one place to the other in a long day, in which you will experience every vicissitude of climate. If you perform the journey in midwinter, starting from Real de Monte at dawn, you will shiver over your *desayuno* in the raw cold atmosphere of an Alpine pass; in the plain beyond Velasco you will think the climate perfect; in the bottom of the *barranca* of Mextitlan you will suffer from a tropical heat; and, before you reach Zacualtipan, your clothes will be soaked through with a mist which would put Scotch mists to shame, and your teeth will be chattering with cold. In a single day, you will have learnt more about the three-fold climate of Mexico than you would have done from a year's reading.

For the first half of the climb from Guadalupe, all went smoothly enough; but, when we had ascended some 3,000 feet, the clouds, which had been threatening all day, began to descend, first in the shape of mist, and then in the more decided form of rain. As we advanced, the air became so raw and cold as to completely chill me through, and I halted to put on all the wraps which I could get at without unlading the pack-mule. What would I not then have given for a little of the heat which could so well have been spared from the bottom of the *barranca*?

As we approached the summit of the pass, the ascent became more and more gradual, which enabled us to push on in spite of the increasing badness of the road. When we reached the watershed, the character of the scenery, which had been monotonous and uninteresting thus far, became so gloomy and severe that there seemed little to choose in point of blackness between earth and sky. As the darkness gathered around us, we found ourselves traversing an undulating wilderness of barren rock, partially covered by a thin crust of dark mould or peat, in the hollows of which pools of stagnant water gleamed out of the surrounding blackness. Had one been in quest of snipe or plover instead of a night's lodging, the scene might have impressed one differently.

At this juncture a clap of thunder burst overhead; and its echoes had hardly ceased reverberating amongst the hills, when it was followed by a second, louder than the first. Never doubting but what we were going to have a severe tempest, I listened attentively for the third clap, which never came—the storm having apparently exhausted itself in its double shot at the outset. The rain, however, unhappily came down faster than before.

Our position was certainly not an enviable one. It was nearly pitch dark, and my *mozo*, who had not been that way for several years, and only twice before in his life, had about as much notion of which way to turn as I had.

To encamp where we were, in the rain, was not to be thought of for an instant, as we had no fodder for our beasts, no shelter for ourselves, and no fuel to make a fire with. So we pushed on as best we could in the dark, and fortunately very soon reached a kind of mud *hospice* in an exposed position, on the highest point of the pass.

This building was wrapped in a thick mist, and the atmosphere outside was so raw and cold that I envied the party of *arrieros* within, who were discussing their *aguardiente* in darkness, made visible by a glimmering rushlight.

At the sight of the *aguardiente* my shivering *mozo*, unable to control himself for an instant, dismounted with great alacrity, and, leaving me outside with the beasts, dived into the drinking parlour, whence he presently emerged, with the dismal intelligence that we were still several miles from Zacualtipan, from which we were separated by a deep ravine. Had the decision rested with my *mozo*, I suspect he would have preferred passing the night at the *hospice*, but I was resolved at all risks to reach Zacualtipan. So we pressed on across the ridge, and presently reached the edge of the ravine, down which we sprawled headlong.

High up on the opposite bank of the ravine, two lamps glimmered through the darkness. Praying devoutly that those might be the lights of Zacualtipan, we plunged into the stream at the bottom of the ravine, which was much swollen by the heavy rains; and, having gained the opposite bank, commenced the difficult ascent which we had before us.

In broad daylight it is not a pleasant sensation to find yourself clambering up slippery places where your beast can with difficulty get a footing, and threatens to topple over with you backwards at every step; but in the dark the excitement was so painfully increased, that I resolved that, if I reached the summit in safety—of which I felt extremely doubtful—the experience should last me for the rest of my life.

When at length we reached the blessed lights, which had been our guiding stars throughout the ascent, we found that they proceeded from two outlying tenements, and that we had still a long stretch of darkness to traverse before reaching the main portion of the town of Zacualtipan.

The bare thought of tearing ourselves once more from the light, which we had reached so painfully, and plunging once more into the outer darkness, seemed to me so terrible, that I besought the occupant of one of the houses to light us on our way, or to sell us his candle, but he would not hear of it, and shut his door in our faces.

When at length we reached Zacualtipan, our case seemed hardly bettered, for, after threading our way for some distance through dilapidated mud tenements, we found ourselves landed at last in a deserted market-place, which was lighted by a single flickering oil-lamp.

Having with some difficulty discovered the residence of Don Ignacio Torres—one of the principal shopkeepers—for whom I carried a letter of recommendation, we presented ourselves at his door, and begged for admittance.

Without asking a single question, and even before I had time to deliver my letter, Don Ignacio opened his gates to us, like a true Christian, and invited us to enter.

Immediately after supper, at which he produced his best bottle of red wine, my host, suggesting that I should probably be glad to retire, most considerately withdrew, and placed his own bed and bed-chamber at my disposition for the night.

In a very few minutes I was in bed, and slept

soundly till about four A.M. when I was startled out of my sleep by a sudden flapping of wings, and a tremendously shrill crow, with which a game-cock, tied close to the head of my bed, defiantly answered a lusty rival, confined in the house over the way, whom he was to meet in mortal combat during the Easter holidays.

I need hardly add, that this noisy dialogue, which continued till daylight, effectually prevented me from getting any more sleep. I felt sorely tempted—for the first time in my life—to see what would come of sacrificing a cock to Æsculapius. Milder measures were worse than useless, for the harder I hit him over the head with my slipper, the louder he crowed.

CHAPTER XXIII.

THROUGH THE HUASTECA TO TAMPICO.

It was still drizzling when we left Zacualtipan, and proceeded cautiously down the slippery descent on the northern side of the town, for Zacualtipan is perched on the top of a ridge, whence the view —if the mist would only let you see it—must be magnificent. So far, in point of scenery, we had experienced nothing worth the trouble of going much out of one's way to see; but for the next day and a half we traversed a region which, for surpassing loveliness, I should imagine unequalled in any part of the world. At any rate, in my own experience of Scotland, Switzerland, and Italy I never saw anything approaching it in point of beauty.

Such is Mexico, a country made up of the most astonishing contrasts, where the scenery is most unattractive or enchantingly beautiful; where the earth produces nothing or three-hundred fold; where the sun never shines, but it scorches unmercifully; where it never rains, but it pours. In Mexico, there is no moderation in anything, and no steady return for honest labour. Thus nature seems to do her utmost to encourage man to become a gambler.

In an Indian village hanging on the brow of the hill, not far from Zacualtipan, I observed for the first time, an Indian woman employed in spinning cotton. So inaccessible to commerce is the Huasteca, that the scanty clothing worn by the Indians is mostly of home manufacture. Further on, I inquired of a half-caste woman, whether she too, like the Indian women, bought raw cotton to spin into calico. To this question she replied contemptuously, "*Nosotros, que tenemos razon, compramos genero. Los Indios, no mas, compran algodon.*" (We people of reason buy ready-made stuff, only the Indians buy raw cotton.)

As we advanced the beauty of the scenery and the badness of the road seemed to increase in about equal proportions. As far as Pinolco—a small farmhouse situated on a green plateau from which the ground falls away rapidly on every side—we followed an undulating path, carried mostly along the edge of the ridge.

This path is bordered on either side by dense tangled masses of luxuriant foliage, compactly bound round by creepers and parasitic plants, which shed a delicious fragrance around. Through occasional breaks in this flowery hedge, we were enabled to catch refreshing glimpses of rich grassy slopes, which stretched away beyond, and where the cattle were browsing in a warm, moist, Devonshire atmosphere.

Was it possible that one was still in thirsty, treeless, milkless, butterless, cheeseless Mexico? One would have thought that those cows must have yielded plenty of rich milk, yet hardly a drop was to be had anywhere for love or money.

In the language of the country we were travelling *cuchillo*—for the edge of the ridge is so sharp, that it goes by the name of "knife"—an advance on the Spanish *sierra*.

As far as Pinolco you have no choice of routes, but from Pinolco to Los Naranjos—an Indian village at the foot of the hills, where the difficulties of the road end—you may choose between keeping up on the edge of the ridge and descending abruptly into the depths and intricacies of the valley below. By adopting the former course you will only postpone the evil day — for the descent in either case will be painful—and therefore I decided on the latter, and took the header at once. And this time it turned out to be a literal header, for we had hardly commenced the descent, when, at a very steep place, I felt my saddle gradually slipping forward on to the neck of the mule, and, before I could recover myself, it turned round, and I was precipitated headlong to the ground, the mule following with the saddle dangling by the girths round its neck.

Happily for me, I fell so flat that I hardly moved from where I fell, but the mule, in its anxiety to avoid treading upon me, swerved so much to one side, that I thought he must have rolled over the slope, which was almost precipitous. When the animal, suddenly stretching out his fore-legs, pulled himself up abruptly on the brink, I felt a great sensation of relief, for the mule had been lent me by Mr. A. and was of great value. If it had not killed itself outright, the poor beast, with all its cleverness, could hardly have done itself a less injury than that of breaking its back.

During the remainder of the descent, which lasted about an hour and was very steep throughout, no further mishap occurred; and at about three P.M. we found ourselves by the side of a rushing stream, which pursued its winding course through the deep narrow valley between precipitous cliffs, whose summits were enveloped in thick mist. So sheer in many places did the rocks come down to the water's edge that, following the windings of the path, which was carried on whichever side there was space for it, we were driven to the unpleasant necessity of fording the stream, which was on an average twenty yards wide, and four feet deep, no less than fifty-three times in the course of three hours. Owing to the slippery nature of the bottom, my beast threatened to lose its footing every moment, in consequence of which I was kept in a state of most unpleasant excitement throughout the afternoon.

Meanwhile, it had been raining continually, so that we were pretty well drenched through by the time we reached Tlacolula—a collection of mud hovels planted on low ground by the edge of the river, where the valley opens out into a wooded amphitheatre, —a spot of surpassing loveliness, seldom more than half disclosed by the mist, which hangs over it constantly.

It was already dusk when we arrived, and as we threaded our way for some distance amongst flimsy bamboo cottages, pervious to wind and rain, and almost floating in slush, I could not help pitying the poor Indians, who were condemned to live in them.

At the same time I began to look about me with some anxiety for the house of Don Cajetano, the principal personage in the place, of whom I had heard in Zacualtipan. After wandering about, seeking in vain for some indication of a more substantial residence than any we had yet seen, we eventually fell in with an obliging Indian, who conducted us through a sea of slush to a thatched cottage, with projecting roof supported on wooden props, so as to form a verandah. This was Don Cajetano's residence.

Dismounting under the verandah, which was less than a yard wide, and afforded very poor shelter from the rain, I put my head into a dimly lighted apartment, and inquired for Don Cajetano. Whereupon a grisly, unwashed, unkempt individual, with a repulsive expression of countenance, came forward and begged to know what I wanted. Having glanced over the letter of introduction, which I presented with some diffidence, Don Cajetano proceeded to declare himself at my disposition, and begged that I would make myself quite at home, observing more than once, "*Que sabe, Vd. que Vd. tiene aqui su casa*," literally, "Your grace must know that this is your grace's house."

Now, considering that the whole house consisted of but a single apartment, in which the Don lived night and day, with an old hag of a wife, a grown-up son and daughter, a cat, and a game-cock, and that the room served as a shop besides, it was not so easy to take him literally at his word. However, reflecting that it would be the height of imprudence to attempt to sleep in the dripping clothes which I had on, I felt the necessity of overcoming my bashfulness, and changing them at once in the presence of the assembled family, and the customers, who dropped in continually. This operation I was enabled to effect without shocking anybody's sense of decency, for when I had divested myself of my upper garments, I had still as much clothing on as my host or any of his friends, whose light and airy costume consisted of a pair of calico drawers, a shirt of the same material, a straw hat, and a pair of sandals.

My next proceeding was, I fear, a more shameless one, for, espying a caldron of hot water bubbling over the fire in an adjoining kind of outhouse, which served the family as a kitchen, I could not resist the temptation of asking for a foot-tub, with a view to getting rid of the arrears of mud, which had now accumulated for two whole days.

Regretting that he had not a tub on the premises—a fact which I might have inferred from the unwashed appearance of the clothes, hands, and feet of the whole family—Don Cajetano was good enough to suggest, that if the caldron would do as well, it was quite at my service. This offer was far too tempting to refuse, and so I closed with it instantly, not without some misgiving as to the strict propriety of using the family cooking utensil as a foot-pan. How Don Cajetano came by that iron caldron, I should be curious to know, as, to the best of my recollection, I never met with another in the whole course of my travels in the country districts, where earthenware utensils prevail exclusively. There is nothing of which the Mexicans, Indians and half-castes alike, are so fond as of decorating their walls with innumerable little earthenware models of every kind of household utensil. These are often arranged in the form of a triangle, of which the constituent units constantly diminish in size as they approach the base, finally becoming hardly bigger than a good-sized pea. There must be some hidden meaning, underlying these tea-cup triangles, with their vanishing bases.

Meanwhile, as I sat taking my footbath, I had ample time to make an accurate survey of the family chamber. In length it certainly did not exceed twenty feet, while it was hardly sixteen feet broad. The floor was of mud—only dryer than the mud outside because of being protected from the rain, but only too ready to relapse into its original state of slush, as I was made painfully aware, when I spilt some hot water over it. In three of the four corners stood a canvas stretcher, intended to do duty as a bed, while the fourth corner, under the window at which customers presented themselves, was used as a repository of candles, maize, beans, &c. and was devoted to the business of the shop.

Immediately facing the door, and filling up the space along the wall, between the beds in either corner stood an altar, hung with dirty embroidery, and decorated with several vases of dingy artificial flowers, a pair of broken-down candlesticks, and a bit of an old looking-glass. In the centre, and supported against the wall, stood a good-sized portrait of our Saviour, surrounded by smaller pictures of saints; while a game-cock was tied by the leg to the lower portion of the altar—unhappily, in the closest proximity to the head of the stretcher which was assigned to me for the night. After my experience of the previous night, the very sight of the bird was enough to fill me with horrid forebodings, to which I suppose my face must have given silent expression, for, before we lay down for the night, Don Cajetano endeavoured to allay my anxiety by assuring me that the cock was a very lazy fellow, and would certainly not begin crowing before four A.M.

On retiring for the night, no member of the family laid aside any portion of their clothing, but just lay down, dressed as they were, on their respective bed-frames, the father and mother occupying one; the son, Don Pedro, a second, while the third was given up to me. As for the daughter of the house, whose appearance was hardly less repulsive than that of her parents, she waited till she thought we were all asleep, and then stole gently up to the altar, as if she was going to pray. However, it soon became evident, that she was not bent upon prayer, for her next proceeding was to take up a small travelling looking-glass, which I had laid accidentally upon the altar, by the side of the cracked one belonging to the family. As she held the polished mirror up before her, and continued gazing fixedly into it, it was not difficult to divine that the girl was now for the first time beholding her own face reflected in an uncracked mirror. Having feasted herself with gazing, she finally put out the light, threw her shawl over her, and lay flat down on the floor, her head resting on the very spot where my foot-pan had stood.

Next morning, long before daylight, the cock began to crow lustily, and the whole family—with the exception of Don Pedro, who continued snoring in his corner—was soon astir. Their dressing, which consisted of rubbing their eyes and shaking themselves, was a much simpler affair than mine, for I had the unpleasant task before me of getting into the damp riding suit, which I had laid aside the evening before. While I was performing this operation, a dirty, drunken-looking fellow, who was introduced to me as the village *curé*, dropped in to make my acquaintance. He had evidently got wind of the *Cognac*, which I carried about with me, and seemed a good deal disappointed at finding, that the bottle was already restored to the packing-case.

On taking leave of my host and hostess I offered them what I considered sufficient payment for my uncomfortable night's lodging, but, seeing that they expected more, I produced a second dollar, and was hesitating whether to give it to the man or his wife, when the latter snatched it unceremoniously out of my hand and plunged it into her bosom.

Having on the previous day had enough of water to last me for the term of my natural life, I determined, even at the cost of a desperate climb of about 2,000 feet, to give up travelling *rio*, literally " river," and take once more to *cuchillo* or ridge travelling. With a view to this we struck into a narrow path, a little beyond the church—which was nothing more than a barn with a thatched roof—and in a few minutes reached the foot of the abrupt mountain wall, which shuts in the valley. After a difficult climb of about an hour, during which it drizzled continually, we reached the summit of the ridge, whence we looked sheer down upon the roofs of the houses of Tlacolula, which appeared no bigger than beehives.

So far the weather had been hopelessly bad, but we had not proceeded far along the ridge, when the sun began to shine feebly through the mist, giving promise of better things. For some time the struggle between sun and clouds continued doubtful, but at last the sun so far prevailed, as to split a great cleft in the misty veil, through which we gazed upon a picture of the most surpassing beauty. From our eyrie in the clouds, upon which we seemed to be walking, we beheld stretched out at our feet a network of deep intricate valleys, choked up to the very brim with an exuberant growth of choice shrubs and flowers, such as are only known in hothouses in our northern climes.

Out of this bright heaving ocean of verdure, patches of a still brighter green gleamed out, wherever the sun's rays happened to fall, and from its depths, the muffled roar of the torrent made itself faintly heard through the dense masses of intervening foliage.

But it was only for a few short moments, that I was permitted to gaze upon this enchanting picture, for, almost before I had had time to engrave its main features on my memory, the remorseless clouds returned, and drew over it an impenetrable veil. With this brief revelation of the Paradise we were traversing, I had to be content. Thenceforth, walking by faith rather than by sight, we continued following the slippery path along the edge of the ridge, which was less like a knife than a constant succession of camels' backs. So slimy and boggy was the path where there was one, and so slippery the face of the rocks where there was none, that the descent to Los Naranjos was even a more arduous affair than our climb from Tlacolula in the early part of the morning. About half-way down, the brown roofs of an Indian village, planted on a natural terrace on the face of the mountain, began to loom faintly through the thick fog. The naked children playing about the puddles in front of the cottages might indeed have been styled " children of the mist."

It was about noon, when we emerged from the last watercourse, and found ourselves landed on a narrow grassy plain, shut in on either side by densely-wooded hills. Here I once more mounted my horse, which had been led so far by my *mozo*, and cantered on to Los Naranjos—an Indian settlement lying at the foot of the hills.

At Los Naranjos—a place of which I shall for ever retain a grateful recollection — our troubles ended, for, although we were not yet half-way on our road to Tampico, we had already accomplished almost the whole of the descent from the table-land to the *Tierra Caliente*.

From Los Naranjos an undulating plain extends with unimportant breaks as far as Tampico. This plain is for the most part densely wooded, and intersected by broad grassy rides cut through forest and jungle, along which you might gallop—almost without once drawing rein—the whole distance to Tampico. Were the heat less suffocating, it would be impossible to imagine more delightful riding-ground than this portion of the *Tierra Caliente* affords.

During the whole three days which I occupied in traversing it, I felt that I was the only living thing there which did not revel in the heat. For I could almost see the things growing about me. I felt that, without leaves to put forth, I had no business there. Around me the woods were alive with the discordant cries of birds of bright plumage; and the rich moist earth was teeming with creeping things innumerable. As for the butterflies, there never were half so many colours in the rainbow, as were revealed whenever the sunlight fell upon the under side of their wings; and they were so big, that when they lighted on the bowl of a convolvulus, as big as a teacup, they quite filled it, and when they flew away, you would have been puzzled to say whether butterfly or convolvulus had taken wing.

As for the trees, their branches for the most part grew downwards, and took root in the soil, while the roots themselves seemed to be growing upwards. Had the monkeys only been forthcoming, there would have been little wanting to complete my ideal of tropical scenery; but they disappointed me to the last, for I did not see a single specimen, nor any wild animal except one solitary hind.

During my passage through this tangled wilderness, which, as I approached the coast, opened out into grassy glades with an abundant admixture of palm groves, I met with none of the adventures which fall to the lot of most travellers in this brigand-haunted region. My nearest approach to an adventure was to find myself at the town of Ozuluama—my last sleeping-place before reaching Tampico—at the mercy of the Juarists, who held the place; but, so far from being in any way molested, I was treated with great kindness by their leader, upon whose hospitality I threw myself. In the course of the evening some boys made their appearance, and were introduced to me by my host as "*Mis hijos—otros defensores de la libertad.*" In this company, for the first and last time during my travels, I listened to the open expression of opinions adverse to the Imperial *régime*, and heard the Mexican question freely and intelligently discussed by Mexicans themselves. But for this accidental encounter, I should have doubted that Mexico could have produced such respectable and moderate Liberals as these specimens before me seemed to be. Against the Emperor Maximilian personally, my host and his friends seemed to bear no ill-will, reserving all their bitterness for the French in general, and Colonel Du Pin in particular—the commander of the contra-guerilla force, which had scoured the Huasteca a few months previously.

Two months after my arrival in England I received tidings of these very Liberals, which somewhat lowered them in my estimation; for I learned from Mr. A—— upon whom the loss fell—he had agreed to purchase my horse of me, if I got him safe to Tampico—that on the return journey the animal had been stolen by the Juarists of Ozuluama.

Early in the afternoon of the sixth day out from Velasco, I reached Tampico el Alto—a clean airy village built upon a lofty ridge, which commands an extensive view of the crocodile-haunted lagoons and rivers, which surround the modern town and port of Tampico. Beyond all, and bounding the horizon, the blue sea-line was faintly visible above a range of low sand-banks, which form a golden fringe to the green carpeting of the *Tierra Caliente*, which extends almost to the margin of the ocean. So high does the village church stand, that its tower serves as a mark, which may be seen far out at sea by mariners as they approach the dangerous shifting sand-bar in the mouth of the Tampico river.

Pushing on rapidly down the slope, which leads to Tampico el Viejo, we reached the wharf-side, whence you embark for the modern town of Tampico, about an hour before sunset, having accomplished not less than forty-five miles since the morning.

Here I took leave of my *mozo*, and the excellent beasts which had carried me so well—little dreaming that my horse, which had so lately been ridden by the side of the Emperor Maximilian, was destined to fall a prize to the partisans of his rival, Juarez.

After a ride of eleven hours, the change from the saddle to the canoe, in which I was paddled over the lagoon and up the river to Tampico, was so enjoyable, that I was almost sorry to reach my destination.

I had arrived in the nick of time, for the packet was due, and actually arrived early next morning, when we were all bustled on board a little steam tug, which took us down the river, over the bar, and out into the open sea to the English packet, which turned out to be my dirty old friend the *Solent*, instead of the hoped-for *Eider*.

The tug in which we had embarked had only lately arrived out from England, and, in happy ignorance of the misery in store for them, a party of elegantly-dressed Mexican ladies from Tampico had taken it into their heads to make a pleasure trip out to the steamer and back again. Poor things! How bitterly they must have rued their resolve, for no sooner had we crossed the bar than they all became ghastly pale, and were soon rolling promiscuously about the quarter-deck horribly sea-sick, quite forgetful of their finery. Meanwhile the sea became continually rougher, and it was with the utmost difficulty that the passengers bound for Europe were transferred to the *Solent* before night-fall. If the poor sick ladies ever got safely back to Tampico I would vouch for it that they will not in a hurry set foot in a vessel again. In our big steamer we had a rough night of it, lying at anchor out in the offing.

On the following day, March 29th, we made for a safer anchorage under the lee of the island of Lobos, where we lay for twenty-four hours, our captain deciding in favour of remaining there, rather than proceeding at once to Vera Cruz, where we were not due till March 31st.

FINIS.

www.ingramcontent.com/pod-product-compliance
Lightning Source LLC
Chambersburg PA
CBHW030553300426
44111CB00009B/969